THE BROTHER OF JESUS

THE BROTHER OF JESUS

James the Just and His Mission

edited by

BRUCE CHILTON AND JACOB NEUSNER

Westminster John Knox Press

LOUISVILLE

LONDON ·LEIDEN

© 2001 Westminster John Knox Press

Book design by Sharon Adams
Cover design by PAZ Design Group

First edition
Published by Westminster John Knox Press
Louisville, Kentucky

This book is printed on acid-free paper that meets the American National Standards Institute Z39.48 standard. ∞

PRINTED IN THE UNITED STATES OF AMERICA

01 02 03 04 05 06 07 08 09 10 — 10 9 8 7 6 5 4 3 2 1

Library of Congress Cataloging-in-Publication Data

The brother of Jesus : James the Just and his mission / edited by Bruce Chilton and Jacob Neusner.— 1st ed.
    p. cm.
    Includes bibliographical references and index.
    ISBN 0-664-22299-4 (alk. paper)
    1. James, Brother of the Lord, Saint. 2. Bible. N.T. James—Criticism, interpretation, etc. I. Chilton, Bruce. II. Neusner, Jacob, 1932–

    BS2454.J3 .B76 2001
    225.9'2—dc21

                      2001026927

Contents

Abbreviations

A.H.	Irenaeus, *Adversus haereses*
AB	Anchor Bible
AnBib	Analecta biblica
ANF	*Ante-Nicene Fathers*
ANRW	*Aufstieg und Niedergang der römischen Welt*
B.C.E.	Before the Common Era
Bib	*Biblica*
BTNC	Black's New Testament Commentaries
BWANT	Beiträge zur Wissenschaft vom Alten und Neuen Testament
C.E.	Common Era
CBQ	*Catholic Biblical Quarterly*
CD	Damascus Document
CurBS	*Currents in Research: Biblical Studies*
ETL	*Ephemerides theologicae lovanienses*
FRLANT	Forschungen zur Religion und Literatur des Alten und Neuen Testaments
FS	Festschrift
H.E.	Eusebius, *Historia ecclesiastica*
HNT	Handbuch zum Neuen Testament
HThK	Herders theologischer Kommentar
JSNTSup	Journal for the Study of the New Testament Supplement Series
JSPSup	Journal for the Study of the Pseudepigrapha Supplement Series
JTS	*Journal of Theological Studies*
LCC	Library of Christian Classics
LCL	Loeb Classical Library
M	the Matthean tradition
n.s.	new series

NIBC	New International Bible Commentary
NIGTC	New International Greek Testament Commentary
NovT	*Novum Testamentum*
NovTSup	Novum Testamentum Supplements
NRSV	New Revised Standard Version
NTOA	Novum Testamentum et Orbis Antiquus
NTS	*New Testament Studies*
ÖTK	Ökumenischer Taschenbuch-Kommentar
Q^M	Matthean form of the sayings source
RSV	Revised Standard Version
SBL	Society of Biblical Literature
SBS	Stuttgarter Bibelstudien
SC	Sources chrétiennes
SNTSMS	Society for New Testament Studies Monograph Series
SUNT	Studien zur Umwelt des Neuen Testaments
SupNovT	Supplements to Novum Testamentum
THK	Theologischer Handkommentar
ThR	*Theologische Rundschau*
TU	Texte und Untersuchungen
VF	*Verkündigung und Forschung*
WBC	Word Biblical Commentary
WUNT	Wissenschaftliche Untersuchungen zum Neuen Testament
ZNW	*Zeitschrift für die neutestamentliche Wissenschaft*

Preface

What better person to represent a dead master's teaching than his brother? For many decades, scholars have investigated the evidence for contending that James—known as both "James the Just" and "James, the brother of the Lord [Jesus]"—was in fact a prominent keeper of traditions concerning Jesus, and a preeminent leader in the movement which came to be called Christianity. Following the lead of Ethelbert Stauffer, researchers have even used the language of a "Caliphate" to speak of the strong line of succession that derived from Jesus through James.

Our purpose in the essays that follow is to draw upon the scholarship of James in order to accord him his deserved place in Christianity's earliest history. We focus on James in his role as "his brother's keeper." Theological fashions have made a balanced assessment difficult in the past. Whether in the form of the Protestant veneration of Paul, or of the Catholic claim of Petrine supremacy, dominant Christian theologies through the centuries have been designed principally for Gentiles, rather than for Israelite followers of Jesus. Further, the New Testament as we have received it—including the Gospels, Acts, and a diverse set of letters from Paul and others that were updated and augmented over the course of decades of transmission—is the product of Christianity at the end of the first century, by which time the Temple in Jerusalem had been burnt in the Roman arson of 70 C.E.

James himself had died in the year 62, but he passed from the scene as a martyr (just a couple of years before Paul and Peter), and there was good reason to believe at that time that his influence would only increase after his death, much as Jesus' had (and as Paul's and Peter's later did). But the natural constituency of James, Jews in Jerusalem who were faithful to Jesus' message, was decimated by the Romans. The Sanctuary, the center of his devotion and the pivot of his reputation, was desolate. The recovery of James, therefore, necessarily involves finding an aspect of Christian identity that has been lost to popular awareness. It is that Jesus' movement after his resurrection, as well as before, stood for the vindication of Israel, and not by any means for the rejection of Judaism. Until we can appreciate the place of earliest Christianity within Judaism, we will understand neither Jesus' own brother nor the origins and the true character of Christian theology.

Our essays engage a sequence of questions, to facilitate what we believe is a sound evaluation of James. Professor Neusner provides an actual itinerary in his introduction, but we should call attention here to the framing conception of the whole. Because James's context was Judaism, and the Temple in particular, the assessment of Judaism in critical terms is an indispensable dimension of analyzing the relevant evidence. Far too often, even today, that is overlooked. Scholars frequently speak of "the Jewish background of the New Testament," apparently forgetting that, for teachers such as James and his brother, Israel was really the foreground of humanity, the focus of all God's aspirations for the world he created. An awareness of that factor explains why we have found the context for our analyses of James (both the person and the epistle attributed to him) within formal considerations of the Judaisms of the first century. Only by those means, we think, can James be recovered.

This volume is the product of several years of work by the Consultation on James. Our considerations to date have been deliberately technical and tightly focused, and here we wish to make our research accessible to a general readership. We convened the Consultation in 1998 at a meeting in Orlando, Florida, where invited scholars systematically assessed all the major evidence concerning James. The result of that was a collection of academic papers called *James the Just and Christian Origins*, which Bruce Chilton edited with Craig Evans. We were delighted when this work was published in 1999 by E. J. Brill, in the series "Supplements to *Novum Testamentum*." The year after our first session in Orlando, we met in Boston to consider the relationship between James and Peter in particular, and that collection of essays is nearing publication. We plan a final meeting in 2001 to assess the relationship between James and Paul.

This volume originates in our meeting in Nashville in 2000. With a systematic program of scholarship both behind us and before us, the collaborators thought it time to provide, for a broader audience, an account of our general assessment of the figure of James and his significance. By approaching the question as we have here, we believe that justice is done both to the complexity of the question and to the force of the evidence for the vital importance of James within primitive Christianity.

The James who emerges from our consideration also has his place within the history of Second Temple Judaism, although his role there is considerably less prominent than it became within the Judaic movement that later emerged as Christianity. James, then, is a case where Judaism and Christianity will be understood in relation to one another, or not at all. For that reason, our Consultation has been the most notable contribution of the Institute of Advanced Theology at Bard College.

The Institute owes its inception to the vigor of the chair of its Board of Directors, Mr. Frank T. Crohn. Mr. Crohn has spurred the Institute to the historical and comparative study of religions, with special reference to the period of ancient Christianity and Judaism, where we believe a great deal can be learned that illuminates the relationships among other religions and their social interactions. The Institute has been able to draw on grants from Bard College and the Pew Charitable Trusts, and most recently from the Tisch Family Foundation, which has permitted Jacob Neusner to be named as the first Senior Fellow of the Institute. Mr. Crohn has seen us through the Consultation on James, not only as its principal donor but as an intellectual stimulus. The title of his master's thesis at Skidmore College, for example, inspired our focus on James as "his brother's keeper"; that is only one sign of his deep engagement in the discussions of the Consultation.

The Consultation has addressed the aims of our larger endeavor: to focus the resources of academic expertise on key questions of religious development, and to engage the public with the results of that inquiry. James, the brother of Jesus, has permitted us to take up that task and to complete at least one aspect of it.

B.D.C. and J.N.

Institute of Advanced Theology
Bard College
Annandale-on-Hudson, New York

Contributors

Richard Bauckham is Professor of New Testament Studies and Bishop Wardlaw Professor in the University of St. Andrews, Scotland. He was previously Reader in the History of Christian Thought in the University of Manchester. He has published widely in New Testament, early Judaism, and Christian theology. His books include *Jude and the Relatives of Jesus in the Early Church* (Edinburgh: T. & T. Clark, 1990) and *James: Wisdom of James, Disciple of Jesus the Sage* (London: Routledge, 1999). He is a Fellow of the British Academy.

Bruce Chilton is Bernard Iddings Bell Professor of Religion at Bard College, Annandale-on-Hudson, New York, and Rector of the Church of St. John the Evangelist. He is an expert on the New Testament and early Judaism, his principal scholarship having been in the understanding of Jesus within Judaism and in the critical study of the Targumim, the Aramaic paraphrases of the Bible. Jesus appears clearly as a rabbinic teacher in Dr. Chilton's analysis, on the basis of his study of the Targum of Isaiah, which he has edited and translated in the first commentary ever written on that book. Dr. Chilton has earned degrees at Bard College, the General Theological Seminary of the Episcopal Church, and Cambridge University. Previous to his chair at Bard College, he held positions at the University of Sheffield in England, the University of Münster in Germany, and Yale University (as the first Lillian Claus Professor of New Testament). His books include *Beginning New Testament Study* (Eerdmans and SPCK), *A Galilean Rabbi and His Bible* (Glazier and SPCK), *The Isaiah Targum* (Glazier and T. & T. Clark), *The Temple of Jesus* (Penn State University Press), *A Feast of Meanings* (Brill), and *Pure Kingdom: Jesus' Vision of God* (Eerdmans). With Jacob Neusner, he has written *Judaism in the New Testament* (Routledge), a trilogy titled *Judaism and Christianity—the Formative Categories* (Trinity Press International), and *Jewish-Christian Debates* (Fortress). His most recent work is *Rabbi Jesus: An Intimate Biography* (Doubleday).

Peter H. Davids is an educational missionary with International Teams, who, together with his wife, lives in Innsbruck, Austria. After twenty years of teaching in North American graduate institutions, he presently teaches mainly in various graduate programs located in Eastern or Western Europe and directed toward Eastern Europeans and third-world students. He has been involved with James since his 1974 University of Manchester Ph.D. thesis and is the author of *A Commentary on James* (NIGTC; Eerdmans, 1982), *James* (NIBC; Hendrickson, 1989), and numerous articles and book chapters on James, as well as being an editor of the *Dictionary of the Later New Testament and Its Developments* (InterVarsity, 1997), which also covered the General Epistles.

Craig A. Evans received his Ph.D. (1983) in New Testament from Claremont Graduate School and is Director of the Graduate Program in Biblical Studies at Trinity Western University, where he has taught since 1981. He has authored many books, including *Luke* (Hendrickson, 1990), *Noncanonical Writings and New Testament Interpretation* (Hendrickson, 1992), *Luke and Scripture*, with James Sanders (Fortress, 1993), *Word and Glory* (JSOT Press, 1993), *Jesus and His Contemporaries* (Brill, 1995), *Jesus in Context*, with Bruce Chilton (Brill, 1997), and *Mark* (Thomas Nelson, 2001). His specialties include the historical Jesus and the Dead Sea Scrolls.

Jacob Neusner is Research Professor of Religion and Theology at Bard College and Senior Fellow of the Institute of Advanced Theology at Bard as well. He also is a Member of the Institute for Advanced Study, Princeton, New Jersey, and Life Member of Clare Hall, Cambridge University, in England. He has been awarded nine honorary degrees, including seven U.S. and European honorary doctorates. He was President of the American Academy of Religion (1968–1969) and founded the European Association of Jewish Studies (1980–1981). He also served, by appointment of President Carter, as Member of the National Council on the Humanities and, by appointment of President Reagan, as Member of the National Council on the Arts (1978–1984, 1984–1990, respectively). He is Editor of the monograph series Academic Studies in the History of Judaism, Academic Studies on Religion and the Social Order, and International Studies in Formative Christianity and Judaism, all at Global Publications, and he is a coeditor of the *Encyclopaedia of Judaism* (3 vols., Brill, 1999), *The Annual of Rabbinic Judaism*, and the Brill Reference Library of Judaism, published by E. J. Brill, Leiden, Netherlands. He also is editor of Studies in Ancient Judaism (University Press of America).

John Painter was born in Bellingen, north coast country, New South Wales, educated in Sydney, Australia. His degrees include the B.D. (London University) and Ph.D. (Durham, U.K.). He is a Fellow of the Australian Academy of the Humanities. He has taught at St. John's College, University of Durham, U.K.; the University of Cape Town; and La Trobe University, Melbourne,

Australia, and is now Professor of Theology at St. Mark's National Theological Centre, School of Theology, Charles Sturt University, Australia. His academic area of interest is Early Christianity and its relationship to Judaism. His
books include *Just James: The Brother of Jesus in History and Tradition* (University of South Carolina Press and Fortress Press, 1997, 1999); *Mark: Worlds in
Conflict* (Routledge, 1997); *The Quest for the Messiah* (T. & T. Clark, 1991;
Abingdon, 1993); *Theology as Hermeneutics* (Almond, 1987).

Wiard Popkes is professor of New Testament at Hamburg University and the
Baptist Seminary at Elstal/Berlin, Germany. He received his Dr. theol. degree
from Zurich University. He is a European Fellow of Regent's Park College,
Oxford University. His books include *Christus Traditus* (Zurich: Zwingli,
1967), studies on the Lord's Supper (Kassel: Oncken 1981) and the church
(Kassel: Oncken, 1984), *Adressaten, Situation und Form des Jakobusbriefes*
(Stuttgart: Katholisches Bibelwerk, 1986), *Paränese und Neues Testament*
(Stuttgart: KBW, 1996), *Der Jakobusbrief* (Leipzig: Evangelische Verlagsan-
stalt, 2001). His articles deal with various New Testament topics, in particular
James and paraenesis.

Robert M. Price, from Jackson, Mississippi, is Professor of Biblical Criticism
for the Center for Inquiry Institute, a Fellow of the Jesus Seminar, and founding editor of *The Journal of Higher Criticism*. He holds two Ph.D. degrees from
Drew University (Systematic Theology, 1981; New Testament, 1993). His
books include *The Widow Traditions in Luke–Acts: A Feminist-Critical Scrutiny*
and *Deconstructing Jesus*. He is also a scholar of the work of H. P. Lovecraft and
Robert E. Howard. Price has published many short stories and edited a score
of fiction anthologies. He works with the Council for Secular Humanism.

1

Introduction

What Is a Judaism?

Jacob Neusner

I

When we study a religion, one important goal is to describe, analyze, and interpret religion in the setting of the social order: how religious ideas relate to the social world of the people who hold those ideas. Attaining that goal requires viewing religion as a cultural system of cogent ideas sustaining the shared life of a social group. Religion as a public, shared activity comes to the surface when we find out how religious ideas and practices form a coherent account: the realization of abstract religion as embodied in the details of a concrete social system. So, defining religion in its this-worldly social setting builds upon the premise that religion not only sets forth abstractions concerning custom and conviction. It also comes to expression in a detailed design of the society meant to live by the rules of custom and account for itself by appeal to the convictions concerning God and the world order. The Pentateuchal design of "Israel" as "a kingdom of priests and a holy people," of which Moses speaks, the "abode of Islam" set forth in the Qur'an by the prophet Muhammad, the City of God contemplated by St. Augustine—these represent cases in point, systematic statements of religious accounts of the social order.

But lacking such systematic statements, how are we to proceed? To describe the religion, we should be able to work upward from the concrete to the abstract: from the details of those convictions and customary practices to the large system of thought that comes to realization in those details. To analyze the system, we ought to pick out the points of connection between the components and the whole. To interpret the system, we require ideas on how the diverse details in many ways turn out to say one important thing. The issue may be simply framed: Do the details repeatedly answer an ineluctable question that

1

the social order confronts at its foundations, and if so, what is that generative question? That points us to the relationship between the religious ideas and practices of a community and the world in which that community seeks to construct its being. At stake, in such an approach to the study of religion, is how we conceive the whole holds together.

What is at stake in such a description, therefore, is the relationship between a religious system for the social order, that is, religious propositions and the practices that realize them, on the one side, and the social order that, in its political context, embodies that system, on the other. So a paramount question is, how do the religious ideas people hold account for the social order in which they dwell? It is an inquiry into relationships, matters of balance, proportion, coherence, and order. Such systemic description, then, aims at seeing religious ideas in the framework of society. How systemic description proceeds is through undertaking three steps of reflection. The first involves identifying the pertinent data and describing those data: the evidence and how it is to be read in detail. The second demands analyzing how the details of a religious system hold together in a coherent theory of society. The third then requires interpreting the system by identifying the generative question, the critical tension, that animates society and demands the answer set forth by a given religious system for the social order.

Now to the task at hand: by "the Judaism of James," therefore, in these pages, we mean to read the evidence concerning James and his community in a particular framework. That is defined by how, in our judgment, seen whole, the structure and system of religious ideas attested in writings by, and references to, James cohere and form a cogent account of the worldview and the way of life of that "Israel" that James through his community contemplates. We propose to define how, in his context, a compelling answer responded to an urgent question. We propose

1. to describe the details as they seem to us to cohere into a cogent whole,
2. to analyze the way in which the details recapitulate a coherent message, and
3. to interpret the system viewed whole by proposing an account of the urgent question and the self-evidently valid answer that, seen all together and all at once, the narratives about, and writings of, James adumbrate.

That is to say, we want to know how the parts fit together. We want to find out how each detail states in its way the main point of the whole. And we want to discern that to which all the details point: the message of the system viewed whole and the question that it answers.

A case in point is Rabbinic Judaism, with its emphasis upon the sanctification of Israel in the here and now and the salvation of Israel at the end of days. The former reaffirms Israel beyond defeat, denying God has rejected his elect. The latter reconfirms Israel's hope, despite subjugation to the idolaters, for vindication at the end of days. So the urgent question of Rabbinic Judaism is the question of Israel, and the self-evidently valid answer invokes God's enduring love for Israel, in the here and now and at the end of days. Other Judaisms ask other questions and come up with different answers to their questions.

These theoretical remarks prepare the way for taking up the question, what "Judaism" do the stories about and writings attributed to James, the brother of Jesus, adumbrate?

II

What accounts for the unfamiliar usage, "the Judaism of James," which is a brief way of referring to the Judaic religious system that is adumbrated by stories told about, views imputed to, and writings of, James, the brother of Jesus? Answering the question requires, first, a definition: when we use the word "Judaism" (or its counterparts, Christianity, Buddhism, Islam, and the like), to precisely what do we refer in the present context of the study of religion and society?

By "a Judaism" in these pages we mean, a religious system put forth by a group that regards itself as "Israel," meaning, as the embodiment in the here and now of that community to which the Hebrew Scriptures of ancient Israel make reference: (1) the way of life and (2) the worldview of (3) an "Israel." The context of discourse for the orthodox—not gnostic—Christian writings that concern the initial century of Christianity speaks of the followers of Jesus in the context of Israel: they either are Israel or form part of Israel, and explicitly so. They furthermore value the Scriptures of ancient Israel and refer to them for knowledge of God and God's plan for Israel. And they maintain that theirs is the right reading of those Scriptures. The way of life subject to definition, the worldview coming to expression—these mark that particular "Israel" as distinctive in that matrix of Israelite society and culture that also envelops the followers of Jesus. These are, as I shall spell out, the indicators that we deal with in a Judaism in the context of antiquity.

Counter-indicators, marking a Christian community and its system as not-Israel, are simply stated. Such a system pronounces God's rejection of "Israel." It makes explicit the dismissal of the Scriptures of ancient Israel and the God made known therein and thereby. A Christian community outside of the framework of a Judaism expresses disinterest in the interpretation of those Scriptures as a sustaining source of the community's convictions. A Christian system that does not qualify as a Judaism is presented for our purpose by many gnostic writings, presenting a religious system explicitly rejecting the God made known to Israel and the Scriptures that convey that knowledge. It follows by the model of description, analysis, and interpretation offered here that in the complex corpus of distinct Christian systems adumbrated in the earliest Christian centuries, some find their context among Judaisms, others do not—in both cases, designated by their own word and self-classification.

In the theory, then, that "a Judaism" forms a coherent account of the social order of the group at hand, we want to describe the details of the way of life and worldview of that group as these are set forth in the pertinent writings and record of that group (the stories they told, the rites that embodied those stories). Further, we want to analyze how those details cohere as a detailed answer to an urgent question. Finally, we want to form a theory to interpret the relationship between the system and the social world formed by those who realized the system: the social ecology of religion in belief and practice. That then comes to brief summary in the phrase: the relationship between the religious ideas a group of people hold and the social order that they realize—and that larger society in which they form their being.

"The Judaism of James" treats details as components of a coherent whole. It then portrays the details as evidence of the working of a religious theory of the social order: a compelling response to a generative question. We propose to find in the way in which they work together the answer to that urgent question that animates and sustains the group in its corporate life. What marks the system for the corporate community as "a Judaism"? And what outer limits do we recognize in providing for the multiplicity of Judaic religions systems? These traits govern, all of them required to characterize a system as Judaic:

1. the privileging of ancient Israelite Scripture;
2. the identification of that community with the "Israel" of which Scripture speaks;
3. the insistence upon the priority of that system over all competing accounts of an "Israel" in context; and
4. the certainty that all who adhere to that community and live by that system of practice and proposition constitute "Israelites."

As to the first, the various Judaic religious systems that antiquity attests all concur on the priority of Israelite Scripture. They differ on details, but invariably affirm the principal parts thereof.

They always insist that they are that "Israel" of which Scripture speaks, its continuators and heirs.

They accord recognition to other "Israels," other systems. That is ordinarily by forming a theory of how the competing "Israels" relate to their "Israel," and that theory is ordinarily exclusive, but always hierarchical. That is to say, the particular "Israel" at hand constitutes the authentic, the true Israel of God.

They afford admission to new adherents to the "Israel" that they constitute. Confident in their community in relationship to God made known through the Torah, they find place for all comers.

In one way or another, we may read in the systemic framework of a generative question and a self-validating answer the various coherent bodies of writings that have come down from antiquity. That is, the evidence concerning distinct groups of Jews and their religious practices and beliefs sustains the conception of competing Judaic religious systems, each of those bodies of writings demanding a reading in its own terms and context. Then we have a three-dimensional relationship between and among Judaisms.

1. Autonomy: Each is autonomous of all others, because it forms a coherent theory of the social order embodied in its corporate community.

2. Connection: Each is connected to (some of) the others, both through common appeal to ancient Scripture and through engagement with competing groups of Jews constituting "Israels," respectively, of the same time and place.

3. Continuity: Some may insist as well, besides autonomy and connection, that the groups form a continuity. But what defines the continuity of all Judaic religious systems remains elusive and subject to debate—especially among the Judaisms of contemporary academic culture. That is, how we may speak of Judaism, not simply Judaisms, forms a critical question facing contemporary scholars of Judaism, the religion. May we speak of Judaism, over and above Judaisms, and if so on what foundation—historical? theological? phenomenological? The difficulty of speaking of one Christianity over and above Christianities here finds its counterpart. And among the many approaches, encompassing the definition of a lowest common denominator among Judaisms, the identification of a single Judaic religious system that forms the model for the rest and the criterion of religious truth, and the specification of indicative traits that all Judaisms do indeed exhibit, it is that third, which I call the phenomenological, that presents the greatest difficulty. But in the end it promises the only descriptive, not-normative solution to defining Judaism out of Judaisms.

III

Such an approach to defining religion, with stress on religion and the social order, begins in the recognition that much conflicting data attests to the condition of a single religious world. That is because diverse groups take shape around Scriptures held in common, and defining the religion that, in one way or another, all of them realize demands both analysis and synthesis. The beginning of analysis is attention to the traits of the various groups that make common cause. The work of synthesis insists on abstraction, the quest for commonalities of conviction and convention. At stake in the approach just now outlined is defining a given genus of religion—Judaism, Christianity, Islam, and the like—in full recognition of speciation by social groups.

But when people speak of "Judaism," "Christianity," "Buddhism," "Islam," or "Hinduism," they commonly have in mind uniform constructs of ideas, yielding "the Judaic doctrine of . . . ," or even (confusing the religion and the ethnic group, "the Jewish doctrine of . . ." These constructs indeed produce neat and simple definitions of matters. But they fall of their own weight when variation and differentiation take over. For just as the ethnic group, the Jews, concurs unanimously on very few propositions, fewer still of consequence, so the writings and other evidences of Judaism yield a mass of conflicting doctrines. To be sure, these generalizations save a whole lot of work; the labor-saving devices are not to be gainsaid. But they also are not to be relied upon.

So when people refer to those religions as though they were easily defined by normative beliefs and practices, they engage in an exercise of selection. This they carry out, whether by theological or some other, less logical rules, choosing some data out of a mass of data. Those are the facts deemed to hold together and define the norm. That exercise, whether logical or arbitrary, is, by definition, not a labor of description, analysis, and interpretation. It is a work of abstraction and simplification. The selected facts are treated as generalizations. They are made to stand for much to which they are not congruent at all. Not only so, but that language invokes the model, for description and explanation, of a single, coherent system of thought and rite. Such a system is represented as the product of a unitary history, readily embodied by the select, uniform beliefs and practices. We speak as though a given religion originated in some one starting point and can be traced back to that point of origin, which then contained within itself all that would take place later on. And, it goes without saying, we then can compare and contrast one religion with some other, secure that the uniformities permit us to use the language, "Judaism maintains" and "Christianity teaches."

The model serves a particular mode of thought, the historical, which traces the sequence by which a body of religious ideas took shape at a particular time and place, to the contingencies to which we refer back to explain the shape and structure of that body of ideas. That agreeable mode of thought affords the sense that if we can explain origins, we understand traits and characteristics. It further appeals to a natural predilection for order in place of chaos and for sequence—first this, then that—as a means of explanation—first came this, which therefore caused that. Here we confront the error captured in the phrase *post hoc, ergo propter hoc*. That is to say, because one thing has followed some other, it has been brought about by that other. When that fundamental logical flaw is raised, no one is much intimidated by it. So we work with language that invokes historical models of description, analysis, and interpretation of what we call "religions" as constructs of religious beliefs and rites, each with its unitary, linear history, all of them with their formation of beliefs and rites into simple constructions: -isms, -ities.

But everyone understands that the -isms and -ities of which we speak serve as laborsaving devices, making unnecessary the work of nuanced differentiation, on the one side, and the recognition of conflict and contradiction, on the other. The simple model of a single religion, starting at some one point and unfolding in orderly sequence, sustaining the contrast of "the Judaic view" with "the Christian view," serves only the unsophisticated. But they are many, because historical thinking continues to influence accounts of culture, including religion, and because pictures of religions with accounts of "beginnings" and "middles," "early Judaism," "middle Judaism," "late Judaism," for example, continue to circulate.

The problems with the historical model of description, analysis, and interpretation of a single, unitary Judaism starting in some one place prove intimidating. First, an account of a one "Judaism" requires that once more we treat all data produced by all regarded as Jews as evidence of a single structure of religious thought deriving from a common point of origin and continuing to develop along a continuous path from then to now. Variations are ignored, diversity obscured. Then when the data conflict in matters of doctrine, or when the rules followed by one body of writing scarcely intersect with those followed by another, e.g., multiple calculations of the calendar of the holy days, or when one set of writings about "Israel" contradict another set of writings, also about "Israel," what is to be done? And how are we to sustain a single, unitary history, when components fall away and new ones claim a place, when one body of writing ceases to command an audience, and another, ignoring much of the past, takes over? There are two solutions to the problem of the diversity of types of evidence speaking about one and the same -ism or -ity. We harmonize and synthesize, or we differentiate and analyze.

Each approach serves in its context. To take a familiar example, harmonies of the Gospels yield synthetic lives of Jesus, and differentiated readings of the Gospels, lives of a "historical Jesus," each the product of a particular process of selection. The merits of each approach need not detain us; it suffices to say, analytical and synthetic readings of complex data need not conflict. But when it comes to the vast and complex corpus of evidence that is supposed to find a place within the -ism or -ity, matters are not so readily sorted out.

Books on "Judaism," comparable to harmonies of the Gospels, either select among the data the more congenial sets, or impose a theological judgment of what was normative and what sectarian, on those same complex collections of data. Either way, arbitrary choice substitutes, in place of the systematic description of pertinent data, the elimination of impertinent ones. Such selections define a single, harmonious Judaism, the outcome of a unitary and continuous history, from start to finish. They then afford no place for sizable parts of the evidence produced by people who thought of themselves as "Israel" and their writings as "Torah." Massive components of the pertinent data gain no entry into the picture, and theological, not phenomenological, considerations in the end predominate to allow for a continuous account of a single, unitary religion.

By "Judaism" people turn out to mean a very particular set of convictions indeed. The other approach finds a lowest common denominator, e.g., a Judaism with which all parties can concur. Here too, a fair part of the evidence produced by a variety of communities claiming to embody "Israel" (in the case of a Judaism) loses all place in the account of matters. So that the answer to the question upon which diverse writings the parties are supposed to concur proves trivial or stupefyingly bland, and Judaism consists of a few doctrines and practices among the many represented by Judaic writings valued by one group or another—a few doctrines and a vast corpus of contradictions best left unremarked upon.

Clearly, a different approach to the description, analysis, and interpretation of the diverse evidence produced in the name of a single religion deserves consideration, one that responds to the problems of the historical, harmonizing, unitary compositions of a single (normative) Judaism or a single (catholic, orthodox) Christianity, and of their counterparts in Islam, Buddhism, Hinduism, and so on throughout the world. That different approach is signaled by the title of this chapter and the book explained herein: not what is Judaism, but what is a Judaism: a species of the genus, Judaism, a way of life, worldview, theory of the social entity "Israel," that all together respond to an urgent question with a (systemically) self-evidently valid answer.

IV

How, in concrete terms, do the essays that unfold in these pages undertake the job of a systemic description of the Judaism of James?

History. We begin with the descriptive question, what, exactly do we know about James: the sources and their data? Professor Painter answers the first question. It is a historical one, for systemic description concerns itself with the facts of the matter, asking what happened and what people thought happened. That account of the context of the system is the work of Professor Painter.

Context in Christianity. In that same frame of reference, papers by Professors Davids, Popkes, and Bauckham place James into its other context, that of the larger, literary community of Israel formed by followers of Jesus as represented by the Epistle of James. Once we know what we know and do not know, then, we ask about the setting defined by kindred Judaic systems of the same time and circumstance.

Worldview. The historical texts and contexts in hand, we want to read as a cogent statement the various stories the community told itself, the propositions it set forth to define the norms of conviction that would mark the community and its boundaries among the competing Israels of the age. We then turn, quite logically, from an account of the historical facts to the first of the three tasks, which is the account of the system's worldview, described by Professor Davids as "James's message." Here the questions addressed by any Judaic religious system of the social order come up: for example, God, Torah, Israel as mediated by the particular convictions of the community at hand.

Way of Life. Then comes the formulation of the data pertinent to the system's way of life. This takes the form required by the nature of the Christian context (variously described by Professor Popkes and Professor Bauckham):

the debate on the imperatives of the Torah in light of that Christian situation that was sustained between James and Peter, on the one side, and James and Paul, on the other. Professor Chilton's essay analyzes that controversy and its implications. The fundamental issues of the Israel contemplated by Paul and debated by Peter and James arise here: what, in fact, does it mean, in practical terms, for an Israelite community to take shape around the life, death, and resurrection of Jesus Christ? Does that fact critical to the community's self-understanding make no difference, little difference, or all the difference in the world, when the community defines its practical affairs?

Definition of the Jacobean Community within and as (an) Israel. It is only when we compare Judaisms—that set forth in the Dead Sea library, that portrayed by the Rabbinic writings, and the one set forth in the record of James—that we gain perspective on the respective accounts of "Israel" that form the foundations of the several systems. Professor Evans sets out that comparison. Knowing how several systems—not contemporaneous but confronted by a common logic—defined the "Israel" that was embodied in their communities allows us to gain perspective on the choices made by each out of a common program of possibilities.

The Judaism of James. Professor Chilton at the end reflects on the methods and findings of our account of the Judaism of James. Seeing that system whole permits us to appreciate the various assessments of Jesus' brother in the Christian tradition. Whether from the perspective of that sector of Christianity which, from then to now, insists that its faith fulfills the faith of Israel and its revealed Torah, or from the perspective of that other sector, that insists upon the opposite—a Christianity autonomous of Israel and in no way a species of the genus Judaism—James remains a focal figure.

2

Who Was James?

Footprints as a Means of Identification

John Painter

Simple questions can have complicated answers. This much is true of the question our chapter seeks to answer. The first thing to note is that James is one of the very common Jewish names in the first century. In the New Testament the name is used over sixty times of as many as eight people. The popularity of the name is partly a consequence of the influence of the great patriarch Jacob. His name in Hebrew, *Ya'aqob*, was transliterated into Greek as Iakob. But the name also appears in hellenized form as *Iakobos*. All twenty-four references to the patriarch Jacob used the form *Iakob*, as do the two references to Jacob the father of Joseph, the supposed father of Jesus (Matt. 1:15–16; contrast Luke 3:23). All other references use the hellenized form *Iakobos*.

WHICH JAMES?

The question "Who was James?" can be rephrased as "Which James?" The simple answer is, "James the Just, the brother of Jesus." The simplicity of the answer conceals complications. The first complication arises because the name James is often used without further clarification. On a few occasions the earliest sources refer to James the brother of Jesus (the Lord), and it is likely that some of the references to James without further qualification refer to him also.

In the New Testament the Semitic form of the name always refers to figures in Jewish history prior to Jesus. This distinguishes them from those who were part of the Jesus movement who are always given the hellenized form. English translators have followed this lead giving the name Jacob to figures in the Old Testament and translating *Ya'aqob* as Jacob. But the hellenized *Iakobos* is used of followers of Jesus and is translated as James. The English names Jacob and James are derived from Latin where *Jacobus* and *Jacomus* are variants of the same name. This variation exists also in other European languages such as Italian (*Giacobbe* and *Giacomo*) and Spanish (*Iago* and *Jaime*). In English Jacob and James have tended to be thought of as two different names. Jacob is thought of as a Jewish name, though it is also used by Christian groups attracted to Old Testament names. Yet there are clues that remind us of the connection between the two names in English. For example, the supporters of the Stuart Jameses are referred to as *Jacobites* and the period is named *Jacobean*.

This linguistic distinction helps to exclude twenty-six references from the discussion of James the brother of Jesus. The remaining references in the New Testament use the hellenized form. About half of these clearly refer to James the brother of John and son of Zebedee. About a third of them probably refer to James the brother of Jesus. The remaining references concern figures often difficult to identify: James the son of Alphaeus, one of the twelve (Mark 3:18); James the "less" (or the "small" or the "younger"), son of Mary and brother of Joses (Joseph; Mark 15:40); James the father (or brother?) of Judas who was one of the twelve (Luke 6:16). This Judas may be identified with Thaddaeus (Mark 3:18) or Lebbaeus, according to the variant reading in Mark 3:18 and Matthew 10:3. There is also James the brother of Jude and author of the Epistle of James, who could be the James mentioned in Luke 6:16 or the brother of Jesus. Alternatively, it can be argued that some of the references normally identified with the brother of Jesus actually refer to one of the other Jameses. Historically, the tendency has been to move in the opposite direction.

The number of Jameses in this group can be reduced from six if it is argued that the same person is referred to in different ways in different places. In the fourth century Jerome developed his distinctive hypothesis by making such identifications. Given the small number of names in use in Judea and the popularity of this name, it is likely that the number of people referred to is more rather than less. This means that care needs to be taken in identifying which James where the name is used without further clarification.

The earliest sources do not refer to "James the Just." Our knowledge of this nomenclature comes from the work of the next generation. Hegesippus tells us of James the brother of the Lord, "whom everyone from the Lord's time till our own has named the Just, for there were many Jameses" (Eusebius, *H.E.* 2.23.4). We have no evidence that "the Just" was used of James before his martyrdom. The reference from Hegesippus suggests that it was. Nevertheless, references to James the Just in this tradition can be taken as references to the James who was "the brother of Jesus." The added identification was made because "there were many Jameses."

Yet, of the many Jameses, there were two who were so prominent that they needed to be carefully distinguished. The James with whom we are concerned is thus clearly distinguished from James the son of Zebedee in Acts 12 where the death of the latter is noted before mentioning the second James. This distinction is also the point of the quotation of Clement of Alexandria recorded by Eusebius (*H.E.* 2.1.2–5). In the New Testament this James is specifically referred to by Paul as the brother of the Lord (Gal. 1:19) and the Gospels mention the brothers and sisters of Jesus (Mark 3:31–35; 6:3; John 2:12; 7:3, 5; and see Acts 1:14). In Mark 6:3 the brothers are named as James, Joseph (Joses), Jude (Judas) and Simon (Symeon). In Paul the explicit reference to James the brother of the Lord (Gal. 1:19) is followed swiftly by reference to James as the first of the three supposed pillars of the Jerusalem church (Gal. 2:1–10), whose influence causes even Peter and Barnabas to conform to his message (2:11–14). Paul also refers to the brothers of the Lord in 1 Cor. 9:5, and the early church rightly understood Paul's reference to the appearance of the risen Lord to James as a reference to the brother of the Lord (1 Cor. 15:7 and thus Eusebius, *H.E.* 1.12.4–5). Given the identification of the brother of the Lord in Gal. 2:1–10, the leading role of James in Acts 15 also concerns the brother of the Lord as does Acts 21:17–26.

WHO WERE THE BROTHERS?

Two approaches to the way to understand the "brothers" can be traced prior to Jerome. With Jerome's intervention the debate reached a new intensity. His work was critical in both senses of the word. He offered a new and critical reading of the canonical evidence concerning the brothers of Jesus. His contribution was also critical, that is, polemical, in response to two major alternative understandings of "the brothers of Jesus." J. B. Lightfoot (1865, 253–91; esp. 254) identified the resulting three positions by reference to their fourth-century advocates, naming them the Epiphanian (after Epiphanius of Salamis, 315–403); the Helvidian (after Helvidius, who wrote ca. 380); and Hieronymian (after Jerome, 347–419/20). Lightfoot does not treat a fourth position which rejects the virginal conception of Jesus and accepts those called brothers and sisters of Jesus as precisely that. Among communities of those who believed in Jesus in the second century, this position seems to be restricted to Jewish believers known as Ebionites who did not accept the incarnation and divinity of Jesus. It is arguably the position presupposed by Mark, John, and Paul, who provide no indication of their acceptance of the teaching of the virginal conception of Jesus by Mary. Of course this does not make them founders of the Ebionite position. Indeed, this "silence" does not prove that Mark, John, and Paul did not know of or believe in the virginal conception of Jesus. All we can say is that they do not mention this view and it is nowhere presupposed by their teaching.

Our question, "Who was James?" finds different answers in each of these four positions. There is also an implied fifth position. Thus the range of answers: (1) Some held that James was a full brother of Jesus. Jesus and those known as brothers and sisters were children of Joseph and Mary. (2) Those who accepted the virginal conception of Jesus affirmed that he was a half-brother of those called his brothers and sisters. Jesus was a child of Mary while they were children of Joseph and Mary. (3) Then there were those who believed that those called brothers and sisters were children of Joseph (but not Mary) by a previous marriage. From this perspective, Mary was the mother of Jesus only and Joseph was not his father. Those called his brothers and sisters were children of Joseph and not actually related to Jesus at all. They were step brothers and sisters. (4) Jerome argued that those called brothers and sisters were children of the sister of the mother of Jesus, whose name was Mary also. This made them cousins via Jesus' mother. (5) Eusebius, claiming the authority of Hegesippus, asserted that Clopas was the brother of Joseph and that Symeon (son of Clopas) was a cousin of Jesus and the second bishop of Jerusalem. If we argue that Symeon was one of the four who were called brothers of Jesus, this would make them cousins in name, but not actually related to Jesus. To answer the question, Who was James? the evidence for these views must be examined.

Lightfoot set out a strong critique of the Hieronymian (Jerome's) view which had prevailed in the West. At the same time, Lightfoot sought to rehabilitate the Epiphanian position. He was deeply impressed by the traditional support for the latter while he emphasized the novelty of Jerome's views. The continuing virginity of Mary had become a symbol of the superiority of celibacy. This found expression in the Epiphanian position. Although Jerome was an advocate of celibacy in the West, he was opposed to the Epiphanian position because it was based noncanonical writings, not on the biblical evidence.

THE EPIPHANIAN POSITION

According to the Epiphanian position, those described as brothers and sisters of Jesus were children of Joseph by a first marriage, prior to his betrothal to Mary. Thus they were not directly related to Jesus or Mary, and Mary remained a virgin after the birth of Jesus. Early advocacy of this view is to be found in the *Gospel of Peter*. Most scholars regard this work as dependent on the canonical Gospels and date it in the second half of the second century, though J. D. Crossan (1985, 125–81) names it as one of his early Gospel sources. Crossan was answered by R. E. Brown (1987). A fragment of this Gospel was discovered in 1886 or 1887 in the excavations of Akhmim (in Egypt). It had been known previously from a reference in a fragment from Serapion of Antioch (late second century) now preserved in Eusebius (*H.E.* 6.12 and cf. 3.3.2) and another by Origen (*Commentary on Matthew* X.17 [on Matt. 13.54–56]). Origen was a supporter of this view, which finds its fullest expression in the *Protevangelium of James*. The earliest explicit evidence for this Gospel is to be found in Origen in his discussion of the brothers of Jesus in his commentary on Matthew, already mentioned. It was probably used by Clement of Alexandria (*Strom.* 7.16.93) and perhaps by Justin Martyr (*Dial.* 78.5).

The *Protevangelium of James* gives us our earliest evidence of the tradition on which belief in the perpetual virginity of Mary was based. That Mary continued to be a virgin in conceiving and giving birth to Jesus is clear from the narrative. That those known as the brothers of Jesus were the sons of Joseph by a first marriage seems clear in that he had sons. There is no mention of daughters of Joseph, implied sisters of Jesus.

The document gained its title from the Latin translation of G. Postel (Basel, 1522). Its title is derived partly from the conclusion, where the author names himself as James (25.1), and partly from its content as an infancy Gospel. The Decree of Gelasius identified the author as James "the less" ("the small" or "younger") of Mark 15:40. Following Jerome this is understood to indicate James the Just, known as the brother of Jesus but in fact being his cousin. Origen referred to it simply as "the book of James." It is not likely to be the work of a Palestinian because the author does not depict the geography and customs accurately.

The earliest manuscript evidence is Bodmer Papyrus V, dated to the third century and already showing secondary developments. The popularity of the work is attested by more than thirty Greek manuscripts. Translations were made into Syriac, Ethiopic, Georgian, Sahidic, Slavonic, Armenian, and Latin though no Latin manuscripts have survived because, following its rejection by Jerome, it ceased to have wide influence in the West. Jerome rejected it because it portrayed the brothers (and sisters) of Jesus as children of Joseph by a previous marriage, prior to his marriage to Mary, a tradition that could not be established from the canonical Gospels. He was harsh in his criticism of the aberrations of these other Gospels which he described as "the ravings of the apocryphal writings." His condemnation of the *Protevangelium of James* led to its rejection in the West. The sixth-century Decree of Gelasius placed it among the rejected apocryphal works.

The *Protevangelium of James* appears to be composite, changing from third-person to first-person narration by James at the end (compare the *First Apocalypse of James*). Joseph also speaks in the first person, as if he were the narrator, in 18.2. No doubt James is identified as one of Joseph's sons (9.2) who led the she-ass upon which the pregnant Mary rode while Joseph followed behind (17.2). Something like this scene is often depicted in art, for example in the crypt of the Benedictine Dormition Abbey in Jerusalem and in the refectory of a monastery outside Jericho. The scene is modified to the extent that in these the baby Jesus is carried on the ass by Mary. (On my most recent visit to the Dormition Abbey in August 2000 I found that this mosaic had been removed.) The scene is the flight into Egypt, with a youthful James leading while Joseph brings up the rear following the donkey bearing Mary and the infant Jesus.

The *Protevangelium* is dependent on the infancy stories of both Matthew and Luke, though attention has now turned from a concentration on the circumstances of *the birth of Jesus* to the virginity of Mary. Her own miraculous birth is first narrated. According to this document, based on the model of the birth stories of Isaac and Samuel (rather than the later doctrine of the immaculate conception), she is born to aged and barren parents. While it is not taught that Mary was born without sin, nevertheless the narrative pays attention to the maintaining of the conditions of purity until she is handed over as a ward of the Temple. Following the pattern of the story of Samuel, she is made a ward of the Temple at the age of three (7.1). When she attained the age of twelve her presence in the Temple became problematic, probably because of a purity issue at the onset of puberty. Joseph, an aged widower with sons by a previous marriage, was chosen by lot to receive Mary as his virgin ward (9.1). As a virgin she conceived (11.1–6) and bore Jesus (18.1–19.3). What is more, after the birth of Jesus, the test conducted by the midwife proved that her virginity remained intact (19.1–20.4).

Because the teaching of the perpetual virginity of Mary had become important, the *Protevangelium* not only espoused the teaching of the virginal conception of Jesus but also of the virgin birth *(in partu)*. It was also necessary to account for those who had become known as the brothers (and sisters?) of Jesus. To this end reference is made to a prior marriage of Joseph and the presence of sons. Of those sons, James is by far the most prominent and gives his name to this, the earliest and probably most influential of the infancy Gospels. By postulating an earlier marriage, and a number of sons as the fruit of that marriage, the picture is painted of Joseph as an older man, though no actual age is mentioned nor are the other children in addition to James named. Joseph asserts "I have sons and am old and she is a girl" (9.2). According to Epiphanius, Joseph was over eighty years of age (with four sons and two daughters) when he was betrothed to Mary. Though a kind of betrothal is implied, it is clear that Mary became the virgin ward of Joseph. In this way the *Protevangelium of James* was to become the model for the understanding of the family of Jesus in Eastern Christianity.

Lightfoot attempted to revive this tradition in the West. Although he drew attention to the novelty of Jerome's theory, Lightfoot allowed the evidence of the Epiphanian tradition from an earlier period, the second half of the second century, to weigh heavily in its favor. He nowhere asks why the earliest references (in the New Testament) to brothers and sisters of Jesus have the appearance of referring to actual brothers and sisters without qualification and why even in Matthew and Luke (and Acts) the brothers appear with Mary the mother of Jesus. There the teaching of the virginal conception of Jesus implies that Jesus and his brothers and sisters have the same mother. We know of no tradition concerning children born to Joseph by an earlier marriage that antedates the *Protevangelium of James*. Had there been reliable traditions asserting that Mary bore no other children after Jesus, Jerome would have welcomed them, as would Origen and others. Had there been early tradition concerning children born to Joseph by a prior marriage, Origen would have welcomed it.

From the two named sources (the *Gospel of Peter* and the *Protevangelium of James*) Origen mentions the view that the brothers of Jesus were children of Joseph by a marriage prior to his marriage to Mary. Origen notes that this view comes from those who "wish to preserve the honour of Mary in virginity to the end." He admits that this view is not found in the canonical sources but shows himself to be in harmony with it. "And I think it in harmony with reason that Jesus was the first-fruit among men of the purity which consists in chastity, and Mary among women; for it were not pious to ascribe to any other than to her the first-fruit of virginity." This argument reveals an awareness of no earlier traditional evidence for the view. The argument arises from what is fitting. That Origen knows no earlier evidence than the sources he cites places a serious question over the argument for the historical reliability of the tradition that seeks to establish that the brothers and sisters of Jesus were children of Joseph (but not Mary) by a previous marriage. Nevertheless this is the position adopted by Origen. (See *On Matt.* X.17 and also his comments in *Joann.* ii.12 and *Hom. in Luc.* 7.)

There is no evidence that this tradition can be traced beyond the infancy Gospels that Jerome repudiated as spurious and fanciful. Both Jerome and Origen were preoccupied with the preservation of the virginity of Mary. On this view it was necessary to find an alternative understanding of those who were spoken of as the brothers and sisters of Jesus. According to the *Protevangelium* they were not blood relations of Jesus at all. They were children of Joseph by a first marriage while Jesus was the child of Mary without a human father. Given that Joseph was the legal father, it is not impossible that all might be described as brothers and sisters. It is just that there is no hint of this complex web of relations in the earliest evidence, and when the tradition does emerge it has a strongly apologetic character. The intent was to preserve and to venerate the virginity of Mary, as Origen acknowledges. We are not able, with any confidence, to identify evidence of this tradition any earlier than the middle of the second century. Its apologetic character undermines the credibility of the tradition, and the earliest expressions of it (the *Gospel of Peter* and the *Protevangelium of James*) bear deep marks of legendary development.

THE HIERONYMIAN VIEW

The latest view to emerge was developed by Jerome (347–419/20) and championed in the West by Augustine (354–430). Jerome was an advocate of Eastern forms of asceticism in the West. The virginity of Mary had become an important symbol of the superiority of virginity. Nevertheless, Jerome repudiated the Epiphanian tradition in favor of a position that he worked out based on canonical evidence in Paul and the Gospels.

It was the position of Helvidius that provoked Jerome to develop his own *distinctive* position; see his *Against Helvidius (Adv. Helvidium de Perpetua Vir-*

ginitate B. Mariae). Jerome consistently defended the perpetual virginity of Mary but did not always do so on the basis of the view associated with his name. Nevertheless, with the support of Augustine, it became dominant in the Western church and remained so until modern times. Thus it is appropriately called the *Hieronymian* view after Jerome. According to this view, Gal. 1:19 taught that James, the brother of the Lord, was an apostle. In the lists of the twelve apostles only two have the name of James (see Mark 3:16–19). Because James the brother of John can be excluded, only James the son of Alphaeus is left. From Mark 15:40, 47 and John 19:25 Jerome concludes that Mary the mother of James and Joses (Mark 15:40) is the wife of Alphaeus, the sister of the mother of Jesus (why not Mary the mother of Jesus?), and [daughter?] of Cleopas (Clopas). Given that James has been identified as the son of Alphaeus, Jerome indicates he cannot explain the connection of Mary the mother of James and Joses to Clopas, though he suggests she may be his daughter (see Mark 15:40; John 19:25). James and Joses are the names of two of the four of those called brothers of Jesus (Mark 6:3). Thus Mary of Cleopas is identified as the wife of Alphaeus and mother of James. Those called brothers were actually cousins of Jesus related through their mothers, who were sisters. Clearly Jerome is right in arguing that the term "brother" can be used of an actual brother, persons of common nationality, a kinsman, or friend. Jerome used the terms *natura, gente, cognatione, affectu*, to designate these categories. The question is, in what sense do the Gospels and Paul speak of the brothers of Jesus?

The details of Jerome's critical theory have been developed in ways not recognized by him. The first is the possibility that Clopas, the name found in John, represents the Aramaic name of which Alphaeus is a hellenized form. While this is possible, there is no evidence that Jerome or anyone from the early church recognized the possibility. Indeed Jerome confesses that he cannot explain the connection of Mary to Cleopas, suggesting that he perhaps was her father or that it is used as a family name. Chrysostom (347–407) was first to suggest that James the brother of the Lord is the son of Clopas though, according to Eusebius, Hegesippus asserted that Symeon was the son of Clopas. While Jerome argued that two of the brothers of Jesus were apostles, later scholars have suggested that another of the remaining two brothers was also an apostle. Luke refers to "Jude as [brother?] of James" (Luke 4:16; Acts 1:13) and the author of Jude refers to himself as "Jude the brother of James" (Jude 1). Jude is mentioned as one of the four brothers of Jesus (Mark 6:3). Then there is Symeon (Simon), who is listed with James the son of Alphaeus and Judas [the brother?] of James (Luke 6:15–16). If we follow this line of argument then three of the four brothers were apostles, understood as the twelve. The earliest evidence suggests that none of the brothers belonged to the twelve.

The strength of this theory is that it combines and makes some sense of a wide range of apparently unrelated details. Nevertheless, it founders badly, having no support from any earlier tradition. It is not enough to show that the term "brothers" *can* be used of those who are not strictly brothers. There needs to be evidence to suggest that this, in fact, is the case with reference to the brothers of Jesus. In the Gospels, those called brothers appear with the mother of Jesus (see Mark 3:31–35; 6:3; John 2:12; Acts 1:14). This does not suggest that "brothers" means "cousins" or anything other than actual brothers.

Jerome's hypothesis depends on the assumption that a repetition of the same names probably refers to the same people. But this overlooks the small number of Jewish names in use in Judea in this period and the popularity of certain names like Jacob and Mary, Judas, Joseph, and Symeon. The recognition that James was an apostle (Gal. 1:19) need not mean that he was one of "the twelve" (1 Cor. 15:5–7). Clearly "the twelve" is a more restricted group than "all the apostles." Indeed, the story of Mark 3:31–35 and Paul's reference in 1 Corinthians 15 imply that the brothers are to be distinguished from "the twelve."

A number of unlikely readings are necessary for the success of Jerome's hypothesis. From a larger group of women mentioned, Mark 15:40 names only three at the crucifixion, Mary Magdalene, Mary the mother of James [the younger? or the small?] and Joses, and Salome. There is no hint of an early tradition concerning a greater James which emerges in later liturgy in relation to James the brother of John. John 19:25 mentions four women of whom two are named, Mary of [?] Clopas and Mary Magdalene. Only Mary Magdalene is explicitly common to the lists of Mark 15:40 and John 19:25. In John 19:25 the first two women are identified as the mother of Jesus and the sister of his mother. Jesus' mother is not named here or elsewhere in John. Her relationship to Jesus is emphasized without using her name. Presupposing that the mother of Jesus is Mary, we have three women by the name of Mary in John's list. Also with the mother of Jesus is her sister. Jerome argued that she is to be identified with Mary of [?] Clopas. Assuming that, in John, Jesus' mother is Mary, Jerome's reading of John 19:25 involves three women named Mary, two of whom are sisters. A way out of this dilemma consistent with Jerome's approach is to suggest that Mary of Clopas was the sister-in-law of the mother of Jesus, being Joseph's sister. Though not adopting the position himself, Richard Bauckham (1990, 21) suggests that this strategy would strengthen Jerome's hypothesis. See the discussion of the identification of Clopas as the brother of Joseph in the reference to Hegesippus in Eusebius *H.E.* 3.11.1. More likely John lists four women, identifying the first two by relationship and the second two by name. If that is the case, we do not know the name of the sister of the mother of Jesus.

The differences between the Johannine and Markan accounts of the women present at the crucifixion warn against Jerome's attempted identification. First, in Mark 15:40 the women watch from afar while in John 19:25 they are standing by the cross, close enough for Jesus to speak to them in intimate terms (19:27). The Beloved Disciple is also present (John 19:26) and the words spoken by Jesus idealize the roles of his mother and the Beloved Disciple. Mark makes no mention of the Beloved Disciple or the mother of Jesus and her sister at the cross. This is enough to warn the critical reader against attempts to harmonize Mark and John at this point. Given that Mark does not name all of the women, it is dangerous to insist that the three named in Mark can be identified with the group named by John.

Jerome's position is not supported by any early Christian sources. Eusebius records details which throw light on Jerome's hypothesis and undermine it at the same time. First, in various places he deals with the succession to the throne of James of Jerusalem. This is the way Eusebius refers to the succession of bishops in Jerusalem. He asserts that the capture of Jerusalem swiftly followed the martyrdom of James and that, after this, the apostles and family of Jesus gathered in Jerusalem and unanimously agreed that Symeon, the son of Clopas, the brother of Joseph should succeed James (*H.E.* 3.11.1). Eusebius attributes the identification of Clopas as the brother of Joseph to Hegesippus and himself notes that Clopas is mentioned in the Gospels (see John 19:25; Luke 24:18). Eusebius notes here and elsewhere that Symeon was the cousin (*anepsion*) of Jesus and that he was the second bishop of Jerusalem in succession to James who was first (see also *H.E.* 3.32.1–6; 4.5.1–4; 4.22.4.). While Eusebius consistently called Clopas a cousin of Jesus, he always speaks of James as a brother, even though he has reservations about the strict applicability of this description (see *H.E.* 2.1.2). His language is consistent with the Epiphanian view of the brothers.

The Gospels name the brothers of Jesus as James, Joseph, Jude, and Simon (Symeon). Jerome identified Mary the mother of James (the younger? the small?) and Joseph (Mark 15:40) with the sister of the mother of Jesus (Mary of Clopas in John 19:25). But there is no mention there of Jude or Symeon! Eusebius makes no mention of Mary as the wife of Clopas or the mother of Symeon. He identifies the cousin of Jesus as the son of Clopas. There is no mention that this Symeon was the brother of James, whom he succeeded as bishop of Jerusalem. Rather, James is always referred to as brother while Symeon is cousin.

There is no reason to think that the brother of Joseph or the sister of Mary had children by the name of James, Jude, or Joseph. Attempts to harmonize Mark 15:40 and John 19:25 are driven by a conclusion held independently of those texts. Jerome was convinced of the perpetual virginity of Mary the mother of Jesus. Given that Mark mentions only three of a larger group of women it is unlikely that those named include the mother of Jesus and her sister. Mark would have identified them.

Jerome's distinctive position was developed in his work *Against Helvidius* in 383. Nevertheless, in his later (387) commentary on Galatians (commenting on 1:19) he writes:

> Suffice it now to say that James was called the Lord's brother on
> account of his high character, his incomparable faith, and extraordinary

wisdom: the other Apostles also are called brothers (John xx.17; comp. Ps. xxii.22), but he preeminently so, to whom the Lord at His departure had committed the sons of His mother (i.e., the members of the Church of Jerusalem). (Quoted in Lightfoot 1865, 260)

While this approach does not express Jerome's distinctive position, it does preserve the virginity of Mary. The quotation also shows the preeminent position of James according to Jerome. His preeminence places him ahead of the apostles and accounts for the Lord committing the Jerusalem church to his (James's) care at his (Jesus') departure.

There are four major weaknesses in Jerome's hypothesis. (1) It is a novelty. There is no tradition to which he appeals in support of his views. (2) The names Mary and Jacob (James) are amongst the most popular Jewish names of the time. The process of identifying the various references to James with a single person is driven by the need to explain away the brothers of Jesus. (3) Jerome himself vacillates in respect to the hypothesis he uses to defend the continuing virginity of Mary. This suggests that the continuing virginity of Mary was the issue for him and that the hypothesis that has become known by his name was just a means for its defense. He was content to drop it in favor of an alternative argument that would produce the same result, the perpetual virginity of Mary. (4) Attempts to harmonize Mark 15:40 and John 19:25 overlook the tendentious nature of the Johannine account in which the mother of Jesus and the Beloved Disciple are depicted as ideal disciples. It also presupposes (a) an unlikely punctuation for John 19:25 to enable the reading that the sister of the mother of Jesus was Mary of Clopas (b) who was also the mother of James and Joses and (c) the wife of Alphaeus. None of these identifications is likely.

THE HELVIDIAN VIEW

Jerome opposed the views of Helvidius, who was critical of the growing claims (in Rome) concerning the superiority of celibacy to the married state. In this debate Jerome used the virginity of Mary to support celibacy as the ideal state. So successful was Jerome in his campaign that Helvidius's writing on the subject did not survive. His views can be reconstructed through Jerome's critique of them. Even from this reconstruction it can be seen that Jerome ridiculed Helvidius without responding to the evidence and argument he put forward.

Helvidius argued that those described as brothers and sisters of Jesus were children of Joseph and Mary subsequent to the birth of Jesus. The language of Paul, the Gospels, and Acts is understood in its natural and straightforward sense. Brothers and sisters are exactly that. Well, almost exactly that. Matthew and Luke affirm that Mary was a virgin when she conceived her firstborn, Jesus. For those who followed this teaching, subsequent children born to

Joseph and Mary were half brothers and sisters of Jesus. Helvidius seems to have made five main points.

1. He argued that Matthew 1:18, 25 imply that, subsequent to the birth of Jesus, Joseph and Mary had other children. That Mary was found to be pregnant through the action of the Holy Spirit "*before*" they [Joseph and Mary] came together" was taken by Helvidius to mean that subsequently they came together. The assertion that Joseph did not "know" Mary "*until*" she bore a son" was taken to mean that he did come to "know her," that is, have sexual intercourse with her, subsequently (see *Against Helvidius* [*Adv. Helvidium de Perpetua Virginitate B. Mariae*] 3).
2. He appealed to Luke 2:7, which refers to Jesus as Mary's "firstborn son," arguing that it implied subsequent children (see *Against Helvidius* 9).
3. He listed the various passages in which the evangelists mention and sometimes name the brothers and sisters of Jesus (see *Against Helvidius* 11).
4. He appealed to older Western tradition (see *Against Helvidius* 17) in which the brothers and sisters of Jesus had been mentioned in a way consistent with his views and specified Tertullian (see his *Adv. Marc.* 4.19; *De carne Christi* 7; *De monog.* 8) and Victorinus of Pettau. The reference was apparently to his now lost commentary on Matthew which was referred to by both Origen (*Homilies on St. Luke*, preface) and Jerome (*Commentary on St. Matthew*, preface).
5. He argued that it was no dishonor that Mary was a real wife to Joseph since all the patriarchs had been married men and that child bearing was a participation in the divine creativity (*Against Helvidius* 18).

Jerome's response was to ridicule the literary deficiencies of Helvidius but without dealing adequately with his arguments. He attempted to nullify Helvidius's appeal to tradition by asserting that Tertullian was a schismatic and that Victorinus did not support Helvidius, while asserting that the majority of the Fathers accepted the perpetual virginity of Mary.

That Jerome conceded Tertullian to the opposition implies that Helvidius was correct in his claim of support. This tends to be confirmed, as Lightfoot notes:

> Though he [Tertullian] does not directly state it, his argument seems to imply that the Lord's brethren were His brothers in the same sense in which Mary was His mother (*adv. Marc.* iv.19, *de Carn. Christ.* 7). It is therefore highly probable that he held the Helvidian view. Such an admission from one who was so strenuous an advocate of asceticism is worthy of notice (Lightfoot 1865, 279).

The evidence of Victorinus cannot be settled because his works are lost and it is the word of Jerome against Helvidius. Jerome's appeal to tradition in this matter provides no grounds for any confidence in his word against that of Helvidius.

Jerome claimed the great weight of tradition in support of his own position against Helvidius. On the point of the perpetual virginity of Mary he could make use of all who adopted what has been called the *Epiphanian* position. He did this, but failed to note that they did not support his own distinctive position but one that he rejected. His appeal to Ignatius, Polycarp, Irenaeus, Justin, and many others was not relevant to *his own theory*. As Lightfoot has shown, in the case of Ignatius, Jerome has seriously misconstrued his meaning. Not only does Ignatius not support Jerome's theory, he nowhere maintains the perpetual virginity of Mary. Where he does refer to the virginity of Mary, which he does in a passage quoted several times by later writers (*Ephes.* 19), it is with reference to the *conception* of Jesus (see Lightfoot 1865, 278 n. 1). This careless use of sources to his own advantage gives no confidence in Jerome's appeal to others on this issue.

LIGHTFOOT'S ADVOCACY OF THE EPIPHANIAN VIEW

Nevertheless, Lightfoot advanced what he considered to be two strong arguments against the Helvidian view. First, Joseph disappears from the Gospel narrative from the early life of Jesus. He last appears when Jesus is twelve (Luke 2:43). Lightfoot concludes, "There can be little doubt therefore that he had died meanwhile" (1865, 270). This, he argued, is consistent with Joseph's advanced years at the time of his betrothal to Mary, providing support for the Epiphanian view. To make the point Lightfoot contrasts the way "Mary comes forward again and again." That Mary and the brothers are mentioned is true but the implied frequency in the Gospels is an exaggeration. At the same time, the mention of Joseph in Matthew 13:55 and Luke 4:22 does not suggest that these authors thought he was dead. But the reference to Jesus as the son of Mary in Mark 6:3 is strange and cannot be explained by the death of Joseph. Here Mark reports the reference (by those who heard Jesus in his hometown) to Jesus as the brother of James, Joses, Judas, and Simon in a way that implies Mary is their mother also. There is no mention of Joseph. Even if he were dead by the time Jesus completed his ministry, this need not imply he was elderly when betrothed to Mary. Average life expectancy for a man was about forty years. The average age of men buried at Qumran was thirty-six or thirty-seven years. If Joseph was twenty when Jesus was born he would have been fifty by the time Jesus commenced his ministry. Had he been dead by that time, it does not follow that he was already an old man when he was betrothed to Mary.

Lightfoot thinks he has struck a more telling blow against the Helvidian view when he notes that Jesus assigned his mother to the care of the Beloved Disciple (John 19:26–27). Lightfoot finds it inconceivable that Jesus would have done this had Mary four other sons of her own. He argues that even had they been unbelievers at the time this would not have overridden "the paramount duties of filial affection." Thus, when she "is consigned to the care of a stranger," he takes this to be conclusive evidence that those called brothers of Jesus were not actually children of Mary (1865, 272). In spite of the peculiar Johannine introduction of the Beloved Disciple and the mother of Jesus into the scene at the cross, Lightfoot does not question whether this theme can be treated as straightforwardly historical. Certainly scholars today are generally reticent to accept the historicity of this detail. This is the major reason for not allowing the weight Lightfoot assigns to this piece of Johannine evidence. The evidence of Mark 3:31–35 and John 2:4 suggests that Jesus may have weakened the importance of family ties in relation to the significance of the eschatological family in his movement. This weakens the force of Lightfoot's argument, and would do so even in the unlikely case that 19:26–27 turned out to be historical tradition.

Further, Lightfoot strangely appeals to Acts 1:14 to argue that, although Mary lived in the same city and joined in common worship with those described as the brothers of Jesus, she was "consigned to the care of a stranger." This is hardly a fair reading of Acts 1:14. Rather, Acts speaks of the disciples (Acts 1:13) being at prayer "with the women and Mary the mother of Jesus and his brothers." See also John 2:12 where it is said that Jesus "and his mother and brothers and disciples" went down to Capernaum. There, as in Acts 1:14, the mother of Jesus is linked directly with his brothers. In these texts Mary is described in relation to the brothers, with whom she is grouped. She is not grouped with the disciples or the Beloved Disciple, who of course, is not mentioned. If "Mary the mother of Jesus and his brothers" seems to be a strange way of speaking of the brothers in relation to Mary, we note that she and they are described in terms of their relationship to Jesus rather than each other. We may add to this that the brothers were known in the church in this way. On this see Mark 3:31; 6:3 and Paul's reference to James in Galatians 1:19. Only Lightfoot's determined introduction of John 19:26–27 into his reading of Acts 1:14 could lead him to the conclusion he adopts. Why did he not rather read John 19:26–27 in the light of Acts 1:14? This text implies the relatedness of the mother of Jesus to his brothers, her sons. It may suggest that John 19:26–27 should not be read as straightforward history.

BROTHERS OF JESUS

Irenaeus (*Adv. Haer.* 1.26.2), Origen (*Contr. Cels.* 2.1; *Princ.* 4.3.8), and other fathers including Epiphanius of Salamis (*Haer.* 30.16.7–9) draw attention to Jewish Christians referred to as *Ebionites* who rejected the virginal conception of Jesus. Thus, for them, the brothers and sisters of Jesus were fully that. The earliest traditions, which can be traced back to the middle of the first century (Paul and Mark), show no knowledge of the virginal conception of Jesus, let alone the continued virginity of Mary. From these sources we have no reason to think anything but that Jesus and his brothers and sisters were children of

Joseph and Mary. Because the evidence in support of this view from Paul and Mark is their *silence* about the virginal conception, we cannot be certain that they did not know or accept this position. All we can say is that they did not find any reason to write of it and nothing that they write implies that they believed in the virginal conception of Jesus. This is true also of the later evidence of John, for whom there is no reason to think that "incarnation" (1:14) implies virginal conception.

JAMES AND JESUS

Given that those known as brothers were children of Mary and Joseph, how are we to think of them, especially James, in relation to Jesus? The critical reader needs to cope with sources, none of which is written from the perspective of James. The epistle of James may be an exception, but even James has been subjected to an interpretative tradition that has dislocated it from its Jewish context, identifying it as a General (Catholic) Epistle.

The critical reader also needs to be aware of a tradition of reading the New Testament that is more negative in relation to James than the documents demand. Three common assumptions have guided the way references to James have been understood. First, James and the brothers are thought to have been unbelievers and opponents of Jesus during his ministry. Second, the evidence of 1 Corinthians 15:7 is taken as a reference to the "conversion" of James from opposition to believer. Third, James's leadership of the Jerusalem church is understood to have been a result of a transition from the leadership of Peter, caused by his need to escape from Jerusalem (Acts 12:17). If we suspend judgment on these traditional approaches to reading the evidence, quite a different view of James emerges. James emerges as the leading figure in the Jerusalem church. This perception of James is strengthened by paying attention to traditions about James outside the New Testament.

James emerges as the first leader of the Jerusalem church, the successor of his brother, Jesus. In this role he was effectively "his brother's keeper." From this perspective, tradition coming from James can be seen as a guide to the understanding of the mission and achievement of Jesus. Before following this line we need to address the common assumptions that distance James from Jesus during Jesus' ministry.

JAMES AS AN UNBELIEVER?

Was James an unbeliever during Jesus' ministry? Evidence for this view is based largely on Mark and John. In Mark 6:3 the people of Jesus' hometown marvel at Jesus' wisdom and works in the light of what they know of him as the carpenter, the son of Mary and brother of James, Joses, Jude, and Simon and of sisters. Indeed they ask, "and are not his sisters here with us?" By its form the question implies that the sisters [but not Mary and the brothers!] were present in the synagogue at the time. The incident described in Mark 6:1–6 indicates that the people of Jesus' hometown were scandalized by him (6:4) and he marveled at their unbelief (6:6). For this reason the incident has been described as "The rejection of Jesus at Nazareth." But the question is, does Mark imply that the family was implicated in the rejection? It is true that it is implied that the sisters of Jesus were present at the time. But nothing is said of the action of any member of the family of Jesus in this rejection. Indeed the role of the family in this incident is to confirm that his known background makes acceptance of his new status difficult for the people of his hometown. What they know of his past overrides what they now find in him and leads to their rejection of this new Jesus.

More significant is the treatment of the family in Mark 3:20–35. In recent commentaries this sequence is understood to begin when Jesus returns "home" and encounters the crush of a crowd that makes it impossible for Jesus and the disciples even to take a meal. News of this causes the family to set out to restrain Jesus (3:21 NRSV, but see RSV) and the mother and brothers of Jesus arrive (3:31). But is this reading justifiable and the most natural reading of what Mark has written?

First, the reference to "his family" in 3:21 translates a much more general expression (*hoi par autou*) which has a wide range of possibilities and can just as easily mean "his friends" (RSV) or "associates" as "his family" (NRSV). Then why has the recent trend of interpretations moved to read this as "his family"? Many commentators appeal to the characteristic Markan sandwich structure formed by 3:20–21 and 3:31–35. In Mark 3:20–21 the family sets out to restrain Jesus, arriving only at 3:31. By breaking the narrative concerning the family with 3:22–30, the hostility of the scribes from Jerusalem has a bearing on the way the actions of the family are understood. For another example of the Markan sandwich structure compare the way the incident of the woman with the issue of blood interrupts the story of the healing of Jairus's daughter (5:21–43).

Recognition of a Markan characteristic suggests that, even on this reading, we are dealing with a Markan construction rather than historical tradition. This conclusion is supported by the recognition that 3:20–21 is found only in Mark and these verses appear to be a Markan composition characterised by Markan vocabulary. We may doubt the historicity of the incident. Thus, even on this reading, it is dangerous to conclude that the family of Jesus was hostile to him during his ministry. But there are also grounds for thinking that this reading is wrong.

Scholars adopting this position treat 3:20–35 as a unit. They do not observe that 3:13 commences a unit that is not complete until 6:13. In 3:13–19 Jesus appointed the twelve *to be with him* and *to send them out* (3:14). But it is only in

6:7–13 that he actually sends them out. Matthew (10:1–15) has brought together, into a single incident, Jesus' choosing of the twelve and his sending them out on the mission. In Matthew this incident becomes the basis of Jesus' great second discourse on mission (the Sermon on the Mount being the first), ending as it does with the formula found in 11:1. See the endings of the other four discourses in 7:28–29; 13:53; 19:1; 26:1. The contrast with Matthew makes clearer that, in Mark, the disciples are chosen to be with Jesus (in 3:13–19) until they are sent out in 6:7–13. Meanwhile, it is implied, they are with Jesus. But on the reading we are considering, the disciples are not mentioned at all in 3:20–35! This implies a strange narrative decision by Mark immediately after Jesus has chosen the disciples to be with him.

An alternative is to return to an older reading of *hoi par autou* (in 3:21) understanding it to mean "his friends" (RSV) or "his associates," that is, his disciples. Indeed, this seems to be the most natural reading. Given that those described by this phrase are not identified, it is most natural to think it refers to the group which has just been chosen to be with Jesus (3:13–19). Because the phrase does not identify any specific group it seems unreasonable to expect the reader to recognize a reference to the family, which has not been mentioned at all in Mark to this point.

But what are the implications for Mark's understanding of the disciples? If we understand the phrase to refer to them, it is they who go out to *restrain* Jesus. This is the force of the term used of their intended action. But why do the disciples act in such a negative way toward Jesus? According to 3:21 it is when the disciples *heard* that they went out to restrain Jesus. The second half of 3:21 could report what the disciples were saying or, on the other hand, it is the only possible report of what they heard. The latter seems more likely. It is characteristic of Mark (about 50 times) to provide the explanation, after the narration of the event, in a clause introduced by *gar*. See here especially 5:7–8; 11:13; 14:1–2; 16:4, 8. When the disciples heard, they went out to restrain Jesus "for they (the crowd) were saying, 'He is beside himself.'" This reading is less negative of the disciples than one that attributes the saying to them, but only a little less so. It attributes to them the intent to protect Jesus but in a way that takes matters out of Jesus' hands. Thus it is a negative view of the disciples. Is this likely of Mark?

The choosing and appointment of the twelve is a high point in the story of the disciples in Mark. Yet this account (3:13–19) concludes with the reference to "Judas Iscariot, who betrayed him" (3:19). This reference to Judas prepares the way for the account of the first failure of the disciples, immediately after their appointment. This pattern continues to be played out in Mark. Peter, having confessed that Jesus is the Christ, immediately becomes the mouthpiece of Satan (8:29–30, 33 and see also 9:19, 34; 10:37; 14:27–31; 16:7–8). Mark's critical attitude toward the twelve is widely recognized.

What then are we to make of Jesus' treatment of his mother and brothers in 3:31–35? First, there is nothing in this narrative that suggests any hostility on the part of the family. They wait patiently outside the house, sending a message to Jesus who is inside the house. The incident provides Jesus with the opportunity of affirming that his [true?] family is constituted by those who do the will of God and identifies this group with those gathered around him (3:34–35). The effect of this narrative is to distance Jesus from the ties of his natural family in the interest of asserting the ties with his followers. This move was essential for the success in any movement that sought to go beyond the boundaries of the "clan" and become a universal movement. The story of 3:31–35 makes no suggestion of the opposition of the family to Jesus. It is only by linking this incident with an identification of the family in 3:20–21 that this can be done. Even when this is done the negative evaluation seems to be restricted to the brothers. Scholars generally do not include the mother of Jesus in their negative evaluation, though she is present in 3:31–35. But as we have seen, this reading of 3:20–21 is improbable. Consequently the negative conclusions drawn concerning the family from this passage are ill founded.

More explicit in its indication of opposition to Jesus is the reference to the brothers of Jesus in John 7:3–5. This text is taken to mean that, at this stage, Jesus' brothers did not believe in him. First, we need to notice that all of the references to the family (the mother and brothers of Jesus) in John are peculiar to John and form part of John's special point of view (see also 2:1–11, 12; 19:26–27). Second, the statement in 7:5 is somewhat more nuanced than a straight indication of the unbelief of the brothers. There is no suggestion that the brothers did not accept that Jesus performed signs. Indeed, when the brothers urge Jesus to go to Jerusalem it is "so that your disciples may see your *works* which you do." Here the brothers use the more positive term *works* which, in John, also covers the signs but frequently draws attention to Jesus' relation to the Father (see 5:17, 36). Further, the use of the imperfect tense with *oude* suggests that "not even his brothers were believing in him." This lacks the definitive sense of unbelief that can be communicated with the aorist tense. It also implies that the suggestion of the brothers that Jesus go to Judea so that his disciples (there?) may see the works he does should not be understood in a cynical sense (thus also C. K. Barrett 1978, 312).

There is no suggestion that the brothers denied that Jesus performed impressive works. Rather, the problem seems to be that they failed to see the connection between Jesus' works and the Johannine understanding of his relation to the Father. They urged Jesus to perform his works openly in Judea and thus to establish his position on the basis of them. But this position falls under the critique of 4:48, "Unless you see signs and wonders you will not believe." Nevertheless there is a sense in which belief is on the basis of the works. But here a double possibility seems to be recognized. The works seem to offer the possibility of a first level of belief. Those who are unable to believe Jesus' self-witness to his relation to the Father are exhorted to believe because of the works themselves (14:10–11). As part of the farewell discourses this is addressed to the disciples! Belief because of the works is a first level of belief and the disciples do not seem to have progressed beyond that. In 10:37–38 Jesus addresses the Jews, challenging them to see in his works the evidence of his relation to the Father (see also 5:17 and 10:30–36).

Recognizing that John allows for at least two levels of belief opens a number of possibilities for the interpretation of John 7:5. The level of belief implied in relation to the disciples in 14:10–11 has already been noted. A more dramatic case occurs in 16:29–31. There the disciples affirm that they believe Jesus has come from God. In response Jesus says, "Do you now believe? Behold the hour comes and has come when you will be scattered each one to his own place." According to Jesus, even the belief of the disciples is put in question by the events about to be narrated. Even they are not believers yet in the full Johannine sense. And yet, although their belief is put in question by the confronting accusation, "Do you now believe?" and the contrary evidence that follows, no one would suggest that the disciples were in no sense believers. This seems to be true of Jesus' brothers. Their belief in Jesus was based on the works he performed but did not (according to John) penetrate the mystery of his relation to God. Nevertheless the narrator says incredulously of them, "not even his brothers were believing in him." Yet readers may point to Jesus' rather negative response to his brothers (7:6–9).

Nevertheless, *five* factors common to this story and the story of the Cana wedding (2:1–11) need to be taken into account. (1) Both concern the family of Jesus, his mother in 2:1–11 and his brothers in 7:3–9. (2) In each story the family makes an implied or explicit request. (3) In each case Jesus apparently rejects the request. (4) The words with which Jesus "turns down" the request bear a close resemblance in each case. In the first, "Woman, what is there between you and me, *my time has not yet come*"; in the second, "*my time is not yet but your time is always ready . . . my time is not yet fulfilled.*" (5) In each case Jesus actually complies with the request. He dealt with the lack of wine and he did go up to Jerusalem on the Feast, even if secretly and not openly as his brothers had requested (7:4, 10). All of this suggests that the brothers were believers but their belief sought a different goal for Jesus than the one to which he was committed, according to John.

Following the first sign at Cana, Jesus "went down to Capernaum and his mother and his brothers and his disciples" (2:12). This is the first mention of his brothers in John. Neither they, nor Jesus' mother are named in this Gospel. The order in which this grouping is mentioned is interesting (compare the order in John 2:1–2, the mother of Jesus, Jesus, and his disciples). The order of Jesus, his mother, his brothers, and his disciples is somewhat surprising. It certainly emphasizes the role of the family among the followers of Jesus. The same point is made by the narrative of John 7:1–10. There it is clear that Jesus' brothers are with him, traveling in his company. All of this confirms that they were followers even if they had not grasped Jesus' own vision of his mission. But as we have seen, the same point is made by Jesus of his disciples. Jesus' brothers are no less believers than the disciples were at the same time. Acts

1:14 continues to support this view by describing "the twelve" at prayer together "with women and Mary the mother of Jesus and his brothers." Again the mother of Jesus is grouped clearly with his brothers and their place amongst the followers of Jesus is stated as a matter of course with no suggestion that this constituted a remarkable change.

THE CONVERSION OF JAMES?

Given that Paul nowhere mentions another James other than the brother of the Lord (Gal. 1:19), it is reasonable to take 1 Corinthians 15:7 as a reference to him. Indeed there is no alternative tradition of interpretation (see Eusebius, *H.E.* 1.12.4–5). Commentators commonly take this reference as an indication of the conversion of James. Thus it is argued that James was an unbeliever until the risen Jesus appeared to him. This event turned unbelieving James into a believer. This reading can only be adopted on the basis of a prior knowledge of James's unbelief. If, as we have argued, the Gospels provide no evidence, nothing in 1 Corinthians 15:1–11 supports this view. Indeed, a careful reading of 1 Corinthians is actually opposed to this view. Rather, James stands in the sequence begun with Cephas in 15:5–7. It is Paul who stands apart from that sequence (15:8–11). He is the last of those to whom the risen Jesus appeared. He describes himself "as one untimely born" because he was a persecutor. The appearance to Paul is presented as the basis of what we may describe as a "conversion" from persecutor (and certainly unbeliever) to apostle. But James is in the regular sequence of appearances, to Cephas and the twelve, to more than five hundred brethren, then to James and all the apostles. Nothing suggests that any of these were converted by the appearance. The contrast of all of these stands out starkly in relation to Paul. Thus, if James is to be considered a convert at this time, then so are Cephas and the twelve, the more than five hundred, and all the apostles. But if we call that conversion, we need to note a much stronger form of conversion in relation to Paul.

As with Cephas and the twelve, it seems better to speak of a deepening of belief with James, brought about by the appearance of the risen Jesus to him reported by Paul. This view is what we find in the evidence outside the New Testament, in evidence reported by Clement of Alexandria, the *Gospel of Thomas*, and the *Gospel of the Hebrews*.

The *Gospel of the Hebrews* was known to Origen and a fragment of it was preserved by Jerome. It records what Jesus did after the resurrection.

> And when the Lord had given the linen cloth to the servant of the priest, he went to James and appeared to him. For James had sworn that he would not eat bread from the hour in which he had drunk the cup of the Lord until he should see him risen from among them that sleep. And shortly thereafter the Lord said: Bring a table and bread!

> And immediately it is added: He took bread, blessed it and brake it and
> gave it to James the Just and said to him: My brother, eat thy bread,
> for the Son of man is risen from among them that sleep. (Wilson 1965,
> 1:165)

There is no doubt that this is a reference to James the brother of Jesus, addressed by Jesus, only here and in the fourth-century Nag Hammadi *Second Apocalypse of James* (50:13), as "My brother." What makes this clearly a reference to the brother of Jesus is that he is also called "James the Just." This is a title reserved for the brother of Jesus.

In this quotation not only is James presented as the first believing witness to the risen Jesus, he is also portrayed as one who was present at the Last Supper when "he had drunk the cup of the Lord." From this perspective, the giving of the linen cloth to the servant of the priest does not count as an appearance. It is simply part of the resurrection process. The narrative attributes no significance for the servant of the priest in this action but is narrated, apparently, for the sake of the reader. The first action of the risen Jesus which has significance for the person for whom it is performed is the action in relation to James. Thus it is clear in this tradition that James was among the followers of Jesus. The importance of the portrayal of him as the first believing witness to the risen Jesus now needs further attention.

Against this background the record of testimonies to the risen Jesus in 1 Corinthians 15:5–11 makes interesting reading. There is little doubt that Paul took over traditional material in 15:5–7 to which he added his own testimony in 15:8–11. From Paul's perspective verses 5–7 stand together over against his own "Last of all . . ." Yet, at the same time, there is reason to think that there is some tension within the tradition within 15:5–7. Interestingly 15:5 does not assert "*first* he appeared to Cephas, then to the twelve" just as 15:7 does not assert "*first* he appeared to James and then to all the apostles." Rather 15:5 and 7 look like rival appearance claims, 15:5 giving priority to "the twelve" with Peter (Cephas) as leader and 15:7 broadening the base of witness to "all of the Apostles" with James as leader. The form of 15:5 and 15:7 suggests that each of them may represent a tradition expressing some rivalry between the supporters of Cephas and James. For whatever reason Paul adopts an arrangement of the order of resurrection appearances giving priority to Cephas. It may be because he perceived in him a position more sympathetic to his own mission.

The first conclusion to draw from this evidence is that it provides no more support for the view that James underwent a radical conversion through his experience of a resurrection appearance than it does for Cephas. Obviously the resurrection appearances had a transforming affect on all who experienced them. The contrast is to be found between, on the one hand, those who were already followers of Jesus, such as "the twelve" and "all of the apostles," groups that included Cephas and James and, on the other hand, Paul who had been a persecutor. Yet there is clearly tension over the question of to whom the risen Jesus first appeared. The reason for this is because the primacy of appearance became the ground for the claim of authority within the Jerusalem church.

JAMES AS FOUNDATIONAL LEADER

Although there is no tradition concerning Peter's leadership *of* the Jerusalem church—such traditions as there are concern Rome—a tradition of reading Acts has assumed his leadership of that church from the beginning. Acts is not explicit about the leadership of the Jerusalem church and in this the reading tradition has its opportunity. There is no doubt that Peter has a leadership role *in* the Jerusalem church. It is less than clear that he was ever the leader *of* the Jerusalem church. The assumption that he was seems to be grounded in a number of characterizations, none of which relates directly to *this* leadership question. First, the Gospels portray Peter as spokesperson among the twelve. A case can certainly be made for Peter's leadership of "the twelve" In the lists of "the twelve" Peter is invariably named first! Even if this were to be described in terms of leadership of "the twelve," it does not translate easily into leadership of the Jerusalem church.

Then Acts certainly does portray Peter in a leadership role. On the day of Pentecost it was Peter who addressed the multitude of pilgrims gathered in Jerusalem. In what follows in Acts, Peter is portrayed as the leader in mission to those who were not believers. Paul's account in Galatians 2:1–10 gives support to this view of Peter's leadership. In 2:7–8 Paul depicts Peter as the one entrusted with the gospel of circumcision and the mission to the circumcised just as he (Paul) had been entrusted with the circumcision-free gospel to the nations. This parallel description of the missions of Peter and Paul suggests that neither of them was the leader of a single church. Rather, each of them was leader of one of the two missions.

Against this background we may read Acts 12:17. It is normally taken to mean that, after Peter's arrest by Herod (12:1–3), he was miraculously released from prison but forced to flee from Jerusalem. Before leaving he came to the house of the mother of John Mark, where the church used to gather. There he passed on a message, "Tell this [news of his release and forced departure] to James and the brethren." How is this message to be understood? It is commonly understood as a cryptic message from Peter, the leader, to James, indicating that James must take over the leadership in the absence of Peter. This is less than clearly the intended meaning. More likely we should understand Peter's message in the context of his report back to James, the leader of the Jerusalem church. Nothing is more natural than that Peter should report to the leader.

If we allow that Peter's leadership was interrupted by his forced departure from Jerusalem, we then need to face the general recognition of James's leadership of the Jerusalem assembly (Acts 15), although Peter was again present in Jerusalem. While Peter plays *a leading role*, it is James who sums up (15:13–21) and gives his *judgment* (*ego krino*, 15:19) which was accepted by the gathering of apostles and elders with the whole church (15:22). Thus it is James who directs the outcome of this assembly. Acts records no debate concerning his judgment and there is no debate among contemporary scholarship concerning the leadership of James at this point. Given that Peter is present, had his leadership been interrupted by his enforced departure, we might have expected the reassertion of his leadership at this crucial gathering in Jerusalem. Instead James clearly and confidently asserts his authority.

In Paul's account of this meeting in Galatians 2:1–10 he names, as the reputed pillars of the Jerusalem church, James, Cephas and John, in that order. That this is James the brother of the Lord is implied by Paul's identification of him already in 1:19. This reference is clear and lies close, just a few verses before the next reference to James in 2:9. No other James has been mentioned by Paul, so that we are right to suppose that this too is a reference to the brother of the Lord.

Named as the first of the supposed pillars in the context of the dispute over the rules applied to mission is a clear indication of the leadership of James among the pillars. This is confirmed by Peter's (Cephas's) response to the messengers from James. He, and other Jewish believers in Antioch (including Barnabas), withdrew from table fellowship with Gentile believers as a consequence of James's intervention. This raises significant questions about what was decided in Jerusalem. Certainly it suggests that James did not believe that there was an equality between the two missions which allowed total freedom of full relationship between Jewish and Gentile believers. From this perspective it appears that, although James acknowledged a mission to the Gentiles that did not involve full law observance, he did not regard that mission to be on equal terms to the Jerusalem mission and consequently full fellowship between the two missions was not possible. That Paul was less than comfortable with the leadership of James is apparent by the way he refers to "the supposed pillars" (see 2:6, 9) putting in question their leading role even when he narrates a situation where he had to take account of their authority.

James's leadership of the Jerusalem church continues to be portrayed in the context of Paul's final visit to Jerusalem (see Acts 21:17–26). Thus we are told that on his arrival "Paul went in to James; and all the elders were present." In response to Paul's account of his mission to the Gentiles, they stress the size of the Jerusalem church and its law-observant character (21:20).

The role of James as leader of the Jerusalem church is uniformly found in early tradition. It is attested in the fourth-century Coptic Nag Hammadi *Gospel of Thomas*, which some scholars date very early. Because three Greek fragments of the Gospel, which cannot be later than 200 C.E., were found in Oxyrhynchus, we can safely say it is not later than the middle of the second century. Some scholars argue that it is somewhat earlier, largely because it is a sayings Gospel comparable to Q, which was used by Matthew and Luke and is thus quite early (see John Dominic Crossan 1993, among others). It is called the *Gospel of Thomas* because the risen Jesus gave him the task of writing down his secret sayings. In spite of this, the *Gospel of Thomas* names James as leader.

> The disciples said to Jesus, "We know that you will depart from us. Who will be our leader?" Jesus said to them, "Wherever you are, you are to go to James the righteous [Just], for whose sake heaven and earth came into being."

Here the appointment of James is directly by Jesus' instruction to his disciples and it assumes their acceptance of his judgment. Indeed, this is implied by their initiative in asking Jesus about the question of succession. After you, who is to be our leader?

A similar tradition is found in a quotation from Clement of Alexandria preserved by Eusebius in *H.E.* 2.1.2–5.

> Then there is James, who was called the Lord's brother, for he too was named Joseph's son, and Joseph Christ's father, though in fact the virgin was his betrothed, and before they came together . . . This James, whom the people of old called the Just because of his outstanding virtue, was the first, as the record tells us, to be elected to the episcopal throne of the Jerusalem church.

Clement, in his *Outlines (Hypotyposes)* book six, puts it thus:

> After the ascension of the saviour, Peter, James, and John did not claim preeminence because the saviour had specially honoured them, but chose James the Just as bishop of Jerusalem.

In book seven of the same work the writer makes this further statement about him:

> James the Just, John, and Peter were entrusted by the Lord after his resurrection with the higher knowledge. They imparted it to the other apostles, and the other apostles to the Seventy, one of whom was Barnabas. There were two Jameses, one the Just, who was thrown down from the parapet and beaten to death with a fuller's club, the other the James who was beheaded.

James the Just is also mentioned by Paul when he writes:

> Of the other apostles I saw no one except James the brother of the Lord.

Here both Eusebius and Clement, in the passages quoted, confirm that James the brother of the Lord was known as James the Just. When Eusebius says he was called this by "the people of old" he may have had Clement in mind. It is unlikely that he restricts his reference to him because he is soon to quote from Hegesippus's account of the martyrdom of James (*H.E.* 2.23.4–18). There Hegesippus reports:

> Control of the church passed together with the apostles, to the brother of the Lord James, whom every one from the Lord's time till our own has named the Just, for there were many Jameses . . . Because of his unsurpassable righteousness he was called the Just and *Oblias*— in Greek "Bulwark of the people and righteousness"—fulfilling the declarations of the prophets regarding him.

Thus it seems that reference to "the people of old" includes Hegesippus and may accept his claim that the title was used of him from the Lord's time, even though it is not used of him in any New Testament writing.

Just how early was Hegesippus and what was his provenance? A straight-forward reading of Eusebius's introduction to Hegesippus's account of the martyrdom of James places him in the first century.

> But the most detailed account of him [James] is given by Hegesippus, who belonged to the first generation after the apostles. (*H.E.* 2.23.3)

He argues that Hegesippus was a Jewish Christian on the basis that he names Jewish sects, draws on the *Gospel of the Hebrews*, on the Syriac Gospel, and on works in Aramaic/Hebrew as well as Jewish oral tradition (*H.E.* 4.22.8). A crit-ical reading of the evidence concerning Hegesippus puts in question any rela-tionship to Palestine and suggests a date in the second half of the second century for his work.

The tradition of the leadership of James in the Jerusalem church is found in diverse expressions. The *Gospel of the Hebrews* and 1 Cor. 15:7 suggest that James's leadership was based on the priority of the appearance of Jesus to him. The *Gospel of Thomas* makes his leadership dependent on the direction of Jesus to the disciples. Clement of Alexandria makes James's leadership dependent on his choice by Peter, James, and John, while Eusebius speaks of appointment by the apostles (*H.E.* 2.23.1), from the savior and the apostles (*H.E.* 7.19.1), and of appointment to the throne of Jerusalem (*H.E.* 3.5.2–3). There is a ten-dency, in the summaries, to add the apostles to the formula stating that James received his leadership directly from "the savior."

Another tradition transmitted by Clement made James the Just, Cephas, and John the recipients of secret knowledge. This tradition of secret teaching to James is known also in the fourth-century Coptic Nag Hammadi *Apocryphon of James*. The tradition of secret teaching in relation to James reveals the asso-ciation of James tradition with Gnosticism. See also the *Gospel of Thomas*, which claims to transmit the secret sayings of the living Jesus which Thomas wrote down. It is probably in response to this that the tradition emerges linking James firmly with the apostles. Nevertheless this tradition is unanimous that James was the first leader of the Jerusalem church, and this is emphasized by the many references to the throne of James.

JAMES AS LEADER AND PETER AS MISSIONARY

The accounts in Acts and Galatians 2:1–10, 11–14 support the view that James remained located in Jerusalem providing leadership for the Jerusalem church while Peter and Paul were occupied in the leadership of the two missions. Just what roles the remainder of "the twelve" played in mission receives little attention in Acts or the rest of the New Testament. Other accounts of their exploits are legendary, intent on filling gaps left by the New Testament writings. The impression built up by Acts 15 and 21 is of James as the strategic leader of the Jerusalem church, located in Jerusalem and concerned with the mission to the Jewish people from the heart of the nation's "capital."

Just how the church's mission came to be centered in Jerusalem is unclear. According to Matthew and Mark, Jesus directed the twelve back into Galilee, promising to meet them there, and according to Matthew this is what happened (28:7, 10, 16–20, and cf. 26:32). In Matthew, the angel who announces the resurrection to the women and sends the message to the disciples ("Then go quickly and tell his disciples that he has risen from the dead, and behold, he is going before you to Galilee: there you will see him"; cf. 26:32) concludes by saying, "Lo, I have told you" (28:7). They run immediately to tell the disciples but were met on the way by Jesus, who repeats the message, "Go and tell my brethren to go to Galilee, and there they will see me" (28:10). While there is no report of the women telling the disciples, Matthew continues, "Now the eleven disciples went to Galilee, to the mountain to which Jesus had directed them. And when they saw him they worshiped him . . ." (28:16–17). This differs considerably from the Markan account. In Mark the message is given only once and by the angel—there is no resurrection appearance in Mark—concluding, "as he told you," referring back to 14:28. Not only is there no account of the women telling the disciples, Mark says "they said nothing to anyone, for they were afraid." Thus there is no account of Jesus meeting with the disciples in Galilee, or anywhere else. Mark's story ends leaving open the question of what happens.

Both Luke and John place the resurrection appearances in Jerusalem and its environs, although John 21 also adds an appearance by the sea of Galilee. Neither Luke nor John makes any reference to Jesus' warning and promise (Mark 14:28; Matt. 26:32), nor does either of them mention the message directing the disciples into Galilee. Thus there is a Jerusalem orientation in both of these Gospels, and Luke, in particular, makes Jerusalem the center for the mission (Luke 24:47; Acts 1:4, 8). Jerusalem centrism is evident throughout Acts. Thus even as the mission moves out from the center to the ends of the earth there continues to be a process of reporting back to Jerusalem, where James continues to be the leading figure. The Acts account of the "Jerusalem decree," which, according to Acts, was probably composed by James, provides a picture of James as one who wields authority not only in Jerusalem but also to the distant reaches of the church's mission.

This general picture is supported by the fragmentary glance provided by some of the letters of Paul. Galatians 1:19 reveals James as a figure too important to be overlooked by Paul in his first visit to Jerusalem following his conversion. More important is the reference to him as the first of the three pillars of the Jerusalem church who seem to be widely recognized as pillars beyond the scope of Jerusalem (Gal. 2:1–10). This is borne out by the incident at Antioch narrated in Galatians 2:11–14. The arrival of messengers from James was enough to cause a change of policy and practice concerning relations with Gentile believers. Here Paul specifically mentions Cephas and Barnabas bending to the will of James, exerted at a distance through messengers. But it was not only Cephas and Barnabas who submitted to James's ruling. Paul indicates that all of the Jewish believers (himself excepted) bowed to James's will. Thus, while Galatians 2:1–10 describes James in Jerusalem while Peter and Paul undertake the mission to the Jews and the mission to the nations, neither of them was free from the overarching authority of James.

THE PSEUDO-CLEMENTINES

While the Pseudo-Clementines contain much legendary material, they are in accord with this perspective. In their completed form these writings are not earlier than the late fourth century. They consist of two main parts, the *Homilies* and the *Recognitions*. The *Homilies* (including two epistles: one ostensibly by Peter [*Epistula Petri*] and the other by Clement, along with instructions concerning the right use of the book entitled the *Contestatio*) are preserved in two Greek codices. The Greek of the *Recognitions* has not survived but the work was preserved in the Latin translation of Rufinus, a contemporary of Jerome. The works were soon translated into Syriac, and a manuscript from Edessa dated to the year 411 C.E. provides evidence of texts from both works.

The *Homilies* and the *Recognitions* overlap in such a way as to throw light on the composition history of the finished work. Systematic study reveals that first one and then the other seems to preserve the more original form of the tradition, suggesting the use of a common source. Georg Strecker identified this as a composite source which was gnostic, Jewish-Christian in character and located it in Syria around 200 C.E. He identifies two underlying traditions as the *Preaching of Peter* (*Kerygmata Petrou*) and the *Ascents of James* (*Ascents*). The latter was a source underlying *Recognitions* 1.33–71 which he dated in the second half of the second century. He distinguished it from a work by this name (*Ascents*), referred to by Epiphanius. The two works have different understandings of "ascents." In *Ascents*, James ascends the Temple steps while Epiphanius refers to the ascent in the steps of instruction. Strecker (1981, 137–254) agrees that the two documents are related but not identical and postulates a common archetype and suggests that the source of *Recognitions* 1.33–71 was written in Pella between 150 and 200 C.E. by the Jewish Christian community that saw itself as the successor to the Jerusalem church. See also R. E. Van Voorst (1989). Some relationship is postulated with the Jewish Christian community at Pella in Transjordan, where the veneration of James was part of a distinctive ethos. Van Voorst (1989, 180) supports this consensus view on the date and place of origin of the *Ascents*, though it is challenged by S. K. Brown (1972).

The Pseudo-Clementines take their name from Clement of Rome, in whose name they are written and whose story they purport to tell. Clement was bishop of Rome at the end of the first century. According to Tertullian, Clement was appointed by Peter, but Eusebius (*H.E.* 3.4.8; 3.15; 3.21; 3.34; 5.6) makes Clement the third bishop after Peter (and Paul) following Linus and Anencletus, dating his death in the third year of Trajan's reign so that his episcopacy can be dated from 92 to 101 C.E.

According to this story, Clement belonged to an aristocratic family in Rome which underwent great misfortunes when the mother of the family, directed by a vision, secretly left the city with Clement's two older twin brothers. When they did not return, the father went in search of them. Eventually Clement also left Rome and in his travels met Peter. He joined his company as a believer, traveling with him on his missionary journeys to cities of coastal Syria. This narrative provides the context for the preaching of Peter, which the *Homilies* contain, and the setting for Peter's confrontation with Simon Magus known to us in Acts 8:9–24. The figure of Simon becomes far more sinister in the Pseudo-Clementines because Paul stands barely cloaked behind him and Peter's confrontation with and triumph over Simon is to be seen as his victory over Paul. Much of this material appears to have been drawn from the *Kerygmata Petrou*.

ASCENTS OF JAMES
AND THE MARTYRDOM TRADITION

The *Ascents of James* (*Ascents*) deals with James's ascent of the steps of the Temple (*Recognitions* 1.66–71) to continue a public disputation over the messiahship of Jesus. This dispute had been initiated with Jewish opponents by Peter and Clement. It is from James's ascent of the Temple steps that the hypothetical source takes its name. It should be remembered that although we speak of this section as if it were the source, we are actually dealing with *Recognitions* 1 on the assumption that it is based on an earlier source.

In the first instance the chief of the opponents is named Caiaphas (1.68).

But, at the point where James had persuaded the multitude to accept baptism, Clement reports that "one of our enemies, entering the Temple," intervened and, although James was able to refute him, he created a tumult and there was great bloodshed through the ensuing violence. The "enemy" threw James down from the top of the steps and left him for dead. From there James was rescued by his friends and supporters (1.70). The account of the throwing down of James from the Temple steps appears to have some relation to the account of the martyrdom of James in Hegesippus. There are major differences. In *Recognitions* (*Ascents*) the top of the Temple steps replaces the pinnacle of the Temple in Hegesippus; Saul is introduced into the narrative in *Recognitions*; James does not die in *Recognitions*.

The "enemy" who threw James down is identified as Saul in a marginal note in one of the manuscripts and this identification is confirmed by 1.71. There we are told that Gamaliel, who has already been identified as a secret believer and secret supporter among the opponents (1.65, 67), brought news that the "enemy" had received a commission from Caiaphas to go to Damascus pursuing believers because it was thought that Peter had fled to this city. There is no doubt that this is a reference to Saul of Tarsus in Acts 9:1–2. There is no hint of his conversion. The motif of the secret supporter among the opponents of James is also found in the *Second Apocalypse of James*, though there the supporter is a priest named Mareim.

KERYGMATA PETROU AND THE *EPISTULA PETRI* ON PETER, PAUL, AND JAMES

The *Kerygmata Petrou* was introduced by the *Epistula Petri*, in which we learn that Moses had made known the true teaching which Jesus had confirmed (*Ep. P.* 2.2, 5). This, the "lawful proclamation" of Peter, is opposed to the "lawless doctrine" of the "hostile man" (*Ep. P.* 2.3). The *Kerygmata Petrou* teaches the reincarnation of the true prophet first in Adam (*Recognitions* 1.47), also in the lawgiver Moses (*Homilies* 2.52.3), and in Jesus (*Homilies* 3.17–19 and *Ep. P.* 2.5). The opposition between true and false prophecy is manifest in the pairs (*syzygy*) where the false, feminine form is first (Eve is the first example) followed by the true and masculine form (Adam is the first example). The last pair in the series of *syzygy* is Paul (the feminine) antagonist of Peter (*Homilies* 2.17.3). Here the portrayal of Simon Magus is a veiled reference to Paul and it is said that the false prophet to the Gentiles appears before the true (Peter). Peter's lawful proclamation is opposed to Paul (*Homilies* 2.15–17; 11.35.3–6 = *Recognitions* 4.34.5–4.35.2; *Hom.* 17.13–19). The conflict at Antioch between Paul and Peter (Gal. 2:11ff.) is in view in *Homilies* 17.19. There is a polemic against visions such as Paul's (Acts 9; Gal. 2:2; 1 Cor. 15:8; 2 Cor. 12:1ff.) which are in contrast to the commission of Peter by Jesus (Matt. 16:17; *Homilies* 17.18f.). It is argued that Paul cannot have been given the teaching of Jesus in a vision because he does not agree with the teaching of Peter and James. Nor can Paul be an apostle, because he is not one of the twelve (*Recognitions* 4.35). His lawless gospel is false doctrine which cannot be approved by James (*Homilies* 11.35.4–6; *Ep. P.* 2.3f.). Here the motif of the primacy of James has an anti-Pauline intent. It is Peter who takes the true law-based gospel to the Gentiles. Thus we have confirming evidence of the role of James in the law-based mission to the circumcision/Jews which is perhaps expressed in the "M" tradition in Matthew, and Peter as the proponent of the circumcision, law-based mission to the nations expressed in the final composition of Matthew. These positions make sense of a nuanced reading of Acts and Galatians. Here also Paul is portrayed as the opponent of James and Peter.

In the *Ascents of James* Paul is identified as the enemy Saul, a representative of high-priestly authority persecuting James, causing his fall from the top of the Temple steps. He was also seeking to persecute Peter, pursuing him to Damascus. Thus Paul's role as persecutor is recalled (Acts 8:3; 9:1–2) but without any reference to his conversion. In the *Kerygmata Petrou*, in the *persona* of Simon Magus, with his lawless gospel, it is actually Paul who is the opponent of Peter. The picture is of James as the bishop of bishops in charge of the Jerusalem church (*Ep. P.*, preface), the judge of true teaching (*Rec.* 1.68.2–1.70.1; 1.70.3; 4.34–35; *Hom.* 11.35.3–5) and Peter as the apostle and missionary of the true and lawful proclamation to the Gentiles. Here the role of Paul the convert is recalled, and to make clear the corrupt nature of his gospel he is portrayed in terms of Simon Magus (Acts 8:9–24). The *Ascents of James* is concerned with the primacy of James (*Rec.* 1.43.3; 1.66.2, 5; 1.68.2; 1.70.3; cf. 1.72.1); as are the *Kerygmata Petrou* (*Cont.* 5.4; *Hom.* 11.35.3–5). This goes beyond the interest in James as the first bishop, asserting that Jesus himself ordained James as head of the Jerusalem church, presiding over the twelve (*Ascents, Rec.* 1.44.1; 1.66.1; cf. 1.72.1 and *Kerygmata Petrou*, preface to *Ep. P.; Hom.* 1.20.2f. / *Rec.* 1.17.2f.; *Hom.* 11.35.3–5 / *Rec.* 4.34–35) and overseeing their missionary labors (*Rec.* 1.17.2f.; 1.44.1; cf. 1.72.1; *Ep. P.* 1.1; *Hom.* 1.20.2f.).

Some aspects of this description appear to echo historical reality. James and Peter are representative of a law-based gospel of the circumcision with James based in Jerusalem while Peter was involved in a law-based mission to the Gentiles. Yet James had authority to veto teaching and action even in the mission situation outside Jerusalem. It could be that Acts was responsible for the presence of these elements. The authority of James over members of the mission from Jerusalem is also attested by Paul in Gal. 2:11–14.

THE PSEUDO-CLEMENTINES
AND JEWISH CHRISTIANITY

The Pseudo-Clementines provide evidence of a Jewish-Christian Gnosticism opposed to Paul. Strangely, Paul takes on the persona of Simon Magus who, from the perspective of "Catholic" tradition, is the father of heresy. That a Jewish-Christian *gnostic* text should portray Paul in this way is ironic, showing that issues related to keeping the Jewish law have become paramount. Only sacrifice is no longer relevant for the gospel of the circumcision, which is not surprising after the destruction of the Temple.

References to James in the Pseudo-Clementines are illuminating. In *Recognitions*, where James was thrown down from the top of the Temple steps by "that enemy," Saul, Peter referred to James on a number of occasions, as "our James" and "James the bishop" twice (1.66). In the process James encountered Caiaphas, who is referred to as "the chief of the priests" while James is called "the chief of the bishops" (1.68) and "our James" (1.69). When James was thrown down the Temple steps, he was rescued and he sent Peter to Caesarea to confront Simon (Magus). James required Peter to send back to him an account of his sayings and doings every year and especially every seven years (1.72). This incident shows the authority of James both in Jerusalem and in the mission beyond. On arrival in Caesarea Peter reports that he was welcomed by "our most beloved brother Zacchaeus" who inquired "concerning each of the brethren, especially concerning our honorable brother James." Peter then informed him of the way the priests and Caiaphas the high priest had called them to the Temple and "James the archbishop, standing at the top of the steps" convinced the people that Jesus is the Christ (1.73). Simon's challenge to Peter followed. When Peter had spent three months in Caesarea, ordaining Zacchaeus as bishop, he instructed Clement to record and to send to James an appropriate account. In his report Clement addressed James as "my Lord James" (3.74). Then (in 3.75) Clement reported to James summarizing the ten books of the teaching of Peter. It is not possible to say if this summary refers to some source used in the writing of the *Recognitions*. Naturally the teaching is consistent with the *Recognitions*, in particular the emphasis on the law of Moses and the role of the true prophet.

Having confronted Simon in Caesarea, Peter and his mission proceeded to Tripolis. Books 4–6 of *Recognitions* are set in Tripolis which is also the location for *Homilies* 8–11, books 4–7 being assigned to the journey from Caesarea. In his discourse Peter cautions his hearers, concerning false apostles, to "believe no teacher, unless he brings from Jerusalem the testimonial of James the Lord's brother, or whosoever may come after him" (*Recognitions* 4.35). Not only does this saying recognize the authority of James (and his successors) beyond Jerusalem, it is anti-Pauline in intent. Paul denied his dependence on Jerusalem even if he did, on his own admission, go up to Jerusalem to lay his gospel before "the pillars" (Gal. 2:1–10). Paul's grudging acknowledgment of the authority of the pillars is evident in Gal. 2:6, 9 and the exercise of the authority of the first pillar (James) leads to conflict between Paul and the second of the Jerusalem pillars, Cephas (Gal. 2:11–14). *Recognitions* ascribes to James the authority to authenticate the credentials of all teachers. With the description of James as "our bishop," "the chief of the bishops," and "the archbishop," this authenticating role sets James as the supreme authority in the early church.

Two epistles have been attached to the *Homilies*, the first attributed to Peter and the second to Clement. To the *Epistle of Peter* is attached the *Contestatio*. Peter addressed his letter "to James, the lord and bishop of the holy Church" and addresses him as "my brother." The stated purpose of the letter was to request that James not reveal the teaching/preaching of Peter to any untried and uninitiated Gentile or Jewish teachers but to follow the practice of Moses who delivered his books to the seventy who succeeded him (see Num. 11:16, 25). The stated reason for this concern was that "some from among the Gentiles have rejected my lawful preaching, attaching themselves to certain lawless and trifling preaching of the man who is my enemy." This strong anti-Pauline motif is related to the special tradition in Matthew often designated "M." In the words of the epistle:

> [S]ome have attempted while I am still alive, to transform my words by certain various interpretations, in order to teach the dissolution of the law; as though I myself were of such a mind, but did not freely proclaim it, which God forbid! For such a thing were to act in opposition to the law of God which was spoken by Moses, and was borne witness to by our Lord in respect of its eternal continuance; for thus he spoke: "The heavens and the earth shall pass away, but one jot or one tittle shall in no wise pass away from the law."

The quotation is from Matt. 5:18, which is from the special M material, a tradition which represents James and Jerusalem and is here affirmed by Peter. The difference between Peter and James in the Pseudo-Clementines is that James maintained the Jewish mission centered in Jerusalem while Peter extended the law-based mission to the Gentiles. That Peter affirms a law-based mission against the Pauline law-free mission is clear. The role of the seventy is also important, linking up with other works related to James. See especially Clement of Alexandria (*H.E.* 2.1.4) and the *First Apocalypse of James*, where Addai, identified with Thaddeus, is named in the chain of transmission of higher knowledge. In the Pseudo-Clementines the explicit link with Moses is spelled out in terms of safeguarding the law-based mission. Underlying the instruction not to reveal the preaching/teaching openly may be the intent to provide an explanation for the late appearance of the pseudonymous apocryphal work attributed to Peter.

In the *Contestatio* the conditions requested by Peter are formalized by James, who, when he had called the elders, instructed them to maintain a six-year proving of those to whom the instruction was to be transmitted. Those receiving the teaching were to be required to agree to strict rules of further transmission. The letter of Clement to James provides a rationale for the *Homilies* that follow. The letter is addressed

to James, the lord [probably "the Lord's brother"], and the bishop of
bishops, who rules in Jerusalem, the holy church of the Hebrews, and
the churches everywhere . . .

Clement acknowledges the leadership of James, not only in the Jerusalem
church, which is described as the church of the Hebrews, but in the churches
everywhere. One of the purposes of the letter is to report the martyrdom of
Peter in Rome and to authenticate Peter's choice of Clement as his successor
and bishop in that place. One of the justifications for this is that Clement had
traveled with Peter from beginning to end, had heard all his homilies, shared
all of his trials, and been proved worthy to succeed to the chair of Peter. The
letter reports Peter's homily on the occasion of the installation of Clement. At
the end of the homily Peter charged Clement to communicate to James something of his own biography, including his hearing of the discourses of Peter
and the circumstances of Peter's death. At the end Clement adds that he had
already sent to James his epitome of the popular preaching of Peter but would
now set forth those sermons as he had been ordered. No doubt we are to think
of the *Homilies* that follow as the fulfillment of his obligation.

Historically it is unlikely that Peter's martyrdom preceded that of James,
though the time of the death of Peter, which tradition locates in Rome, cannot be fixed with any certainty. It is unlikely that Peter was martyred before
62 C.E. But it was important that Clement, in whose name the tradition of
these works was published, should have the explicit approval of Peter and also
the implicit support of James, who, according to this tradition, was the bishop
of bishops with authority over the churches in every place.

The tradition of the wider primacy of James must have its origin in the history of the Jerusalem community, where his primacy was recognized until the
time of his death. It is unclear whether any formal succession continued from
James or if those who succeeded to the leadership of the Jerusalem Church
enjoyed the same authority as he had beyond the boundaries of Jerusalem.
Certainly that is the position portrayed and advocated by the Pseudo-Clementines. Eusebius obscures the gap between the death of James (in 62 C.E.) and
the time after the "capture" of Jerusalem (70 C.E.), after which Symeon, the
cousin of Jesus, was appointed the second bishop of Jerusalem (*H.E.* 3.11.1;
4.22.4). Eusebius says that the capture "instantly followed" the martyrdom of
James. Because we can date each of these events we are aware of the gap
between them when, according to Eusebius, the Jerusalem church was without a bishop. It is also unclear how Eusebius reconciled this view with the tradition of the flight of the Jerusalem church to Pella. It may be that reference
to assembling "from all parts" implies the regathering of the Jerusalem church
(3.11.1). But Eusebius gives us no evidence upon which he might base such
a view.

James emerges, especially in the section dependent on the *Ascents*, as the
bishop and leader of the Jerusalem church (1.62.2; 68.2; 70.3), whose author-

ity derived directly from the risen Lord and encompassed the twelve (1.44.1) including Peter (1.72.1). While not denying the leadership of James, the tradition of the great church was eager to couple the apostles with the Lord as the source of the authority of James, as can be seen in Eusebius *H.E.* 7.19. But in the *Ascents*, James also has responsibility for the early Christian mission and he is depicted as an apologist to the Jews, seeking their conversion (1.70–71). Characteristically James is opposed by Saul of Tarsus (1.70–71), and this motif has played an important role in the history of the study of a distinctive Jewish Christianity, becoming one of the defining characteristics. While this is unambiguously so here, it must be recognized as having its roots in earlier, probably historical, tradition.

There are puzzling features concerning the *Ascents*. On the one hand its identification as a Jewish-Christian source suggests that it might provide access to early and reliable information about James and the early church. On the other, there are features that put in question the Jewishness of the source. R. E. van Voorst notes that *Ascents*, in locating the Temple debates, grossly overestimates the size of the Temple sanctuary and overlooks that the space identified was restricted to priests and Levites. The depiction of the Temple as open to the public, including Samaritans, confirms "that the Temple debates (1,55–71) have no good claim to historicity." (van Voorst, *Ascents*, 170–71). Of course *Ascents* is from the second half of the second century at a time when memory of the Temple was remote. But this need not mean that no tradition relating to debates located in the Temple precincts underlies *Ascents*.

Van Voorst also rejects as unhistorical the attack on Paul in which he is blamed for the failure of the mission to the Jewish nation. To substantiate his view he appeals to Acts 21:17–26 and Romans 9–11 (van Voorst, *Ascents*, 171–72). While he acknowledges that Acts 21 refers to the rumor that Paul had taught Jews in the Diaspora not to observe the law, he notes that James does not blame Paul for the failure of the mission to the Jews and in fact affirms that the mission in Jerusalem had been successful. Such conclusions arise from a partial "face value" reading by van Voorst. No attempt is made to raise any question about the historicity of the Acts account or the tendencies of its author to obscure conflicts. Indeed such evidence of conflict as remains in the Acts account is obscured by van Voorst. For example, did the Jerusalem community accept the collection brought by Paul? Why does Acts not refer to this? Why is there no mention of any advocacy on behalf of Paul by the Jerusalem church after his arrest? Thus even the Acts account reveals real tension between Paul and the Jerusalem church.

Paul's account shows that he was anxious about his reception in Jerusalem and was uncertain of how the collection would be received (Rom. 15:22–32). He asked the Romans to pray that he might be delivered from the unbelievers in Jerusalem and that his service (the collection referred to in 15:25–27) might be acceptable to the saints, the believers, that is, the Jerusalem church. Subsequent events showed that Paul's anxiety was well founded, probably on both counts. Paul's account of the mission to Israel is also at odds with van Voorst's reading of Acts, where the success of the mission of the Jerusalem church is stressed to show that Paul would not have been blamed for failure, because the mission was a success.

Although van Voorst recognizes that Paul acknowledges "the overwhelming failure of the mission to Israel" (*Ascents*, 172), he does not allow the observation to cast doubt on the historicity of *his reading* of Acts. Instead he responds by arguing that Paul did not blame himself and his law-free mission for the failure. Rather, the failure is attributed to "the mysterious purposes of God" (Rom. 9:6–33). There is no doubt that this is true to Paul's *argument* in Romans. This is Paul's expressed point of view. It does not mean that his point of view was shared by all others, including James and the Jerusalem church. Indeed, in Romans there are clues that suggest Paul was arguing against those who have accused him of disloyalty to his own people, lacking natural affection for them (9:1–5; 10:1). What is more, his answer shows that he was sensitive to this charge, and much of Romans is well understood as Paul's answer to it. It was necessary for him to show the continuing place of Israel in his understanding of the plan and purposes of God from the perspective of a law-free mission to the Gentiles. Thus, contrary to van Voorst, the evidence of both Acts and Romans suggest that Paul was accused of threatening the mission to the Jewish nation. That Paul repudiates the charge does not mean that it was not made or that he did not feel the force of it. On the contrary, the manner in which he responds tends to confirm his sensitivity to the charge. Contrary to the views of van Voorst, the point of Acts 21:20–26 is to make clear the way the Pauline mission threatened the success of the Jerusalem mission. It was for that reason that Paul was called on to show proof of his Jewish credentials. The view that Paul encouraged Jews in the Diaspora not to observe the law was probably well based and the strategy to prove otherwise failed.

Van Voorst also argues that "*Ascents's* portrait of the pre-eminence of James . . . is not historical" (van Voorst, *Ascents*, 172). He rightly notes the inconsistency of referring to James as the "head bishop" and the "*only*" bishop" and the anachronism of referring to James as a bishop at all. Granted that the title of bishop is probably anachronistic, what of the claim that James was appointed leader of the Jerusalem church by Jesus himself (*Ascents* 1.43.3)? Here van Voorst argues that James was not the first leader, that Acts and Paul depict the shared leadership of James with the twelve, and that this is confirmed by Hegesippus according to Eusebius (*H.E.* 2.22.1). This reference is obviously a mistake, as there is no reference to either Hegesippus or James here. In *H.E.* 2.23.1 there is a reference to the election of James by the apostles to the throne of the bishopric of Jerusalem. This summary by Eusebius fits his view of the pattern of leadership transmission in the early church in which Jesus chose the twelve and the twelve ordained the first bishops. Thus 1 Clem. 42; 44.1–2; and Irenaeus in *A.H.* 3.3.2–4. But Eusebius does not attribute this to Hegesippus, or to anyone else for that matter. It may be that Eusebius thought that he was drawing on the tradition quoted from Clement of Alexandria in *H.E.* 2.1.3 which says, "After the ascension of the savior Peter, James and John chose James the Just as bishop of Jerusalem." Contrary to van Voorst, this implies that James was leader from the first. The other tradition reported from Clement (*H.E.* 2.1.4) asserts a direct link between the risen Lord and James the Just, asserting that "After the resurrection the Lord gave the tradition of knowledge to James the Just and John and Peter . . ." By naming James first, this tradition already implies his leadership, prior to the ascension and perhaps prior to the recognition of his leadership by Peter and the sons of Zebedee. That recognition is associated with the ascension of Jesus.

Thus, contrary to van Voorst, *Ascents* confirms the original leadership of James. The depiction of that leadership in terms of the bishop's throne and the appointment of James by the twelve is to be seen as an expression of the ideology of the emerging great church. While the role of the *Mebaqqer* at Qumran means we cannot be certain that the early Christian movement did not establish bishops (*episkopoi*) from the beginning, the description of the role of James in *Ascents* goes somewhat beyond this. Nevertheless, the leadership of James should not be denied, being too firmly entrenched in a wide variety of traditions. The church of the second century made his leadership dependent on the authority of the twelve, the mediators of the authority of Jesus. In doing this, they retrieved the authority of James from Christian Judaism, which sometimes manifested gnostic tendencies.

Van Voorst rightly argues that *Ascents* exhibits a positive view of the observance of the Mosaic law, including circumcision (1.33.3–5; 1.35.2; 1.43.2). Only sacrifice is excluded, and this position was developed in relation to the teaching of Jesus, the prophet like Moses. While the teaching of the prophet like Moses does not appear outside *Ascents*, the teaching of the true prophet provides a similar basis in the rest of the Pseudo-Clementines. Overall the Pseudo-Clementines insist on law observance while being antisacrificial and anti-Pauline. On this basis van Voorst argues that the church of *Ascents*

> is Jewish in ethnic origin; it promotes an identification with the Jewish people as "our people." In practice, the community of the *Ascents* is composed of law-observant Jews. They keep Jewish feasts and customs; they may practice circumcision. In belief, they are Jewish-Christian as well. Their christology, that of the Mosaic Prophet, is rooted in Jewish belief. . . . [A]side from its acceptance of Jesus as Messiah and what follows from it, the community of the *Ascents* is one with Judaism. (*Ascents*, 177)

Nevertheless it is clear from 1.44.2; 1.62; and 1.70–71 that the community of *Ascents* "underwent persecution at the hands of the Jewish authorities."

Given that this form of Jewish Christianity was manifest in the second half of the second century, the question is raised as to its relationship to the original Jewish Christianity of the Jerusalem church. Johannes Munck and

S. G. F. Brandon argued that authentic Jewish Christianity did not survive the fall of Jerusalem in 70 C.E. (Brandon 1957 and Munck 1960, 103–16). Against this absolute break van Voorst argues for some continuity between Stephen and the Hellenists as depicted in Acts (van Voorst 1989, 180). This is surely mistaken, overlooking the fact that, according to Acts, it was the scattered Hellenists who began to preach a law-free gospel in Antioch (Acts 11:20). A greater continuity exists between James and the Pharisaic believers of Acts 15:1, 5 and the Jewish Christians of the Pseudo-Clementines.

JAMES AND THE TEACHER OF RIGHTEOUSNESS

At least since 1983 Robert Eisenman has made a literary connection between the Pseudo-Clementines and the Qumran texts and an association between James the Just and the Teacher of Righteousness. Concerning the latter he says, "[It] was a comparatively easy task to link the events and teachings of the Righteous Teacher in the Habakkuk Pesher to those of James the Just in the early 'Jerusalem Community'" (Eisenman 1986, vii, viii, xii, 38). To do this he puts in question the single-line reconstruction based on the paleographic evidence of F. M. Cross (*Maccabees*, xvi); claims to identify in the texts individuals and groups known outside the texts by names other than those used in the texts (*Maccabees*, xi–xii; *James the Just*, vii); claims that the *pesher* was not common until the mid-first century C.E. (*James the Just*, 37–38), and that the Habakkuk *pesher* gives the impression of being written soon after or even at the time of the events of 68 C.E. and "almost every turn of phrase in the Habakkuk *pesher* . . . can . . . [be] put into real historical settings relating to real and important people contemporary with the fall of the temple about 70 C.E." (*James the Just*, 49, 75). Thus he places the activity of the Teacher of Righteousness and the writing of the Habakkuk *pesher* in the mid-first century C.E. and likens the events described to those surrounding James the Just in the early "Jerusalem Community."

In *James, the Brother of Jesus*, Eisenman argues that "the Scrolls allow us to approach the Messianic Community of James with about as much precision as we are likely to have from any other source." He also says, "Whether James is to be identified with the Righteousness Teacher at Qumran or simply a parallel successor is not the point" (1997, 963). The argument used asserts that overlapping language identifies the same people in different sources (44, 112, 115, 208, 955, 958). Thus, according to Eisenman, James is either the Teacher of Righteousness or one of his successors and Paul is identified with the "spouter of lies (126–27) and the wicked priest with Ananus (170–72). The War Scroll is said to be Jamesian (212–13) implying that James and his followers were Zealots of the warlike kind (9, 194, 374–75, 381, 389, 490, 983). The brothers of Jesus—Simon, Judas, and James—are identified with Zealot figures and, as these names appear among the twelve, Eisenman argues that

Zealot members of the family are concealed there (xx, 7, 44, 117–18, 139, 143, 534, 958). Having made this Zealot association for James and two of the other brothers, Eisenman concludes that Jesus was also to be identified with the Zealot movement.

The reason for treating Eisenman's interpretation of James at this point is that it depends on the anti-Pauline tradition found in the Pseudo-Clementines. Without this there would be no basis for identifying Paul with the spouter of lies." Because there Paul is identified as the enemy of James who hurls him down the steps, Eisenman identifies the account of the martyrdom of Stephen, in which Saul/Paul was involved, as a reference to the martyrdom of James. Eusebius preserves references to the election of James by the apostles as the first bishop of Jerusalem and Eisenman takes the election of Matthias to replace Judas as a reference to James.

Eisenman understands Paul is to be a Roman sympathizer, a supporter of the house of Herod. Paul turned the zealot movement of Jesus and James into a Roman mystery cult. Eisenman shows no awareness that the mystery cult hypothesis concerning Paul was fully tested in the last one hundred and fifty years and found to have nothing to commend it. To turn James into a Zealot, Eisenman turns to the reference to the many Jerusalem believers who were "zealous for the law" (Acts 21:20). He conveniently ignores the full phrase and takes it only as an indication of the Zealot character of the Jerusalem church under James. This he connects with his interpretation of the Zealot character of the Qumran sect. According to Eisenman the sect was part of the Zealot wing of the Sadducean movement. About this there is no room for discussion here. There is, however, no evidence that James was a Zealot or that the Jerusalem church was of that character. That James was zealous for the law and that the Jerusalem church generally was of this disposition seems clear.

Eisenman is on safer ground in arguing that what James was, is likely to be a good indication of what Jesus was. Perhaps we should say that what James was, opens up one possible understanding of what Jesus was. Here I identify the teaching and normal practice of Jesus which was, it seems, law observant. But there is also the exceptional practice of Jesus described in those events where Jesus was not scrupulous about purity issues, or the sabbath or relations with those who were not Jews. James followed what was for him the normative Jesus. Jesus' contact with sinners and outcasts as well as with those who were not Jews is somehow recognized but without allowing it to disturb a commitment to scrupulous law observance.

THE MARTYRDOM OF JAMES

Studies have shown that the account of the martyrdom of James in Hegesippus has some sort of relation to the *Ascents of James*. But was Hegesippus dependent on *Ascents*, or *Ascents* on Hegesippus, or were both dependent on a common source? Similarities are stressed by F. S. Jones in his argument that *Recognitions* 1 was dependent on Hegesippus ("Martyrdom," 328–31). Jones notes that the dominant view is that *Recognitions* 1 and Hegesippus were dependent on a common, now lost, source. His purpose was to argue the dependence of *Recognitions* on Hegesippus. To this end he lists thirteen points of similarity but fails to note important differences. Luedemann also lists points of contact but notes differences (*Opposition*, 175–77). Three important differences suffice to show that the case for direct dependence has not been made. In *Ascents* James ascends the Temple steps; in Hegesippus it is the Temple pinnacle. In *Ascents* the opponents are not the scribes and Pharisees as in Hegesippus but the high priest and the one known as "the enemy." In Hegesippus James is martyred while in *Ascents* he is not killed. There are other important differences also, some of them at the very point where contact seems to be indicated. Thus while the issue of Jesus' messiahship is at stake in each of these documents, it is not presented in the same terms.

Ascents does not deal with the martyrdom of James but with a serious point of conflict. Josephus provides the most reliable evidence of the death of James. Eusebius records this (*H.E.* 2.23.21–24) in words that agree closely with what we now find in *Antiquities* (20.197–203). The use of this material by Eusebius makes likely the common use of it by early Christians. Nevertheless scholars accept its reliability because it mentions Jesus only in passing as a means of identifying James as "the brother of Jesus who was called (*tou legomenou*) the Christ." Interestingly, this quotation describes James as the brother of Jesus, without qualification, but says of Jesus, not that he was the Christ, but "who was called the Christ." This is precisely the qualification we would expect a Jewish writer rather than a Christian writer to make. The reference to James by Clement of Alexandria (*H.E.* 2.1.2) introduces him thus: "Then there is James, who *is called* the Lord's brother, for he too was named Joseph's son . . ." Thus Clement qualifies the reference to James as the brother of Jesus, which Josephus does not. He refers to Jesus as the Lord, which Josephus does not. Instead Josephus qualifies the reference to Jesus as the Christ, which a Christian writer would not have done. Here is how Eusebius introduces the quotation from Josephus:

> The same writer [Josephus] also narrates his death in the twentieth book of the *Antiquities* as follows:

> Upon learning of the death of Festus, Caesar sent Albinus to Judaea as procurator. The king removed Joseph from the high priesthood, and bestowed the succession to this office upon the son of Ananus, who was likewise called Ananus. . . . The younger Ananus, who, as we have said, had been appointed to the high priesthood, was rash in his temper and unusually daring. He followed the school (*hairesin*) of the Sadducees, who are indeed more heartless than any of the other Jews, as I have already explained, when they sit in judgement. Possessed with such a character, Ananus thought that he had a favorable oppor-

tunity because Festus was dead and Albinus was on the way. And so he convened the judges of the Sanhedrin and brought before them a man named James, the brother of Jesus who was called the Christ (*tou legomenou Christou*), and certain others. He accused them of having transgressed the law and delivered them up to be stoned. Those of the inhabitants of the city who were considered the most fair-minded and were strict in the observance of the law were offended at this. They therefore secretly sent to King Agrippa urging him, for Ananus had not even been correct in his first step, to order him to desist from any further such actions. Certain of them even went to meet Albinus, who was on his way from Alexandria, and informed him that Ananus had no authority to convene the Sanhedrin without his consent. Convinced by these words, Albinus angrily wrote to Ananus threatening to take vengeance upon him. King Agrippa, because of Ananus' action, deposed him from the high priesthood which he had held for three months and replaced him with Jesus the son of Damnaeus.

We may note that Josephus, whose views were negative in relation to the Zealots and positive toward the Jewish leaders (high priest) in his work on the *Jewish War*, is somewhat negative in relation to the high priest and Sadduccean leadership in *Antiquities*. Nevertheless, this change of perspective does not seem likely to have distorted his account of the martyrdom of James.

In this account, James and certain others are brought before the Sanhedrin by the high priest, the younger Ananus, and accused of having transgressed the law. Evidently they were convicted because they were delivered up to be stoned. With what crime against the law they charged is not stated. There is no suggestion that James or the others were stoned because of their witness to Jesus. Indeed, nothing suggests that those stoned with James were Jewish *believers*. Josephus notes, "Those of the inhabitants of the city who were considered the most fair-minded and were strict in the observance of the law were offended at this." Quite likely Josephus referred to the Pharisees in this way as this group seems to be distinguished from the Sadducees. This strict law-observant group objected, but it is unclear whether they objected to the verdict or to the punishment. The suggestion that what the group objected to was Ananus taking the law into his own hands when Roman authority was required for the imposition of the death penalty (see John 18:31) does not fit an objection raised by "the most fair minded and . . . strict in the observance of the law." This has the ring of Jewish law observance, for which Roman authority is irrelevant. Nor would an objection based on a conflict between Pharisees and Sadducees concerning which offenses were punishable by stoning justify this language. Rather, it suggests that those who were fair-minded and strict in their observance of the law regarded as unjust the verdict that James and the others had transgressed the law.

If the verdict was unjust, and the objection was not only to the form of punishment, we need to ask what was the real reason Ananus moved against James and the others who were stoned with him? In the narrative that follows in *Antiquities* 205–207 Josephus tells of the exploits of Ananus after he was deposed for his part in the execution of James and the others. He bribed both Albinus and his own successor (Jesus the son of Damnaeus) to allow him to take the tithes of the priests who now starved to death. This seems to draw attention to the exploitation of poor rural priests of Pharisaic inclination by the aristocratic Sadducean high priest. If this were the case these events might be more intricately intertwined than is at first apparent. James and the fair-minded citizens were opposed to the exploitation of the poorer priests and this led to the execution of James and others associated with him. S. G. F. Brandon (1967b, 67) is probably right in seeing this as a factor in the situation but wrong in not also relating this to a struggle between Pharisees and Sadducees.

The evidence of Paul and Acts associates the poor with the Jerusalem church and there is reference to the conversion of many priests (Gal. 2:10; Rom. 15:22–32; Acts 6:7; 21:20). James's conflict with Ananus was a result of his opposition to the exploitation of the poor by the rich aristocratic ruling class and in particular the exploitation of the poor rural priesthood by the aristocratic urban chief priests (see Josephus, *Antiquities* 20.180–181, and E. M. Smallwood, 1962, 14–34, and 1981, 272–84, 314). J. Jeremias (1967, 256–58) outlines evidence to show that "a large number of priests were Pharisees." If we allow that the poor rural priests serving in the Temple were more closely aligned to the Pharisees than to the Sadducean aristocratic chief priests, then we have a scenario in which to understand the conflict between James and Ananus, as described by Josephus. At this point Hegesippus has obscured the real opponent of James (the high priest Ananus) by portraying the scribes and Pharisees as responsible for his death. It may be that he simply transposed the traditional opponents of Jesus to the conflict with James.

The account reinforces our understanding of James and his association with believing Pharisees (Acts 15:1, 5) who affirmed the continuing relevance of the Jewish law (Acts 21:20). James and the Jerusalem church supported a mission to other Jews based on the continuing validity of the law including circumcision (Gal. 2:1–10; 11–14). The execution of James by Ananus does nothing to undermine this understanding.

Perhaps Eusebius leaves the quotation from Josephus until last because he has given priority to the Christian tradition. The account by Hegesippus is featured and emphasized. It makes the points that are important for Eusebius concerning the righteousness of James and his courageous witness to Jesus in the face of martyrdom. In contrast to this, the account in Josephus, unless read with care, might be thought to cast doubt on the righteousness of James. It gives no hint of his witness to Jesus in the face of martyrdom. Both of these aspects are emphasized by Hegesippus (*H.E.* 2.23.3–18) along with a number of legendary elements.

But the most detailed account of him is given by Hegesippus, who belonged to the first generation after the apostles:

Control of the Church passed [presumably after the ascension of Jesus] together with the apostles, to the brother of the Lord James, whom every one from the Lord's time till our own has named the Just, for there were many Jameses, but this one was holy from his birth; he drank no wine or intoxicating liquor and ate no animal food; no razor came near his head; he did not smear himself with oil, and he took no baths. He alone was permitted to enter the Holy Place, for his garments were not of wool but of linen. He used to enter the Sanctuary alone, and was often found on his knees beseeching forgiveness for the people, so that his knees grew hard like a camel's from his continually bending them in worship of God and beseeching forgiveness for the people. Because of his unsurpassable righteousness he was called the Just and *Oblias*—in Greek "Bulwark of the people and Righteousness"—fulfilling the declarations of the prophets regarding him.

Representatives of the seven sects (*haireseon*) already described by me asked him what was meant by "the door of Jesus," and he replied that Jesus was the Savior. Some of them came to believe that Jesus was the Christ: the sects mentioned above did not believe either in a resurrection or in one who is coming to give every man what his deeds deserve, but those who did come to believe did so because of James. Since therefore many even of the ruling class believed, there was an uproar among the Jews and Scribes and Pharisees, who said there was a danger that the entire people would expect Jesus as the Christ. So they collected and said to James: "Be good enough to restrain the people, for they have gone astray after Jesus in the belief that he is the Christ. Be good enough to make the facts about Jesus clear to all who come for the Passover Day. We all accept what you say: we can vouch for it, and so can all the people, that you are a righteous man and take no one at his face value. So make it clear to the crowd that they must not go astray as regards Jesus: the whole people and all of us accept what you say. So take your stand on the Temple parapet, so that from that height you may be easily seen, and your words audible to the whole people. For because of the Passover all the tribes have foregathered, and the Gentiles too."

So the Scribes and Pharisees made James stand on the Sanctuary parapet and shouted to him: "Just one, whose word we are all obliged to accept, the people are going astray after Jesus who was crucified; so tell us what is meant by 'the door of Jesus.'" He replied as loudly as he could: "Why do you question me about the Son of Man? I tell you, he is sitting in heaven at the right hand of the great power, and he will come on the clouds of heaven." Many were convinced, and gloried in James's testimony, crying: "Hosanna to the Son of David!" Then again the Scribes and Pharisees said to each other: "We made a bad mistake in affording such testimony to Jesus. We had better go up and throw him down, so that they will be frightened and not believe him." "Ho, ho!" they called out, "even the Just one has gone astray!"—fulfilling the prophecy of Isaiah: "Let us remove the Just one, for he is unprofitable to us." Therefore they shall eat the fruit of their works.

So they went up and threw down the Just one. Then they said to each other "Let us stone James the Just," and began to stone him, as in spite of his fall he was still alive. But he turned and knelt, uttering the words: "I beseech Thee, Lord God and Father, forgive them; they do not know what they are doing." While they pelted him with stones, one of the descendants of Rechab the son of Rechabim—the priestly family to which Jeremiah the prophet bore witness, called out: "Stop! what are you doing? the Just one is praying for you." Then one of them, a fuller, took the club which he used to beat the clothes, and brought it down on the head of the Just one. Such was his martyrdom. He was buried on the spot, by the Sanctuary, and his headstone is still there by the Sanctuary. He has proved a true witness to Jews and Gentiles alike that Jesus is the Christ.

Immediately after this Vespasian began to besiege them.

Because there were many Jameses, Hegesippus makes a number of important points to establish which James, to make clear the significance of his martyrdom. First this is James the brother of the Lord. No qualification is made to this statement such as "called" or "known as." This is the primary identifying qualification. Second, from the time of the Lord this James was known by everyone as James the Just or Righteous. The description fits one of meticulous Jewish law-observant piety, even if some elements overlap aspects of Hellenistic piety. Because of his piety he is described in the role of the high priest, making supplication for the people. "Because of his unsurpassable righteousness he was called the Just and *Oblias*—in Greek 'Bulwark of the people and Righteousness'—fulfilling the declarations of the prophets regarding him."

In this account James's witness to Jesus led many to believe that he was the Christ. Because of the disturbance, the scribes and Pharisees ask James to speak to the people from the parapet of the Temple, where he can be seen and heard by all. They assert that the people have been led astray in the belief that Jesus is the Christ but, at the same time, acknowledge the righteousness of James. Because of this, all will believe him and, they tell him, they will accept whatever he says. Clearly there is the expectation that, at the Passover, where the crowds gathered dangerously, James will put the people right on this matter. Given that the people have come to their belief because of James, this is an unrealistic expectation which signals a legendary motif. It is a motif that testifies to the righteousness of James even in the eyes of the scribes and Pharisees.

When James gives his witness he does so in terms reminiscent of Jesus (Mark 14:62) and Stephen (Acts 7:56). The result was that many believed and the scribes and Pharisees realized they had made a mistake. They threw James down from the parapet and when this did not kill him they stoned him.

But he turned and knelt, uttering the words: "I beseech Thee, Lord God and Father, forgive them; they do not know what they are doing."

While they pelted him with stones, one of the descendants of Rechab the son of Rechabim—the priestly family to which Jeremiah the prophet bore witness, called out: "Stop! what are you doing? the Just one is praying for you."

As they were stoning him he was praying for them in words reminiscent of Jesus' words from the cross (Luke 23:34) and of Stephen (Acts 7:60).

Still he was not dead, so he was finally killed by a single blow from a fuller's club. This account has the appearance of being a complex of traditions. Eusebius has accentuated our awareness of this by collecting together the brief quotation from Clement with the extended account of Hegesippus and the less detailed account of Josephus. Eusebius pointedly (if inadvertently) raises the question of the literary relationship between the three. The account of Josephus could have been used as a source by Hegesippus, or elements from it could subsequently have been interpolated into his account. Some literary influence seems likely. There is also overlap with the short account of Clement. This has been obscured by the ideological interpretation that has driven Hegesippus.

In book 7 of the same work [*Hypotyposes*] the writer (Clement) makes this further statement about him:

> James the Just, John, and Peter were entrusted by the Lord after his resurrection with the higher knowledge. They imparted it to the other apostles, and the other apostles to the Seventy, one of whom was Barnabas. There were two Jameses, one the Just, who was thrown down from the parapet and beaten to death with a fuller's club, the other the James who was beheaded.

The grounds for thinking that Clement's brief account is dependent on Hegesippus are far from convincing. Clement writes of James being thrown down from the parapet of the Temple and then being clubbed to death. The description implies multiple blows. There is no mention of stoning. This seems to be drawn from Josephus's account. But there is no reference there to James being thrown down from the parapet of the Temple or beaten to death with the fuller's club. Thus there is a case for thinking that Clement gives us access to an early independent Christian tradition of the death of James which Hegesippus has combined with Josephus's account. The motif of throwing James down is found also in the *Ascents of James*. There James is thrown down the Temple steps and, though injured, he is not killed in this incident. No stoning or beating with a fuller's club follows in *Ascents*.

In spite of obvious knowledge of Josephus, from whom he may have derived the motif of the stoning of James, Hegesippus has produced his own account with irreconcilable conflicts with Josephus. At every point of conflict it seems likely that the account of Josephus is to be preferred. Contrary to Robert Eisler in *The Messiah Jesus and John the Baptist* (1931, 141–43, 182, 289,

518–20, 540–42, 596), the account of Hegesippus is ideologically driven and cannot be harmonized with Josephus. On this matter modern scholarship tends to follow J. B. Lightfoot (1865, 348–50) and Johannes Weiss (1917) in accepting the account of Josephus as the most reliable historically.

If Josephus gives us evidence of the circumstances of the death of James, the early Christian traditions of his death have been embroidered by an account or accounts of the exploits of James in Jerusalem that focused on his witness to Jesus. Josephus suggests that James died because of a serious intra-Jewish problem which was not specifically Christian. Those who regarded James as a righteous martyr reworked this tradition to portray James as a witness to Jesus, making use of the tradition of the righteous sufferer, the tradition of the trial of Jesus, and the tradition concerning the martyrdom of Stephen. *Ascents* suggests that the early Christian tradition concerning the death of James may have been combined with tradition dealing with the witness of James to Jesus in a conflict with Jewish authority that did not lead to his death. In Hegesippus this becomes joined to the tradition now found in Josephus.

The words that come at the end of the quotation from Hegesippus, "Immediately after this Vespasian began to besiege them," may be the words of Eusebius, adding his own conclusion to the words of Hegesippus. There is no clear indication of where the quotation ends.

JAMES AND THE LAW

The account of the martyrdom of James in Josephus puts in question the characterization of James as a law-observant messianic Jew. But we have argued that Josephus rejects the charges brought against James and those executed with him. Josephus tells of the objection by the most fair-minded, law-observant (Pharisees?) to the conviction of the group on the charge of having transgressed the law. Thus it would be unwise to reject the picture, built up elsewhere, of James and the Jerusalem church as law observant.

The sources that provide a basis for this are, in the first instance, Acts and Galatians. Acts 15 and 21 describe James as the head of the Jerusalem church. In both chapters of Acts, James shows concern for the continuing law observance of Jewish believers. Indeed, there is also some expression of the need to apply the law to Gentile believers. There is certainly the appeal to Paul to modify his behavior because of the presence of many Jewish believers in Jerusalem who were zealous for the law (Acts 21:20–21). That picture of James is confirmed by Paul in Galatians 2:1–10, 11–14.

The Epistle of James calls for observance of the whole law (2:10) and observance involves "doers of the law" (1:22–25; 2:14–26). Many scholars have noted the intertextual relationship between James and Matthew, especially the Sermon on the Mount (Matt. 5:1–7:29). In particular James reflects the language and teaching of Jesus expressed in the tradition found only in Matthew and known by the symbol M. There is also the tradition Matthew shares with Luke which James resembles in the form known in Matthew. This can be described as Q^M. The symbol Q represents the sayings source used by Matthew and Luke while Q^M indicates the Matthean form of this which has been modified by its relationship to M.

Following B. H. Streeter, there is a case for recognizing M as the embodiment of Jamesian tradition which has been combined with Petrine tradition, Q. In Matthew these two traditions are combined to express the views of the law-observant mission. At the same time, the final form of Matthew reflects the Peter's perspective of a law-observant mission to the nations and not James's preoccupation with the mission to his own people, though this remains in such passages as Matthew 10:5–6. The final redaction of Matthew is formally indistinguishable from M because it is found only in Matthew. Nevertheless, in its final form, Matthew reflects the authority of Peter (Matt. 16:17–19) and the law-observant mission to the nations (Matt. 28:19–20). It is rightly noted that Jesus here mandates a mission to the nations. It is often missed that the terms of the mission require law observance. Jesus instructs his disciples to make disciples of all the nations, baptizing them and "teaching them *to observe* all that I have commanded you." Nowhere in Matthew does Jesus break a scriptural law or teach what is contrary to that law. Rather, he intensifies the demands of the law. The intensification represents the position of James (as well as Jesus) and his influence finds expression in this Petrine Gospel (see my *Just James*, chap. 4). What is Petrine about the final form of the Gospel is the leading role given to Peter (16:18) and the orientation of the the Gospel to the mission to the nations (28:19–20).

In the Sermon on the Mount, the M and Q^M traditions give expression to the continuing role of the law and the requirement of the greater righteousness involving the observance of the law plus the additional demands of Jesus, which go to the heart of the motivation for action. In particular we should notice that Matthew 5:17–20 lays a foundation for understanding the law-observant mission of James. Here Jesus affirms the enduring authority and application of the law. He did not come to destroy ("tear down"; compare the use of the same verb in 24:2) the law and the prophets but to fulfill. Clearly what is in view is the commandments in Scripture (the law and the prophets), not simply some summary view of the law. The relevance of the law continues beyond the survival of heaven and earth. Jesus' role was not to destroy but to fulfill the law in the sense of bringing the revelation of the will of God, begun in the law of Moses, to its completion in his own extension of the claims of the law. Thus Jesus in Matthew teaches nothing contrary to the law, nor does he break any scriptural law. He demands of those who would enter the kingdom of heaven: "[U]nless your righteousness exceeds the righteousness of the scribes and Pharisees you will certainly not enter the kingdom of heaven." Because the scribes and Pharisees sit on the seat of Moses, Jesus instructs the disciples to do all that they say. But because they fail to do what they teach, the disciples must not follow their example (23:2–3). Here Jesus also calls for the greater righteousness that exceeds the righteousness of the scribes and Pharisees.

What exceeds concerns that which fulfills the law and brings its demands to completion. Certainly this involves *doing* what is commanded. The greater righteousness also entails additional demands that are expressed in the six antitheses that follow. In none of them does Jesus teach the breaking of a scriptural law. Had he done so, he would have been condemned by his own critique. "Therefore whoever breaks the least of these commandments and teaches these practices to people, will be called least in the kingdom of heaven; but whoever does [keeps the commandments] and teaches [the keeping of them], he will be called great in the kingdom of heaven."

The antitheses of Matthew 5:21–48 suggest to some readers that Jesus is opposed to the law because of the antithetical form in which the demand of Jesus is set over against the command in the law. But in no instance does Jesus demand what the command of the law excludes. Rather, where the law commands, "You shall not murder," Jesus goes further, warning that anger against the brother is covered by the command (5:21–26). Certainly the law does not command anger against the brother, so Jesus is not contradicting the law. In the same way, the law commands, "You shall not commit adultery," but Jesus says the person who looks at a woman with lust commits adultery with her in his heart. The law does not command lust, so Jesus does not contradict the law but extends it. Again, "Whoever dismisses his wife, let him give her a bill of divorce" does not command divorce (5:31–32). Rather the legal status of the wife was protected by the issue of the bill of divorce. The requirement of the bill of divorce was necessitated by husbands dismissing their wives. The provision did not commend the husbands but protected the wives. Jesus takes further the critique of husbands who put away their wives. Anyone who dismisses his wife for reasons other than unchastity causes her to commit adultery, and anyone who marries her commits adultery. But nowhere does Jesus say that the man who divorces his wife commits adultery if he remarries unless (it is implied) he marries a married woman. While there are problems with this view, it does not oppose the commandment to give a bill of divorce to wives who have been dismissed by their husbands. Similarly, the command not to swear falsely addresses the problem that people do not deal honestly with each other (5:33–37). For this reason oaths were developed to bind people where their word alone could not be trusted. But this only led to false swearing. Hence the command. Jesus went back to the fundamental problem, the trustworthy word, "Let your word be 'Yes Yes, No No.'" The command "An eye for an eye and a tooth for a tooth" does not command retaliation but limits the extent to what is just, "an eye for an eye" (5:38–42). It is a command set against the spiral of violence. Jesus went further, "Do not repay evil for evil," which is not a contradiction of the command limiting the scope of retaliation. Finally there is what was said to those of old, "Love your neighbor and hate your enemy" (5:43-48). Certainly Jesus commands, "Love your enemies," which contradicts "hate your enemies." But the command to "hate your enemies" is not scriptural (though see the command at Qumran in 1QS 1:3–4, 9–10), while the command to "Love your neighbor" certainly is (Lev. 19:18). Thus Jesus' command extends the command "Love your neighbor" to include "your enemy" and this contradicts the tradition of "hating your enemy" but contradicts no scriptural law.

The Jesus of Matthew extends the scope of the law but contradicts or breaks no scriptural commandment. All of this material throws light on the position of James the brother of Jesus, who was known as James the Just in the early church. The title in English obscures the relationship of James to the figure of the righteous sufferer in Jewish tradition. No doubt the title was given to James not only because of his law-observant piety but also because ultimately he suffered and died as one for whom faithfulness to the law was more important than life itself. In this regard James the Just was like his greater brother who also was declared to be a righteous man at the moment of his death (Luke 23:47). In preserving this strand of tradition now found in Matthew, James may well have been "his brother's keeper." Without his influence the church of all nations might have obscured the Jewishness of Jesus more comprehensively than was the case.

WHO WAS JAMES?

James was apparently the eldest of the brothers of Jesus. His seniority can be adduced from the fact that, in the list of the brothers, his name appears first (Mark 6:3). His seniority probably also contributed to his emergence as the leading figure from the family of Jesus. On the reading of the evidence developed in this chapter, James was the younger brother of Jesus, born to Mary and Joseph subsequent to the birth of Jesus.

James and the brothers of Jesus were followers of Jesus during his ministry. None of them belonged to the group Jesus appointed as "the twelve." The appointment of that group was a symbol of Jesus' intention to renew Israel. Nevertheless the family of Jesus is frequently reported to be in the company of the followers of Jesus. Their reported presence among the believers in Jerusalem immediately after the resurrection confirms their participation in the Jesus movement from the beginning.

It is likely that they, like "the twelve," needed to adjust their understanding of Jesus and his mission as a consequence of his crucifixion and resurrection. But this should not be taken to mean that they were opposed to Jesus during his ministry. This conclusion is rarely drawn concerning the mother of Jesus, even though she is part of the group in Mark 3:31–35 that is commonly (but incorrectly) thought to have come to restrain Jesus. The brothers are not portrayed as unbelievers any more than the mother of Jesus and "the twelve" are.

From the beginning the mother and brothers of Jesus are present with the disciples in Jerusalem, where the continuation of Jesus' mission was established. Early tradition names James as the first leader of the Jerusalem church. There is no other early tradition of leadership. Traditions vary in their accounts of the way James was established as leader, through the initial appearance of the risen Jesus to him; by the instruction of Jesus to the disciples; by his appointment by the disciples.

If James is depicted as the leader of the Jerusalem church, the primacy of the Jerusalem church is depicted in various ways. In particular the events of the Jerusalem assembly (Acts 15; Gal. 2:1–10), the extension of the authority of James to Antioch (Gal. 2:11–14), and the collection for the poor saints in Jerusalem (Rom. 15:25–32) show the central role of the Jerusalem church and the continuing authority of James (see Acts 21:17–26).

In conjunction with Galatians 2:1–10, 11–14, this picture of the leadership of James in Jerusalem is combined with his leadership in the two missions represented by Peter and Paul. They led the actual missions but they reported back to James and the Jerusalem church. This picture of James in Jerusalem directing the mission is strongly developed in the Pseudo-Clementines. This work appears to have captured an important aspect of the role of James in the early church, an aspect that was reluctantly acknowledged even by Paul. But there is also an anti-Pauline streak in the Pseudo-Clementines. There Paul is the enemy of James, who hurls James down the steps. He is also the thinly veiled opponent of Peter represented by Simon Magus. James authenticates the lawful gospel as proclaimed by Peter in opposition to the lawless gospel of Paul. This extreme opposition to Paul is grounded in tensions already evident in the New Testament, in Acts 15 and 21:17–26.

The anti-Pauline tendencies are further developed in the Epistle of James (2:14–26), where righteousness based on works is affirmed over against righteousness based on faith alone and Abraham is used as the example of works-based righteousness. This is clearly an attack on what is understood to be Pauline teaching (see Rom. 4). The language used in James echoes Paul's words and uses the text concerning Abraham to which Paul appeals to clinch his case. Had James not been responding to Paul, this text would not have been used, because it specifically says "Abraham believed God" where James seeks to establish that Abraham was justified by works (Jas. 2:21–23). The teaching of Jesus in Matthew 5:17–20 also seems to be aimed at Paul. First the binding and enduring nature of the law is affirmed. Then it is affirmed:

> Whoever then relaxes one of the least of these commandments and teaches men so, shall be called least in the kingdom of heaven; but he who does them and teaches them shall be called great in the kingdom of heaven. For I tell you, unless your righteousness exceeds that of the scribes and Pharisees, you will never enter the kingdom of heaven.

While Paul, who neatly fits the person who does not keep the law and teaches others to follow his teaching, is not excluded from the kingdom of heaven by the first part of the saying (he is least in the kingdom of heaven), he does seem to be excluded by the latter. Clearly Matthew 5 and the Epistle of James reflect conflict with the Pauline position.

When James was martyred in 62, both Peter and Paul were probably still alive. By then Paul would have been in Rome and Peter might well have been there also. Tradition implies that their martyrdom took place soon after the death of James. This means that there was a break of about four years between the death of James and the outbreak of the Jewish War in 66 and a further four years before the destruction of Jerusalem in 70. The tradition, possibly from Hegesippus, preserved by Eusebius asserts that "Immediately after this [the death of James] Vespasian began to besiege them" (*H.E.* 2.23.18). This is certainly a foreshortening of the events.

Eusebius implies this foreshortening in his own words in *H.E.* 3.11.1. Here he makes the point that, after the destruction, the apostles and disciples of the Lord assembled with the family of Jesus, presumably in Jerusalem. There Symeon, son of Clopas and cousin of Jesus, was unanimously appointed the second bishop of Jerusalem in direct succession to James. See also the list of the fifteen Hebrew bishops down to the time of the second siege by Hadrian in 135 C.E. (*H.E.* 4.5.1–4). The impression given is of an unbroken tradition of the Jerusalem church with no significant break in the succession of bishops, thus glossing over the break in continuity between James in 62 C.E. and Symeon in 70 C.E. (after the siege). Eusebius gives no hint of the flight of the Jerusalem church to Pella at the time of the Jewish War sometime between 66 and 70 C.E., a tradition known to us from Epiphanius (*Pan.* 29.7.7; 30.2.7).

The martyrdom of James was the consequence of an intra-Jewish problem. While he and a group of others were charged with lawlessness, this was clearly a controversial charge. It roused strong objection from those Josephus describes as "the most fair-minded and strict in the observance of the law." The charge is also inconsistent with the law-observant piety attributed to James elsewhere. More than likely James antagonized the wealthy, aristocratic high priest of the time, Ananus. The early Christian legends concerning martyrdom have shaped the traditions of his death along the lines of those concerning Jesus and Stephen. Thus, James dies for his witness to Jesus and dies praying for those who killed him. This can hardly be reconciled with the terse account given by Josephus, which bears the marks of authenticity.

Apart from the letters of Paul, the writings of the New Testament come from the period following the destruction of Jerusalem and emanate from the church of all nations. Thus they do not represent the perspective of the earliest church in the period in which James and the Jerusalem church were dominant. Because James is the leading figure of the mission directed to the nation of Israel, his dominant role has been obscured in texts that assume the centrality of the mission to the nations. Yet even in texts that express this point of view, evidence of the influence and authority of James breaks through in surprising ways from time to time (see especially Gal. 1:19; 2:1–10; 11–14; Acts 15; 21 and 1 Cor. 15:7). With the destruction of Jerusalem the dominant role of the Jerusalem church came to an end. Tradition representing the position of James continued to influence pockets of Jewish Christianity, which seems often to have developed in potentially gnostic directions.

From the second century, the later traditions concerning James flow in three main directions. Sources outside the "mainstream" show that James remained the single most powerful figure in law-observant Jewish Christianity. From the time of the destruction of Jerusalem this position was increasingly marginalized.

After the destruction of the Jewish War, James is made the architect of the mission to the nations. In the process, tradition from James was embodied in Matthew as the basis of a Gospel establishing a law-observant mission to the nations (see Matt. 28:16–20). In doing this the position of James is merged with that of Peter. In time Matthew came to be read and/or understood in a way that obscured that Gospel's advocacy of the continuing validity of the Jewish law. In this transition Peter, who had led the law-observant mission to the nations, was understood to be the apostle of a mission that leaves Judaism behind and turns to the nations. That is, Peter is interpreted in terms of Paul! This common reading of Matthew does not do justice to a careful reading of the text. At the same time, tradition stemming from James and addressed to Jewish believers in the Diaspora became identified with the message of James to believers generally. Thus the Epistle of James came to be understood as a Catholic Epistle addressed to the church of all nations in every time and place.

Tradition also identified James as the recipient of the higher knowledge. Because the authority of James was obscured by emerging Gentile Christianity, the way was opened for Jewish and gnostic groups to appeal to James as their own authoritative leader. This emerges in the *Gospel of the Hebrews*, the *Gospel of Thomas*, and especially in the *Apocryphon* and two Apocalypses of James discovered at Nag Hammadi. The popularity of James in these texts probably came about because they, and other traditions about James, were isolated from what was becoming mainstream Christianity. Nevertheless, a number of things made it impossible for the early church of the second century to repudiate James and the traditions honoring him.

First, he was widely known as "the brother of the Lord," even in books commonly recognized as scripture. Second, he was known as James the Just because of his piety and his faithful witness as a martyr. For this reason, in the second century, the emerging great church had to reclaim James. This is clear in the evidence Eusebius collects from Hegesippus (*H.E.* 2.23.3–18) and Clement (*H.E.* 2.1.3–5). The emerging great church did this by making his leadership dependent on the apostles and linking them with him in the exercise of his leadership. James was also linked with Peter and John as the recipients of the higher knowledge. That higher knowledge was passed on to the other disciples and to the seventy. (See *H.E.* 2.1.3–5.) In this way James was reclaimed by the great church, though he was soon totally over-shadowed by the growing importance of the role of the twelve and especially Peter. The death of James, shortly followed by the demise of the Jerusalem church, destroyed the context in which the leadership of James had its roots. The growing strength of the church of all nations had little place for a law-observant mission and its gospel, or for the figure who symbolized the cen-tral place it once held in the earliest church.

When, in the second century, the view developed that Mary had not only conceived as a virgin but had remained a virgin, the status of James and the brothers was significantly downgraded. The view now known in the *Protevan-gelium of James* portrays the brothers as children of Joseph but not Mary. If Jesus was conceived by Mary as a virgin, those called brothers were no natural relatives of Jesus at all. In the fourth century Jerome argued that the brothers were actually cousins of Jesus, being children of the sister of the mother of Jesus, who was also called Mary. In both of these views Mary was venerated as the very model of ascetic virtue. For Jerome, Joseph too became an ascetic model, as he was not the father of Jesus or of those known as brothers and sis-ters of Jesus. The distance placed between James and Jesus contributed to James's fall into obscurity, and he became known as James the less, over against James the brother of John, the greater James. This was not the intention of Jerome, who honored James as the second of the famous men whose lives he praised.

At the same time, the Epistle of James was moving out of obscurity. Because it began as a message to believing Jews in the Diaspora, evidence of its circu-lation and use is scant in the early period. Only through the reclamation of James by the emerging great church was the epistle rescued from obscurity and eventually recognized as canonical. While Eusebius recognizes it as the first of the General Epistles (*H.E.* 2.23.24–25), it is not until the Easter Festal letter of Athanasius in 367 that we have evidence of it being listed as a canon-ical work. To do this, the Jewish roots of the epistle were obscured and it was accepted as a letter addressed to the church of all nations.

Modern studies have begun to recover the role of the family of Jesus in the early church. Here the paramount figure is that of James. His leadership is still visible in texts in the New Testament, though they come from traditions that do not set out to honor him. Apart from the Epistle of James, which has been subverted to appear as a General Epistle, there is no writing in the New Tes-tament that takes the part of James. The second-century evidence is kinder to James. It recognizes his eminence and also bears witness to the diverse groups that appealed to him. But from this time on, the streams flowing from James begin to dry up. The historical processes worked against him. What had begun

BIBLIOGRAPHY

Early Fathers. *Patrologiae Cursus Completus.* Edited by J. P. Migne.
——. 1953. *Early Christian Fathers.* Edited by Cyril C. Richardson, LCC. Philadelphia: Westminster.
——. 1899–1900. *The Ante-Nicene Fathers.*, Edited by A. Roberts and J. Donaldson. Grand Rapids: Eerdmans. 10 vols.
——. 1899. *The Ante-Nicene Christian Library.* Vol. xvii, "The Clementine Homilies, The Apostolic Constitutions." Edited by A. Roberts and J. Donaldson. Edinburgh: T. & T. Clark.
——. 1899. *Constitutions of the Holy Apostles. Ante-Nicene Fathers* 7.
——. 1912. *The Apostolic Fathers.* Translated by Kirsopp Lake. 2 vols. LCL. Cambridge, Mass., and London: Harvard University Press and William Heinemann, 1912–1913.
——. 1968. *Early Christian Writings.* Translated by Maxwell Staniforth. Harmondsworth: Penguin Books.
——. 1956. *Documents of the Christian Church.* Edited by Henry Bettenson. Oxford: Oxford University Press.
——. 1968. *A New Eusebius.* Edited by J. Stevenson. London: SPCK.
——. 1954. *Alexandrian Christianity.* Edited by Henry Chadwick. LCC. Philadelphia: Westminster Press.
——. 1956. *Early Latin Theology.* Edited by S. L. Greenslade. LCC. Philadelphia: Westminster.
Jerome. 1977. *Commentaire sur S. Matthieu.* Translation and notes by Emile Bonnard. Livres I–II. SC 242. Paris: Cerf.
——. *Against Helvidius (Adv. Helvidium de Perpetua Virginitate B. Mariae).*
——. 1896. *De viris illustribus.* Edited by E. C. Richardson. TU 14.
Origen. 1980. *Contra Celsum.* Edited by Henry Chadwick. LCC. Philadelphia: Westminster.
——. 1969. *The Ante-Nicene Fathers: Original Supplement to the American Edition (Peter, Tatian, Commentaries of Origen).* Vol. 10. Edited by Allan Menzies. Grand Rapids: Eerdmans, reprinted 1969.
Josephus. 1930–1965. *Jewish Antiquities.* Translated by H. St. J. Thackery, Ralph Marcus, and Louis Feldman, completed and edited by Allen Wikgren. 7 vols. LCL.
——. 1927, 1928. *The Jewish War.* Translated by H. St. J. Thackery. 2 vols. LCL.
——. 1970. *Josephus: The Jewish War.* Translated with an introduction by G. A. Williamson. 2d ed. Harmondsworth: Penguin Books.
Barrett, C. K. 1978. *The Gospel According to St John.* 2d ed. London: SPCK.
Bauckham, R. 1990. *Jude and the Relatives of Jesus in the Early Church.* Edinburgh: T. & T. Clark.
——. "James and the Jerusalem Church," in idem, ed., *The Book of Acts in Its First*

Century Setting, vol. 4, The Book of Acts in Its Palestinian Setting. Grand Rapids: Eerdmans, 1995.

Brandon, S. G. F. 1957. The Fall of Jerusalem and the Christian Church. London: SPCK.

———. 1967a. Jesus and the Zealots. Manchester.

———. 1967b. "The Death of James the Just: A New Interpretation." Pages 57–69 in Studies in Mysticism and Religion, presented to G. Scholem. Jerusalem: Magnes Press.

Brown, R. E. 1987. "The Gospel of Peter and Canonical Gospel Authority." NTS 33:321–43.

Brown, S. K. 1972. James: A Religio-Historical Study of the Relations between Jewish, Gnostic, and Catholic Christianity in the Early Period through an Investigation of the Traditions about James the Lord's Brother. Ph.D. diss., Brown University. Ann Arbor: University Microfilms.

Crossan, J. D. 1973. "Mark and the Relatives of Jesus," NovT 15:81–113.

———. 1985. Four Other Gospels. Minneapolis: Winston Press.

———. 1993. The Historical Jesus: The Life of a Mediterranean Jewish Peasant. San Francisco: Harper.

Eisenman, R. H. 1983. Maccabees, Zadokites, Christians and Qumran. Leiden: Brill.

———. 1986. James the Just in the Habakkuk Pesher. Leiden: Brill.

———. 1991. "Playing on and Transmuting Words: Interpreting Abeit-Galuto in the Habbakkuk Pesher." Pages 177–96 in Papers on the Dead Sea Scrolls in Memory of Jean Carmignac, edited by Z. J. Kapera. Krakow.

———. 1997. James the Brother of Jesus: The Key to the Unlocking of Early Christianity and the Dead Sea Scrolls. New York: Viking.

Eisenman, R. H. and M. Wise. 1993. The Dead Sea Scrolls Uncovered. Element Books.

Eisler, R. 1931. The Messiah Jesus and John the Baptist. London: Methuen.

Elliott, J. K. ed. 1993. The Apocryphal New Testament: A Collection of Apocryphal Christian Literature in an English Translation, Based on M. R. James. Oxford: Clarendon Press.

Jeremias, J. 1967. Jerusalem in the Time of Jesus. London: SCM Press.

Jones, F. S. 1990. "The Martyrdom of James in Hegesippus, Clement of Alexandria, Christian Apocrypha, Including Nag Hammadi: A Study of the Textual Relations" Seminar Papers Society of Biblical Literature, 1990. Atlanta: Scholars Press, 322–35.

Lightfoot, J. B. 1865. "The Brethren of the Lord" in idem, Saint Paul's Epistle to the Galatians. London: Macmillan.

Luedemann, G. 1984. Paul, Apostle to the Gentiles. Philadelphia: Fortress.

———. 1989. Opposition to Paul in Jewish Christianity. Minneapolis: Fortress.

Munck, J. 1959. Paul and the Salvation of Mankind. London: SCM.

———. 1980. "Jewish Christianity in Post-Apostolic Times," NTS 6:103–16.

Painter, John. 1997. Just James: The Brother of Jesus in History and Tradition. Columbia: University of South Carolina Press.

Robinson, J. M., ed. 1988. The Nag Hammadi Library in English. 2d ed. New York: Harper & Row.

Smallwood, E. M. 1962. "High Priests and Politics in Roman Palestine." JTS 13:14–34.

———. 1981. The Jews under Roman Rule: From Pompey to Diocletian. A Study of Political Relations. 2d ed. Leiden: Brill.

Strecker, G. 1971. Der Weg der Gerechtigkeit: Untersuchung zur Theologie des Matthäus. 3d ed. Göttingen: Vandenhoeck & Ruprecht.

―――. 1971. "On the Problem of Jewish Christianity." Pages 241–85 in W. Bauer, *Orthodoxy and Heresy in Earliest Christianity.* Translated by R. A. Kraft and G. Krodel. Philadelphia: Fortress.

―――. 1981. *Das Judenchristentum in den Pseudoklementinen.* TU 70/2. Berlin: Akademie.

Streeter, B. H. 1929. *The Primitive Church: Studied with Special Reference to the Origins of the Christian Ministry.* London: Macmillan.

―――. 1934. *The Four Gospels: A Study of Origins Treating of the Manuscript Tradition, Sources, Authorship and Dates.* London: Macmillan.

Voorst, R. E. van. 1989. *The Ascents of James: History and Theology of a Jewish-Christian Community.* SBL Dissertation Series 112. Atlanta: Scholars Press.

Weiss, J. 1917. *Das Urchristentum.* Edited after the author's death by R. Knopf. Göttingen.

Wilson, R. McL. 1963, 1965. *New Testament Apocrypha.* Translated and edited by W. Schneemelcher. 2 vols. Philadelphia: Westminster Press.

―――. 1960. *Studies in the Gospel of Thomas.* London: Mowbrays.

3

James's Message

The Literary Record

Peter H. Davids

I. INTRODUCTION

The short (105-verse) letter known as the Epistle of James has suffered from neglect in both the church that generated it and the academy that has studied it, particularly when it comes to looking at its message. (Bruce 1979, Chester and Martin 1994, and the recent work of Bauckham 1999, are some notable exceptions.) In this chapter we do not intend to go into the reasons for that neglect, interesting as they are, but to look at the message of the letter itself. We shall do this bracketing questions about authorship, such as whether James the Just, the brother of Jesus of Nazareth, either wrote the letter or was the primary source of its content, for we are looking at the literary record, the text that we have before us, rather than the historical background of that text. From the literary point of view the implied author is James, brother of Jesus. Naturally, one cannot discuss literature totally separate from the context that surrounded it, since culture is the determiner of the meaning of words, so we will assume a general historical context (see Davids 1999 for detailed argument) and relate our observations to that general setting (even though much of this setting is discussed in the other chapters in this book); it is a cultural context of which James is quite aware. Thus, because this is a "general" letter and therefore separate from a known dialogue between an author and a recipient group, we do not have to go into the issue of author and recipients as we would if, for example, a Pauline letter were under discussion.

As we commented above, just as James is aware of the cultural world around him, he is also aware of structure in his work, even though it is not the structure that we might have used. It is our view that the work is an edited collection of sayings and sermons attributed to James (and his brother Jesus), and that that process gives it a certain unevenness. (Davids 1989:6–7) Yet even then the work is not without its logic. In fact, there are at least two types of logic found in the work: the logic of the letter structure (salutation, opening, body, closing) and the logic revealed by discourse analysis (often that of contrasts; Tollefson 1997). This means that topics may be taken up more than once in the work, depending on the particular contrast that is being intended. For example, the "rich" are mentioned in 1:9–11 in contrast to the humble/poor believer, indicating that, in contrast to the "rich," the believer has an honorable future; the "rich" are mentioned again in 2:6 in contrast to the justice of God toward the poor, as the "rich" are presented as those who practice injustice, which contrast challenges the believing community as to its behavior; the "rich" are mentioned a final time in 5:1–8 as those who persecute their (poorer) workers and "the righteous," giving the reason why the "brothers and sisters" need to practice "patient endurance." Thus we have three contrasts with the "rich" as one member of the pair, the first having to do with status, the second with community behavior, and the third with God's eschatological justice. There is a constant in all three of these sections, but they are not mere repetition. These connections and contrasts are the province of discourse analysis. For our purposes, we will more assume these connections than argue for them, since such a demonstration of discourse structure would distract us from presenting the logic of James's thought as a whole.

We begin, then, by noting that James presents itself as a letter in the genre of Diaspora letters sent from Jewish leaders in Jerusalem to Jewish communities outside "the land," however the particular Jewish group may have defined the boundaries. That the communities addressed are viewed as Israel is clear from "to the twelve tribes scattered among the nations" (1:1). If the communities addressed are "scattered" (literally "in the Diaspora"), then the sender is not part of this Diaspora. He is identified as "James," who was known as the Jerusalem leader of that Judaism which acknowledged Jesus of Nazareth as the Messiah of their expectations. We word this carefully. That this group acknowledged Jesus of Nazareth as "Lord" is clear in James 2:1, in some of the references to "the Lord" elsewhere in the letter (also "the good/honorable name" of 2:7), and in the many allusions to (or, with Bauckham's chapter later in this work, wisdom sayings built on the model of) his teaching (5:12 likely being a quotation; cf. Matt 5:33–37).

That the community this letter represents is a Judaism is clear, not only from the self-reference to the communities as "the twelve tribes" (i.e. Israel), but also from the unselfconscious use of the Jewish scriptures. Of course, it would be anachronistic to call them "Jewish-Christian." First, the letter shows no consciousness that there are other groups who are not Israel but still follow Jesus. In James's view, as far as he reveals it, all followers of Jesus were in some sense Israel. Second, while James and his community may or may not have recognized themselves in the term "Christian" (Acts 11:26 dates the first use of the designation in Syrian Antioch to the early '40s, so it may well have been known all over the eastern Mediterranean later in the first century), but they certainly did not think of "Jewish" and "Christian" as separate categories. They were a variety of Judaism, and in their own eyes surely the "true" variety, the renewed Israel awaiting the return of their Messiah, who was even now "at the doors" (5:9).

This tells us two things about the community generating the letter and likely the recipient communities as well. First, as Israel they recognize the formation narrative of Israel, the Torah, as their scripture. Not only can James refer to stories from the whole of the Jewish scriptures, but he also specifically cites the narrative of Abraham from the Torah (Jas 2:21), referring to him as "our father." Earlier he has quoted parts of the Decalogue as divine in origin (2:11; cf. 2:8). When it comes to citing his basic creed, he cites the *Shema'* (2:19; cf. Deut. 6:4). Nor is our author shy about mentioning the Torah (law) in general. The law is "the perfect law, the law of liberty" (Jas. 1:25). It is "the royal law" (2:8). There can be no doubt but that James's community was part of a movement that valued the Torah. He would have approved of Matthew's sayings, "Do not think that I have come to abolish the law or the prophets; I have come not to abolish but to fulfill. For truly I tell you, until heaven and earth pass away, not one letter, not one stroke of a letter, will pass from the law until all is accomplished. Therefore, whoever breaks one of the least of these commandments, and teaches others to do the same, will be called least in the kingdom of heaven; but whoever does them and teaches them will be called great in the kingdom of heaven" (Matt. 5:17–19).

Second, given the number of echoes (at least 36) of the teaching of Jesus of Nazareth (Davids 1982, 47–48; Hartin 1991), James's community saw him as the authoritative interpreter of the scriptures (we could say, "Jewish scriptures," but for James there were no other scriptures) and of the will of God. This, of course, is what we would expect, for since each Judaism called upon these scriptures to justify its claims in some way, each group would likewise need to identify at least to insiders the basis for their interpretation, whether it was the "Teacher of Righteousness" (for those who produced at least some of the Dead Sea Scrolls) or the various "fathers" that another strand of Judaism would later enshrine in the *Mishnah* tractate *'Abot*. For James the one authority other than the scriptures is Jesus of Nazareth, whom James refers to as "Lord" (in 1:1 and 2:1 also adding "Jesus Christ").

Having said the above, we do not wish to imply that James demonstrates a clear "canon consciousness" with Jesus as the expositor of this canon. It is clear that he does not have clear canonical boundaries, as was fitting for a community for which scripture was not a readily available reference work but an oral reading during community gatherings ("synagogue" is James's term, 2:2). Neither are they yet concerned about the issue of which works might not be given up to authorities seeking to confiscate them (which led to later reflection on canonical issues by some Jews) nor which works should or should not be read in the communal assemblies (which was the basic question for later Christian canonical reflection). Thus the boundaries between the scriptural narratives (as we know them today) and the expansions on those narratives in oral tradition were not set. While there is evidence of this phenomenon in his citations of Abraham and Elijah, the clearest case is that of Job in James 5:11. The Job of scripture certainly refuses to turn on God and endures in the sense that he constantly maintains his own rightness, but at the same time the poetic part of the work is a long lament in which Job accuses God of dealing unfairly with him, while the other voices charge Job with being the cause of his own misery. No extant Greek translation of the Hebrew Job uses the word for "patience" that James uses, which indicates patient, trusting endurance. James, however, apparently knows the tradition later enshrined in the *Testament of Job*, the whole of which revolves around James's very word for patient endurance. James shows no consciousness of where the scriptures leave off and where the oral expansions begin. Both scripture and oral expansion are Job or Elijah or Abraham for him (and likely for the communities he addresses as well; "you have heard" indicates a belief in a shared understanding of the narrative), without his concerning himself with what is what.

This, then, sketches out James expressing a Judaism, a form of Judaism that he would likely have believed to be the truest and best Judaism, one that expressed God's intentions for, and calling upon, Israel better than any other. However, in our letter we do not get a full description of that Judaism. What we get is James speaking from within the system (which is why we have described the rough outlines of the system, to the extent that James indicates what they are) to address certain problems within the community. The focal issue is that of communal solidarity. The trigger issue is that of the rejection of the community by the surrounding elites. And the symptoms are internal conflict and a tendency to find security in such wealth and possessions as one had rather than to share within the "family." It is to a fuller presentation of this system that we now turn.

II. TRIALS AND THEIR RESULTS

1. A community under pressure

James begins with a reference to the community's being under pressure: "My brothers and sisters, whenever you face trials of any kind, consider it nothing but joy, because you know that the testing of your faith produces endurance; and let endurance have its full effect, so that you may be mature and complete, lacking in nothing" (Jas. 1:2–4). What are the trials that the community faces? The Greek term for "trials" appears 21 times in the New Testament. In each occurrence it means something that tests one's trust in and commitment to God. In Matt. 6:13 the request for preservation from trials parallels the request for deliverance from the Evil One. In Matt. 26:41 (paralleled in Mark 14:38 and Luke 22:40, 46) it refers to the arrest/crucifixion of Jesus that would cause his disciples to abandon their commitment to him (cf. 1 Cor. 10:13). In Acts 20:19 persecution is the reference (so also 1 Pet. 4:12 and Rev. 3:10). A close parallel to our verse is found in 1 Peter 1:6 ("In this [salvation] you rejoice, even if now for a little while you have had to suffer various trials"). Where are these tests/trials in James?

The first source of trials is the "rich," the cultural and economic elites of the surrounding community. James says about them, "Is it not the rich who oppress you? Is it not they who drag you into court? Is it not they who blaspheme the excellent name that was invoked over you?" (Jas. 2:6–7). Later in 5:1–6 we learn that these people (1) kept back by fraud the wages of laborers working for them and (2) "have condemned and murdered the righteous one." We do not learn why the "rich" do these things. Interestingly enough, only one of the charges (slandering "the excellent name" called over them) is specifically religious; the rest are socioeconomic. But it is precisely these trials occasioned by the "rich" that lead to the summary call to patient endurance in James 5:7.

There is a second source of trials in James, and that is the internal conflict in the community. We are tipped off to the problem in James 1:19–20: "You must understand this, my beloved: let everyone be quick to listen, slow to speak, slow to anger; for your anger does not produce God's righteousness." Our author becomes more explicit in chapter 3, where with special reference to teachers he notes the destructive power of the tongue, the fact that it is used to curse other human beings, and the existence of party spirit (sometimes translated "selfish ambition"). Then he becomes very explicit indeed: "Those conflicts and disputes among you, where do they come from? Do they not come from your cravings that are at war within you? You want something and do not have it; so you commit murder. And you covet something and cannot obtain it; so you engage in disputes and conflicts" (4:1–2). A bit later he exhorts, "Do not speak evil against one another, brothers and sisters. Whoever speaks evil against another or judges another, speaks evil against the law and judges the law; but if you judge the law, you are not a doer of the law but a judge. There is one lawgiver and judge who is able to save and to destroy. So who, then, are you to judge your neighbor?" (4:11–12). He returns to the topic in his summary, "Beloved, do not grumble against one another, so that you may not be judged" (5:9). To make it clear that these are part of the trials that he is speaking of, James integrates this material into the topic of trials at two points: 5:9, which is part of the summary, the response to the trials by the "rich" in 5:1–6, and 4:1–2, which roughly parallels 1:12–15, where trials are explicitly mentioned.

In the world of James, then, the community is under external pressure from those he labels "rich." Some of this pressure may be related to the community's consisting of the "poor," which includes the laborers that the "rich" are perceived to wrong. Some of it appears related to their religious stance, their commitment to Jesus (the "honorable name" named over them in baptism), whom these social elites slander. (Whether this reality is limited to the literary world of James, modeled on scriptural oppression of the poor by the rich, or whether it corresponds to external historical phenomena is not a topic that we are discussing here; our concern is with the rhetoric of the literary world itself. We have discussed this elsewhere, e.g., Davids 1999.) Furthermore, this external pressure is related to internal discord as community members struggle with one another and critique one another. In other words, there is no refuge within the community as the community draws together in the face of external pressure, but instead within the community there is division and criticism that make it an unsafe place. We note that at the very least this is a psychologically accurate portrait in that economic pressure often does lead to internal conflict within a social system, whether that system is a family or a large community. James portrays his community as family, using family language when addressing his readers. There are 17 verses in which he refers to community members as "my siblings" or "a brother" or "a sister." We do not learn whether this simply indicates common membership in the extended family of "Israel" or whether this is to be taken as indicating a closer "familial" relationship among members of the community within "Israel." (In other documents in the New Testament there is more varied family language, such as references to someone being a "father" and to the exchange of a kiss, that normally did indicate close family or friends, but our short letter does not happen to contain such a reference.) What is clear is that the "family" is at present dysfunctional.

2. Reasons for failure

What does James see as the reason for this internal breakdown under pressure? We do not learn the answer to this question the first time he brings up the issue of trials, but he certainly does discuss it the second time the topic appears: "Blessed is anyone who endures temptation [trials, tests of faith—the same word as in 1:2]. Such a one has stood the test and will receive the crown of life that the Lord has promised to those who love him. No one, when [undergoing trials], should say, "I am being [tried] by God"; for God [should not be put to the test by evil people] and he himself [tests] no one. But one is [tested] by one's own desire, being lured and enticed by it; then, when that desire has conceived, it gives birth to sin, and that sin, when it is fully grown, gives birth to death" (Jas. 1:12–15 NRSV, the parts in brackets being the author's changes in that translation to better reveal the sense of the underlying text). Here we see quite a different picture of trials than that present in Matthew 6:13. There the agency of testing is external. One is "led" into the testing situation or one is delivered from "the Evil One." James is aware of such a view of testing, for he refers to the devil in James 4:7 and to the demonic origin of certain tendencies in 3:15. But he does not believe that this is a sufficient explanation for one's failure under trial. External pressure is, after all, external. The reason for failure is internal. It is found (to use a modern expression that conveys his meaning) in one's own self-talk and even more centrally in "desire" within the human being. There are plenty of enemies, both human and diabolic, outside the individual, but the real culprits that cause one's failure are found lurking in his or her own body.

It is, however, at the point that we try to describe this internal force that we encounter a series of difficulties. The first is that the self-talk that James labels improper ("I am being tested by God") appears to be calling upon a scriptural tradition. Genesis 22:1 says, "After these things God tested Abraham" and Exodus 15:25 states, "There he [God] put them [Israel] to the test." In fact, the associated place name, Massah, is interpreted as "testing." The Massah narrative may not have been a problem for James, since the way God tests in the wilderness is more by caring for Israel and observing their behavior than by setting up a situation of difficulty, but the Abraham narrative is certainly within James's purview, for he will cite it explicitly in James 2:21. However, it is clear that James is reading it differently, probably reading it more like the story of Job, as is done in *Jub.* 17:15–18:19:

> And it came to pass . . . that words came in heaven concerning Abraham that he was faithful in everything which was told him and he loved the Lord and was faithful in all affliction. And Prince Mastema came and said before the Lord, "Behold, Abraham loves Isaac, his son. . . . Tell him to offer him (as) a burnt offering upon the altar. And you will see whether he will do this thing. . . ." And the Lord was aware that Abraham was faithful in all of his afflictions. . . . And his soul was not impatient. And he was not slow to act because he was faithful and a lover of the Lord. [Then follows the narrative very similar to the Genesis narrative, except for the comment in 18:12 "And Prince Mastema was shamed," showing that this story is read as an honor contest between Prince Mastema and God.]

Naturally, we cannot be sure that James knew precisely this tradition. Others will be found in different Jewish literature, most of it much later than James. *Targum Ps.-Jonathan* attributes the test to an honor contest between Ishmael and Isaac, so God is honoring Isaac's request by calling for the offering of Isaac. *Ber. R.* 55:4 suggests Abraham's own concerns initiated it. But *Ps.-Philo* 32.1 and *b. Sanh.* 89b both attribute the incident to an honor contest between God and angelic beings/Satan. (Josephus, *Ant.* 1.222–236, reads it as a test, but the test is mitigated by his belief that being free of the body and going to God is good. For Philo, *Quod Deus immutabilis sit* 4, Isaac is "self-taught wisdom" and so might better have been offered than simply bound.) Thus, while we cannot know exactly what reading of the tradition was familiar to James, we do know that several explanations of the narrative existed both before and after James. One that is multiply attested is a reading of the Abraham narrative in light of Job in which the cause of the command to offer Isaac is some form of honor contest between God and another being. Given his references to the devil in James 4:7 and his liking for Job, it would not surprise us if this were how James read the Abraham narrative. What is clearer is that he does not read it as God's being the cause of the test.

The second difficulty is determining what the concept of "desire" meant for James and his community. It is clear that for James desire is what makes a test into a test. Without desire the outward circumstances would not be experienced as testing one's commitment to God. But what is this desire? First of all, it is clear that "desire" is not the polar opposite of "mind" or "rational thought" as it is in *Wisdom of Solomon, 4 Maccabees,* and Philo's works. We are not talking about the "higher" and "lower" parts of a human being, the "lower" having to do with the body and its desires and the "higher" with pure rationality. For James the solution to the problem of desire comes from God, not from a more rational part of the human being. When one repents, one receives "grace." There is an ability to make a choice, but the choice is a choice to submit to God, who then exalts one. To put it another way, salvation is attributed to God, God's word, or God's wisdom, not to a human faculty. What, then, is desire? It appears to be a translation of what at least some Judaisms termed *yeṣer,* or the internal impulse in the human being. We see this idea long before James in Sirach 15:11ff.:

> [11]Do not say, "It was the Lord's doing that I fell away";
> for he does not do what he hates.
> [12]Do not say, "It was he who led me astray";
> for he has no need of the sinful.
> [13]The Lord hates all abominations;
> such things are not loved by those who fear him.
> [14]It was he who created humankind in the beginning
> [and appointed him in the hand of his spoiler],
> and he left them in the power of [his *yeṣer*].
> [15]If you choose, you can keep the commandments,
> and to act faithfully is a matter of your own choice.
> [16]He has placed before you fire and water;
> stretch out your hand for whichever you choose.
> [17]Before each person are life and death,
> and whichever one chooses will be given.
> [18]For great is the wisdom of the Lord;
> he is mighty in power and sees everything;
> [19]his eyes are on those who fear him,
> and he knows every human action.
> [20]He has not commanded anyone to be wicked,
> and he has not given anyone permission to sin.
>   [Text from the NRSV modified from the
>   Hebrew version of Sirach]

What one has here is the juxtaposition of the thoughts/impulses of the human individual and the Torah. One can either live according to one's inner impulses or one can choose to follow the Torah. This combination of pessimism about human nature and optimism about God's remedy is found throughout Sirach (5:1–2; 17:31; 21:11; 27:5–6; and probably 37:3). The vocabulary in Greek (LXX) and at times in Hebrew as well varies over a series of synonyms, showing that we do not yet have a fully technical language. We are instead in a process that recognizes that the inner impulses of the human being, the drives within, tend toward sin, and yet acknowledges that God has provided the necessary remedy. And, given that God has created the human being, it appears as if the human is defective without the Torah. Without Torah he or she is a ship without a compass and thus likely to go on the rocks. In the Judaism of Qumran, especially in the Thanksgiving Hymns (1QH), a similar contrast is seen between the human being as created weak and God's grace, using *yeṣer* terminology for the former (Davids 1974, 13–56)

There is precedent, then, in the language of various Judaisms for the idea of a tendency in the human being toward evil, one that is inbuilt from creation. The various Judaisms have different answers as to why some individuals seem given over to evil and others do not. For Sirach, God has provided the Torah and it is up to the human being to choose to accept the remedy. For at least some of the Dead Sea Scrolls, the reason lies at least in part in divine determinism, the grace according to which a good spirit or otherwise is put into the human being. Nevertheless, the belief in this tendency toward evil appeared long before the later developments of rabbinic thought on the nature of the *yeṣer* in the human being.

How does this impulse in the human being function in James? For James this impulse is "desire," not "evil desire" (as expanded in many translations), but desire pure and simple. It appears to be similar to Freud's term "Id," or, in later psychological terminology, the "drives" within the human being. The problem with "desire" is that it lacks a compass and boundaries; it simply wants something without considerations of right and wrong. So, according to James, the person is soon enticed (the image is of a baited trap) into transgressing boundaries (James does not indicate where the boundaries come from, perhaps from the Torah, but inherent in the concept of sin is that of boundary transgression). And that, of course, is the way of death, whether one looks in the Hebrew scriptures, the New Testament, or the Apostolic Fathers (e.g., both the *Didache* and the *Epistle of Barnabas* have two-ways sections with the way of life contrasted with the way of death). This is the message of James 1:14–15.

The role of desire in producing sin is pictured another way in James 4:1–3. Here the issue is not so much general failure under testing as internal community conflict, "wars" and "conflicts" in James's language. James traces the problem back to desire "in your members" (probably within the individual, for he never mentions a concept of the "body of Christ" or otherwise indicates that he thinks of the community of believers as a body). The inner struggle with desire leads to outer struggle in the community over scarce resources: "you 'kill and covet'" and "you 'fight' and 'war.'" Neither Torah nor faith (in the sense of commitment to God) come into the picture. Prayer does appear, but it is prayer in the service of desire. Here James does not speak of desire leading to death, but to estrangement from God (seen in the language of adultery in 4:4), and therefore enmity with respect to God, probably with the implication of divine judgment (reason enough for the need of grace in 4:6 and the call to repentance starting in 4:7).

Therefore, whether we look in chapter 1 or chapter 4 we see a consistent picture. Desire left to itself leads to estrangement from God or, as 1:15 puts it, to death. Somehow boundaries need to be put on desire so that it cannot take control, so that it is not unbounded, so that it does not lead to death. Yet the chain desire–sin–death has said one thing clearly, which is that God is not responsible for human sin. Testing, which does not come from God, hooks into a problem within the human individual, and that is what makes the test a test.

III. RESPONSES TO TRIALS

1. Eschatological anticipated joy

We have seen how one should not respond to trials, that is, by giving in to the urgings of desire; how then *should* one respond? James states this quite clearly in the first words of the letter opening: "consider it all joy." We must not mistake this for some form of masochism. James is neither asking the reader to enjoy painful situations nor is he instructing the reader to rejoice that "brother Ass" (St. Francis's description of the human body) is being humbled or destroyed. James is not against the body nor for pain. Difficult situations just happen (therefore one "falls" into various trials in 1:2). It is the response that James is concerned about. The response of joy is an eschatological response, or, to use a term coined by Johann Thomas, "eschatological anticipated joy" (Thomas 1968). While James is structurally and/or verbally parallel to Romans 5:3–5 and 1 Peter 1:6–7 (the former is a chain saying like Jas. 1:2–4, while the latter has more verbal parallels), he is not literarily dependent upon either of them; instead, all appear to be applications of, or sayings built upon, the tradition enshrined in the beatitudes of the Jesus tradition, especially the concluding two in the Matthean form (although all are relevant to James in one place or another):

Blessed are the poor in spirit, for theirs is the kingdom of heaven.
Blessed are those who mourn, for they will be comforted.
Blessed are the meek, for they will inherit the earth.
Blessed are those who hunger and thirst for righteousness, for they will be filled.
Blessed are the merciful, for they will receive mercy.

Blessed are the pure in heart, for they will see God.
Blessed are the peacemakers, for they will be called children of God.
Blessed are those who are persecuted for righteousness' sake, for theirs is the
    kingdom of heaven.
Blessed are you when people revile you and persecute you and utter all kinds of
    evil against you falsely on my account. Rejoice and be glad, for your reward is
    great in heaven, for in the same way they persecuted the prophets who were
    before you. (Matt. 5:3–12)

While the first few beatitudes could include people who are undergoing trials (and clearly do in their Lukan form), the last two demonstrate James's point
of view. Those who are persecuted will receive "the kingdom of heaven" and
those who suffer "on my account" can rejoice because "your reward is great in
heaven." Since the beatitude form pronounces one "blessed," "fortunate," or
"happy" (all alternative translations of the Greek term), it is really no step at
all from that form to instructing those declared "blessed" to "rejoice and be
glad," not in their present suffering, but in the coming reward to which the
present trial is a prelude and toward which it points. In other words, the joy is
eschatological in that it is based on the final verdict of God and it is anticipated
because the present joy is in anticipation of the coming reward.

While James is certainly not unaware of the coming reward and also believes
that it is not far off ("the Judge is at the door," Jas. 5:9), he presently sees hope-
ful signs in the more proximate future in that the products of enduring trials
are "endurance," a key Christian virtue, and a mature character, the type of
maturity that followers of Jesus are called to in Matthew 5:48, "Be perfect,
therefore, as your heavenly Father is perfect." (The word translated "mature"
in James is the same term translated "perfect" in Matthew.) These virtues, of
course, also have their own reward later, but the very act of endurance becomes
for James a marker of the coming reward and thus a cause of rejoicing.

The other way that James has of stating this same truth is "Blessed is anyone who endures [testing]. Such a one has stood the test and will receive the
crown of life that the Lord has promised to those who love him" (Jas. 1:12,
NRSV modified for consistency). Here James uses the beatitude form itself,
shifts the noun (endurance) to its corresponding verb and then states the
reward, "the crown of life." This crown (most likely a crown that is life itself)
is also mentioned in Revelation 2:10, so it may have been a known expression
in Christian communities. The combination of test + endurance + statement
of approval + reward appears first in the Torah. Abraham, in the Genesis 22
narrative known to James, shows his endurance by going to the appointed
place, binding his son Isaac, and laying him on the altar with the intention of
offering him as a sacrifice. Then comes the formula of approval, "Now I know
that you fear God, since you have not withheld your son, your only son, from
me" (Gen. 22:12), followed by the promise of reward, "By myself I have sworn,
says the Lord: Because you have done this, and have not withheld your son,
your only son, I will indeed bless you . . ." (Gen. 22:16–18). In our passage in

James we look forward to passing an analogous test: Gain the approval ("has stood the test" = "becoming approved") and you will receive "the [eschatological] crown of life."

This same eschatological perspective is reflected in the summary in James 5:7–8, "Be patient, therefore, beloved, until the coming of the Lord. . . . Strengthen your hearts, for the coming of the Lord is near." These exhortations are a response to trials, the most proximate trials being the exploitation of peasant laborers by the "rich" and perhaps the latter's judicial murder of "the righteous." Whether one thinks of the community in terms of its identifying itself as the poor or in terms of its identifying itself as righteous, 5:1–6 sets up a situation of trial/testing to which the response is patient endurance due to an eschatological perspective. To this exhortation are appended the stories of the prophets and especially of Job. With reference to the latter, James refers to "the purpose" (NRSV) or "the end result" of the Lord. That is, patient endurance does lead to reward.

2. Wisdom

Not only is having an eschatological perspective a needed response to the situation of testing or trials, but also asking for wisdom is an appropriate response. While the result of enduring trials is that the person might be "mature and complete, lacking in nothing," we have also seen that there is within the individual that which is certainly far from mature and complete. Rather, what there is within him or her is that which makes the trial a real test; in its boundarylessness it tends to seduce the individual toward sin and death. Because this weakness is within the individual, to endure in the various tests or trials one needs an outside force to counteract it. Thus James says, "If any of you is lacking in wisdom, ask God, who gives to all generously and ungrudgingly, and it will be given you" (Jas. 1:5). In saying this, James stands squarely in the wisdom tradition of Israel. In Proverbs wisdom is personified as lady wisdom, the good woman who issues an invitation that leads to life:

> Wisdom has built her house,
> she has hewn her seven pillars.
> ²She has slaughtered her animals, she has mixed her wine,
> she has also set her table.
> ³She has sent out her servant-girls, she calls
> from the highest places in the town,
> ⁴"You that are simple, turn in here!"
> To those without sense she says,
> ⁵"Come, eat of my bread
> and drink of the wine I have mixed.
> ⁶Lay aside immaturity, and live,
> and walk in the way of insight."
>
> (Prov. 9:1–6)

God gives freely in James and wisdom offers herself freely in Proverbs. In Proverbs as in James, the wrong way leads to death (in Proverbs this is symbolized in the adulterous wife, who entices "the simple" and whose way leads to death). In both Proverbs and James the right way leads to life, or, to put it in the words of wisdom in Proverbs 8:35–36, "For whoever finds me finds life and obtains favor from the Lord; but those who miss me injure themselves; all who hate me love death." This same theme is found in later literature, such as Sirach, the body of which begins with, "All wisdom is from the Lord" (Sir. 1:1). The author then goes on to argue, "The fear of the Lord is the beginning/ fullness/ the crown/ the root of wisdom" (Sir. 1:14, 16, 18, 20) in that she is granted to the pious. She is indeed both generous and the source of life: "Wisdom teaches her children/ and gives help to those who seek her. Whoever loves her loves life . . ." (Sir. 4:11–12). Wisdom of Solomon puts it in this way:

> Wisdom is radiant and unfading,
> and she is easily discerned by those who love her,
> and is found by those who seek her.
> She hastens to make herself known to those who desire her.
> One who rises early to seek her will have no difficulty,
> for she will be found sitting at the gate.
>
> (Wis. 6:12–14)

Wisdom is indeed a spiritual force from God:

> There is in her a spirit that is intelligent, holy,
> unique, manifold, subtle,
> mobile, clear, unpolluted,
> distinct, invulnerable, loving the good, keen,
> irresistible, beneficent, humane,
> steadfast, sure, free from anxiety,
> all-powerful, overseeing all,
> and penetrating through all spirits
> that are intelligent, pure, and altogether subtle.
> For wisdom is more mobile than any motion;
> because of her pureness she pervades and penetrates all things.
> For she is a breath of the power of God,
> and a pure emanation of the glory of the Almighty;
> therefore nothing defiled gains entrance into her.
> For she is a reflection of eternal light,
> a spotless mirror of the working of God,
> and an image of his goodness.
>
> (Wis. 7:23–26)

There is much more that Sirach, Wisdom of Solomon, and others had to say about the nature of wisdom, but this should suffice to point out that in books circulating in James's day wisdom was viewed as a personified spiritual force from God leading to life. She was also viewed as generous. The person-ification, at least, also holds true for the sayings of Jesus, e.g., "Yet wisdom is vindicated by her deeds" (Matt. 11:18; cf. Luke 11:49).

For James, then, it is the "wisdom from above" that brings virtue: She is "pure, then peaceable, gentle, willing to yield, full of mercy and good fruits, without a trace of partiality or hypocrisy" (Jas. 3:17). This is what one should ask for in the situation of testing, for this is what will provide the necessary virtue.

In Proverbs, Sirach, and Wisdom it is the nature of wisdom to be generous, but in James that generosity is attributed to God. James says of God that he "gives to all generously and ungrudgingly" (Jas. 1:5); in a parallel section he points out, "Every generous act of giving, with every perfect gift, is from above, coming down from the Father of lights, with whom there is no varia-tion or shadow due to change" (1:17). This statement also forms the reason why God cannot be behind trials/testing. His character does not change. Per-fect gifts and generous giving come from him. Thus, due to his unchanging character, things that are less than perfect or generous, things even positively evil, cannot come from him. Therefore, the origin of human evil cannot be found in him. James goes on to give an example of God's goodness: "In ful-fillment of his own purpose he gave us birth by the word of truth, so that we would become a kind of first fruits of his creatures" (1:18). His images are unusual (e.g., God giving birth), but his meaning is clear. God produces life, not death. He makes believers into "a kind of first fruits of his creatures." That God produces life is not an accident on his part, but "in fulfillment of his own purpose"—it is a deliberate choice and thus an expression of his nature. James clearly intends to contrast this with the effects of desire and sin in 1:14–15, for here in 1:18 he says God "gave us birth," a unique use of birthing language for God (indeed, for anything gendered male) designed as a deliberate contrast to the use of the same verb in 1:15 for sin (feminine in Greek). If sin births death, God births us to new life. Thus we end up with two parallel chains:

Desire (in the human being) → sin → death

God → via "word of truth" → life

God's nature is for James, then, that of the generous, life-giving one, who does not change and sometimes bring something less than life. For James this does not contradict the idea that God is jealous (Jas. 4:5), can be an enemy (Jas. 4:4), opposes the proud (Jas. 4:6), or is associated with final judgment (e.g., 5:4–5 in context). What James stresses for his readers is that God is life-giving, generous, gives only good, heals, gives more grace, forgives, draws near, and lifts up, all assuming that they are part of the community of believers and follow James's directions to humble themselves and repent as needed. This picture of God is often forgotten in James, for his prophetic denunciations are often assumed to require a quite different picture of God.

Interestingly enough, when God himself is introduced, wisdom language disappears. It is as if in James one can speak of wisdom or of God but not of both in that they are equivalent. In James, the intermediary that is associated with God language is that of *logos* (word) or law. In 1:18 we discover the "word of truth." In 1:21 (also in a context mentioning God) we encounter "the implanted word." In 1:25 this expression is shifted to "the perfect law, the law of liberty" (the latter expression also appears in 2:12). He can refer to the "royal law" in James 2:8. These references raise questions: What does he mean by these terms? How does the word or law relate to wisdom? What is James's view of the law?

The problem with posing these questions is that we do not have enough of James's system to answer all of them conclusively. While for most Jews both wisdom and Torah were true (in the scriptures the prophetic word was associated with truth in 2 Sam. 7:28; Jer. 23:28; wisdom is true in Eccl. 12:10; the Torah is more assumed than argued to be true), it was mainly Philo who identified Torah with *logos*. Yet for him it would have made no sense to speak of the *logos* being true (which implies that there could be one that is false), for the *logos* was by definition true. Thus James differs from Philo in speaking about some word, some message that both is true and leads to a type of birth. Given the Christian context of the letter, he must mean the gospel (a meaning also found in Pauline literature, e.g., Eph. 1:13; Col. 1:5; 2 Tim. 2:15), i.e., that message which not only was true but led to birth into the Christian community. The language of implantation is more difficult. While some (e.g., Martin 1988) believe that it is a baptismal reference, there are in fact no clear parallels. Someone implants (perhaps sows, as in the parable of the Sower in Matt. 13:4–15, 18–23) a word in a person, much as the poet in the Dead Sea *Hodayoth* speaks of God's laws being implanted in his heart (1QH 4:10). This implantation is received (as the word of the gospel is received in 1 Thess. 1:6; 2:13; in a sense the seed in the parable of the Sower is also received) and the result is salvation. While the language is unique, using imagery that may stem from James's community, the reference is probably to the gospel. (James apparently sees the redemption of believers as one aspect of the redemption of the whole of creation in that he terms the believers a "kind of first fruits" in 1:18. While this picture of a redemption of the world could fit with the expectations found in many contemporaneous Judaisms, James does not elaborate on what the full harvest would look like.)

When we turn to ask what James means by "law" we find ourselves in a much more difficult semantic situation. On the one hand, the language of James 1:25 would not have sounded strange to most Jews, for, however they interpreted it, the various Judaisms did look to the Torah as their foundation narrative and from the scriptural period onward found joy and freedom in its observance (Davids 1982, 99). On the other hand, in James this comes at the end of a passage that starts with a reference to the "implanted word" or the gospel. Does this mean that for James the gospel and the Torah are coterminous? That is, does it mean that the gospel continues and completes the Torah, that Jesus is the authoritative teacher who explains the true meaning of the Torah? That would not sound strange in the context we posit for James, as a Judaism among other Judaisms; unfortunately, James never makes his thought explicit. All we are told is that the "law of liberty" will be the standard for the final judgment, at least that of the members of his community (the "those" of 2:12—he does not inform us if others will be judged by the same law). Likewise he is not explicit when we come to the "royal law" in 2:8. Is this "royal" because God is a king and the giver of the law, because Leviticus 19:18 is the chief of the laws, or because Jesus explicitly cited and so reissued this law? The use of "law" rather than "commandment" appears to point to the whole of the Torah being in view. Furthermore, it is clear that James thinks within the context of the kingdom of God (Jas. 2:5; cf. the beatitudes quoted above), so it is easy to see how he would think of God as the king who issues the law of the kingdom, the Torah. Yet James can use the term "law" absolutely when he means simply the Torah (Jas. 2:9–11; 4:10–12), so perhaps Martin is right when he argues:

> However, when he is referring to the Christian understanding of "law" . . . he qualifies *nomos*, as in 1:25 and 2:12: "the law of freedom." In our present verse the term "law" is equally qualified. There is nothing in our passage to speak against taking the "law of freedom" to be the "supreme law." . . . What James is implying is that obedience to the "love commandment" fulfills the royal law, which refers to the entire will of God, especially as revealed in the teaching of Jesus. (Martin 1988)

Whether or not we accept Martin's argument (we do not have the data to either prove or disprove it conclusively), it is clear that for James the law is a good thing. He never speaks negatively of "the works of the law" nor objects to those in his community observing the law. In fact, every time there is a reference to the law it is positive. God is the lawgiver, so he alone may judge (4:11–12). The assumption is that judgment will be according to the law. The law is not something that one should break (2:8–13). It is assumed that observing the commandments is good and being a lawbreaker is bad. There is no sensitivity to the idea that someone might object to this assumption. Thus we see that James does indeed use his language consistently with our belief that his community was Torah observant. Jesus is probably the interpreter of the Torah for them, much as we find he was for another community in Matthew 5, but it was still Torah, the law of Israel now applied to the renewed Israel.

3. Generosity

As mentioned above, the "rich" are one of the sources of the trials in James's community. This perception leads in three different directions. First, the community perceived itself as the poor. While this is never stated directly, James expresses it in three ways. (1) The person called a community member in 1:9 is "humble" or poor. (2) It is the poor who have the kingdom promised to them (Jas. 2:5). In fact, it appears that the poor are "those who love [God]." (3) In 5:1–6 it is peasant laborers whom the rich oppress, but then James turns to the *community* and calls them to endure patiently. Thus wherever we look in James the community is identified with the poor, even while James is urging the poor to maintain an eschatological perspective and realize that they have in fact a high status (1:9), are rich in what counts (2:5), and will have their rights restored when the day of judgment comes (5:7ff.).

The other side of this coin is that the "rich" are always pictured as outside of the community: (1) they fade away (1:10–11), they persecute the community (2:6–7), and (3) they are the oppressors of their workers and "the righteous" (5:1–6). The eschatological perspective on them is that they are in a pitiful state, for they are doomed. (Again, we remember that "rich" is a term for the social elites who are perceived as oppressing the community.)

Second, one danger to the community was that they would identify with the "rich." A community experiencing oppression often identifies with the values of the oppressors. This is the warning of James 2:1–13. The community is pictured as discriminating for the rich and against the poor (the language and images probably designed to call up a judicial setting; Ward 1969). When members of the community so behave, they have become "judges with evil thoughts" (Jas. 2:4) and are in fact behaving like their rich oppressors in their dishonoring the poor (Jas. 2:6–7). (This is one context where James assumes the validity of the Torah, for he assumes that being a "transgressor of the law" is bad, probably with respect to final judgment [Jas. 2:11–12]. Indeed, the showing of mercy [i.e., care for the poor] is presented as setting up the standard of one's own judgment.)

The picking up of the values of the "rich" (or the values of the unbounded human impulse) is associated with these critical attitudes toward the poor. It is in James 1:6–8 that we first read that prayer should come from singlehearted trust in God. This theme continues in 4:1–10 in that when prayer is an attempt to manipulate God to fulfill the unbounded human drives, it is a siding with "the world" (this age) and thus sets one in opposition to God. The language is the dualistic language we find in Jesus' "You cannot serve God and [Mammon]" (Matt. 6:24; cf. Luke 16:1–13). This explains the woe in James 4:13–17, for the issue is not one of evil activities, but of whether the heart is singlemindedly devoted to God, about a "boasting" that is not in God. It is not about doing evil deeds, but about not doing the good that one knows to do (4:18), whether that good be consulting God about life plans or about giving the surplus one has to the poor—James does not explain which of these he intends. To pick up the values of the "rich" is to value "the world" and thus to try to serve both God and a foreign god, just as Mammon serves for Jesus' sayings, much as Baal does for the eighth-century B.C.E. prophets.

Given such a condemnation of their uneschatological (this-worldly) perspective, i.e., their absorbing the values of the "rich," one could anticipate that those so accused might think, "We are doomed, just as Israel was in the scriptures!" Such contrition is surely what James hopes for. However, James's picture of God is that of a good God. Thus James hurries on to point out that God is willing to offer more grace, if one repents; the picture of repentance looks like the cleansing from idolatry or similar pollution in the scriptures with the one twist that the only foreign "god" named is "the devil" (Jas. 4:6–10). Interestingly enough, neither here nor in 5:15 is the basis of forgiveness named. There is no reference to atonement, just a promise that God will forgive and restore. Thus forgiveness appears to be more a function of divine sovereignty or an expression of the divine nature than the result of an act external to God.

Third, another danger to the community was that, perhaps as a result of economic pressure, they would forget their obligations to fellow community members. James 2:14–26 connects to the showing of mercy in the previous passage (Jas. 2:13). The issue at hand is whether faith must of necessity involve deeds consistent with that faith. While one would be hard pressed to find a Judaism that did not teach care for the poor, what James sees happening is the care being limited to the sphere of faith, of prayer: "[May you] keep warm and eat your fill" (2:16). Perhaps the idea is that faith and deeds of charity are separate gifts (although James does not use the language of gifting). James goes to lengths to argue that faith and actions cannot be separated. Actionless faith is useless; when it comes to the *Shema*‘ (which, as noted above, serves as the basic creed in James's community) even the demons have faith, but this faith does not save them from judgment, as their action of shuddering shows. On the other hand, the community ancestors Abraham (also known in Jewish tradition for his great care for the poor) and Rahab (the archetypal proselyte) were proclaimed righteous after they had acted on their faith, not before. Thus the community cannot expect approval from God for their faith if they are not actually caring for the poor. This is also the message of 1:21–27, although here the language is not that of faith, but, in line with 1:21, of hearing "the word." The point is the same, however, for hearing the word is useless unless it leads to action, with care of the poor being the one specific action recommended.

4. Speech and anger

The second source of trials mentioned in James is internal conflict. Given his rootedness in the wisdom tradition as well as his concern for communal solidarity, one would expect James to address such an issue. He does not disappoint.

We must realize, of course, that James is only concerned with outward action. Thus when he speaks of anger, he is speaking, not of internal emotions, but of verbal outbursts, since the parallel terms are hearing and speaking, which are likewise behavioral terms (1:19). James is, therefore, concerned with behavior, not with internal states such as one would find in some Greco-Roman descriptions of the virtuous person (e.g., one undisturbed by external events; Strom 2000, 60–62). He is more in tune with the Jesus tradition than with Stoicism.

One side of the teaching in James is an application of traditional speech-ethics: One should not speak much, one should listen carefully, one should not express anger, one should not complain, one should not criticize another community member. All of this can be found in the Hebrew scriptures, as well as in other ancient literature, both Near Eastern and Greco-Roman (Baker 1995). James places this in a theological context. On the one hand, the actions coming from human anger cannot establish God's type of righteousness (that of the eschatological age to come). On the other hand, such actions have the effect of (1) blocking the providence of God (4:1–3), since they are really motivated by the person's unrestrained drives, and (2) setting aside God as the eschatological judge (4:11–12). Thus, community conflict turns out to be far more significant than it might seem on the surface. There is good reason not to be engaged in it if "the Judge is standing at the doors" (5:9) and more reason to repent if one is already guilty.

At the same time, there are positive uses of speech in James. The blessing of God is one such approved action (Jas. 3:9—"Lord and Father" being an unusual title), prayer (about the problems of life) is another such action, so long as it comes from a heart singularly committed to God (see above on the absorption of the values of the "rich"). Finally, a third positive action is prayer for the sick, accompanied by the confession of sins. The prayer in James 5:14 is the opposite of the prayer in James 4:3 in that in the earlier passage the prayer was not motivated by trust in God (i.e., faith) but by unbounded human drives. The result there was nonresponse, as 1:6–8 warned. In 5:14 the prayer is characterized by trust in God. (The anointing with oil is probably acted prayer modeled in Mark 6:13. It is neither medicinal nor magical in the sense that one action is recommended for all situations.) James avoids any language that would imply that God is forced to act, but rather speaks of the right attitude leading to the divine response. It is not human righteousness (indeed, not only elders, but all persons, can pray for "one another" with equivalent results) or prayer formulas (none are named) that trigger the action of God, but as the example of Elijah shows, singleminded trust in God. This produces not only physical healing but also the forgiveness of sins. Here is James's "realized eschatology," the benefits of the eschatological reward coming to people in the present age.

James, then, counters the pressure being put on his community by pointing to the eschatological realities toward which they were headed and which they to some extent were already receiving. (By replacing the typical health wish of a letter closing with an exhortation on prayer for healing, James is certainly underlining an ongoing practice of his community rather than introducing a novel idea.) That reality will keep them from identifying with the "rich" and indeed help them identify with the poor. That reality will keep them from attacking one another and instead help them to leave judgment with God. This is theology, principally a theology close to that of the Matthean Jesus, in the service of community. Without the Johannine language of love and without the concrete examples of caring for the poor in the Lukan tradition, James aims at some of the same goals.

IV. CONCLUSIONS

What, then, can we say in terms of summarizing what we have established in this chapter?

1. James's context is a Jewish movement that followed Jesus as their "Lord" (see the definition earlier in this book of what a Judaism is), the whole work being written from this perspective. Thus, as a Judaism, Torah piety in some form characterized his community. We notice references to this assumed piety throughout the work. Because of this the law is referred to several times in a positive sense. There is no sense of the Pauline tension between faith and Torah piety, for James's community is in a different context.

2. James writes the work to a community under stress, externally by the "rich" and internally by conflicts among individuals and groups belonging to the community. The purpose of the work is to assist the community in coping with this stress, which he refers to as "trials." This means that for James the testing tradition in the Hebrew scriptures was relevant, especially as that tradition was reflected in the teaching of Jesus.

3. The root of failure under trying situations, and especially of conflict within the community, is desire, meaning the inborn human drives, which are by nature without boundaries. The cause of failure is definitely not God, who does not test human beings. Thus God does not test; our human drives are the basic cause of the test; and the devil apparently can also play some undefined role (although not a decisive one, since he can be resisted and since the real root of the test is within).

4. The proper response to trials is the maintaining of patient endurance due to one's eschatological perspective. One anticipates future reward and can therefore rejoice and endure in the present. Indeed, endurance in the present situation is part of the eschatological reward, for one sees a virtue that is highly esteemed in the Christian community developing through testing.

5. One receives the needed help in overcoming desire from the generous, life-giving, only God, whose gift is virtue-giving wisdom. This same God

is the giver of law or Torah, which apparently includes the teachings of the gospel. Torah for James's community is a positive gift, unlike Paul's, where it is a mixed gift. Because God is unchanging as well as generous and life-giving, he cannot be the source of testing.

6. James's community is a community that views itself as poor, but our author sees it in danger of adopting the values of the "rich" and both shaming the poor and failing to assist them. He calls on them to repent of this friendship with "the world," pointing out that God is gracious and will forgive them. The outlook of the "rich" or "the world" is a way of death; the eschatological perspective or way of faith that he recommends is a way of life. Thus slipping into the mind-set of the "rich" is a dangerous thing to do.

7. Adopting the speech-ethics typical of Proverbs and related literature, James warns against angry, judgmental, or critical words. Instead, alongside a listening posture, speech is to be used for the type of prayer that flows out of single-minded commitment to God. This makes speech community-building. It, along with generosity, creates community solidarity. Thus James is arguing for the rejection of community-destructive forms of speech in favor of those that are community building.

In pursuing each of these goals James presents a consistent picture of God as a gracious giver and forgiver. Yet he is also the God who gave the Torah and gives life through "the word," and if these are ignored, one is surely choosing the way of death. It is by following the warnings found in James that one can avoid this way of death. Therefore, James is not afraid of strong language and sharp warnings, for he is using this language in the service of turning people from mortal danger. In the end, then, the literary letter we designate James is indeed fulfilling its own purpose statement:

> [19]My brothers and sisters, if anyone among you wanders from the truth and is brought back by another, [20]you should know that whoever brings back a sinner from wandering will save the sinner's soul from death and will cover a multitude of sins. (James 5:19–20 NRSV)

BIBLIOGRAPHY

Baker, William R. 1995. *Personal Speech-Ethics in the Epistle of James*. WUNT 2.68; Tübingen: Mohr (Siebeck).

Bauckham, Richard. 1999. *James: Wisdom of James, Disciple of Jesus the Sage*. New Testament Readings. London: Routledge.

Bruce, F. F. 1979. *Peter, Stephen, James and John: Studies in Early Non-Pauline Christianity*. Grand Rapids: Eerdmans.

Chester, Andrew, and Ralph P. Martin. 1994. *The Theology of the Letters of James, Peter, and Jude*. New Testament Theology. Cambridge: Cambridge University Press.

Davids, Peter H. 1982. *The Epistle of James*. NIGTC; Grand Rapids: Eerdmans.

———. 1989. *James*. NIBC; Peabody, Mass.: Hendrickson.

———. Davids, Peter H. 1974. "Themes in the Epistle of James That Are Judaistic in Character." Ph.D. thesis, Victoria University of Manchester.

———. Davids, Peter H. 1999. "Palestinian Traditions in the Epistle of James." Pages 35–57 in *James the Just and Christian Origins*, edited by Bruce Chilton and Craig A. Evans. SupNovT 98. Leiden: Brill.

Hartin, Patrick J. 1991. *James and the Q Sayings of Jesus*. JSNTSup 47. Sheffield: JSOT Press.

Johnson, Luke Timothy. 1995. *The Letter of James*. AB 37A. New York: Doubleday.

Martin, Ralph P. 1988. *James*. WBC 48. Waco: Word Books.

Maynard-Reid, Peterito U. 1987. *Poverty and Wealth in James*. Maryknoll, N.Y.: Orbis Books.

Penner, Todd C. 1996. *The Epistle of James and Eschatology*. JSNTSup 121. Sheffield: Sheffield Academic Press.

Strom, Mark. 2000. *Reframing Paul: Conversations in Grace and Community*. Downers Grove, Ill.: InterVarsity Press.

Thomas, Johannes. 1968. "Anfechtung und Vorfreude." *Kerygma und Dogma* 14: 183–206.

Tollefson, Kenneth D. 1997. "The Epistle of James as Dialectical Discourse." *Biblical Theology Bulletin* 21: 62–69.

Ward, Roy Bowen. 1969. "Partiality in the Assembly: James 2:2–4." *Harvard Theological Review* 62: 87–97.

4

The Mission
of James in His Time

Wíard Popkes

The following observations and considerations are based solely on the Epistle of James. "James" thus indicates the author of this early Christian document. His relation to the "historical" James mentioned especially by Paul (in Gal. 1–2; 1 Cor. 15:7) and Luke (Acts 15)[1] is of no relevance for the present investigation. Of course, in connection with the dating of the epistle its relation to the figure of James mentioned elsewhere cannot remain completely disregarded. But we do not start from that angle. For the time being it may suffice to say that the epistle probably was written at a time late in the first century C.E. This assessment is the result of several arguments which cannot and need not be expounded here in detail.[2] In any case, the vantage point of comprehending the "time" of James lies within the epistle itself, not outside.

In line with the title of the present publication, we shall ask for James's mission in his particular situation. The question presupposes the methodological validity of such an approach. Differing from the influential position of Martin Dibelius, who regarded the epistle as a collection of disconnected paraenetic material,[3] we assume that James followed a pragmatic intention in composing his epistle.[4] Certainly the situational immediacy is of a lesser degree than, for example, in 1 Corinthians, as is indicated already by the much more general address "to the Diaspora" (1:1). Nevertheless, there are good reasons to abandon both of Dibelius's so-called "prohibitions," viz., with regard to context and situation, which means that the text has enough coherence in itself and that its message has an "actual" (and not merely "usual") relevance (to use Dibelius's words).[5] If this holds true, then what can be said about James's situation and his message, addressing that situation? Posing this question implies, of course, moving in a hermeneutical circle. Naturally, James's own background and tradition exert a considerable influence upon his message. But he is doing more than just passing on tradition. He wants to accomplish, to achieve something which is informed both by what he regards as a current need and by what he has been adhering to himself. The two elements together constitute his mission. In order to grasp James's interest, a helpful heuristic device is to find out what he is not writing about. Although *argumenta e silentio* have to be handled with care, the absence of certain elements sharpens the focus in perceiving someone's intention; by carefully reducing the scope we shall be able to arrive at the crucial issues.

I

Clearly James writes on a Jewish background. This becomes evident immediately from his address "to the twelve tribes in the Diaspora" (1:1). There can be little doubt that James actually means here the Christian church universal. But the very fact that he is using this language indicates that for him the church stands in the continuity of Israel's salvation history. Moreover, the formulation presupposes the (eschatological) fulfillment of the expectation that the tribes of Israel will be restored to their full number (which is rooted in old prophecies such as Isa. 49:6; cf. also Rev. 7). The address also accounts for a (at least preliminary) definition of the genre of the epistle; it is a "diaspora letter."[6] There are some other examples of such literary outreaches from the center of Israel to one's fellows living in foreign countries (Jer. 29:1–23; 2 Macc. 1:1–10a; 1:10b–2:18; Ep. Jer.; *syrBar* (*2 Bar.*) 78–86; *Par. Jer.* (*4 Bar.*) 6:19–25; 7:24–34; rabbinic letters; writings by Bar Kokhba; cf. also Acts 15:13–29.[7] How far does this aspect take us in assessing James's situation? Not too much information can be drawn from the term "diaspora" as such. Jews in the Diaspora were living "abroad"; but this fact did not necessarily imply feeling homesick. In Jewish texts of that time the term "diaspora" occurs mostly as an object in "contexts which emphasise the ommipotence, righteousness and mercy of God."[8] The term "is not used to describe the pitiful situation of people who live abroad, but to praise the power and mercy of God who has gathered or will gather them."[9] The situation faced by James is not identical with the one in 1 Peter. In its wording James 1:1 is akin to the similar opening of 1 Peter (1:1), but the element of "estrangement/alienation" there (also 2:11)[10] is not pursued by him. Rather, he has to admonish his recipients to keep a clear distance over against the "world," lest they become "friends of the world," not of God (4:4). James 1:1 thus indicates a general Jewish frame but has no real bearing on the particular situation.

The Jewish background becomes further apparent in James's references to holy scripture (2:8–11; 2:21–23; 4:6), which is a primary source of authority both for himself and for his recipients. Likewise James inserts references to a few figures of sacred history (Abraham, Rahab, Job, Elijah: 2:20–25; 5:11, 17f.). Possibly James received this material from secondary sources.[11] There is no doubt, however, that this material indicates a Jewish (or Jewish-Christian) frame of reference. James uses the references to scripture in a combative context; hence they reveal something about his situation (we shall return to this later). The personal examples contribute little in this respect. Job is for James a paradigm of endurance (5:11), in a very general sense, however. In addition it may be asked what circumstances the wording of 5:11 has in mind.[12]

II

On the backdrop of this overall Jewish frame it becomes the more conspicuous that James does not refer to a number of items in connection with (first-century) Jewish life, unlike many parts of the New Testament. The terms Israel, Israelites, Jews are absent; there is no mention of Moses, Jerusalem (not even in 5:12, unlike Matt. 5:34–37; 23:16–22),[13] the Temple or its cult, priests and high priests; nor of sabbath, circumcision,[14] food laws, purity regulations, fasting, Passover and other festivals; nor of contemporary Jewish groups (such as the Pharisees) and figures (such as John the Baptist). Whatever may be inferred from this on James's tradition (possibly the absence of cultic and ritual items is partly due to the Diaspora situation of the addressees),[15] it certainly indicates that these items were not of interest in his present mission in relation to his addressees. Obviously they played no role in the situation which James is facing. Moreover, there are no clear indications of a Palestinian situation of either the author or his recipients. In particular, the often mentioned reference to "early and late (rain)" (5:7)[16] is in no way limited to the land of Israel but holds true also for other regions of the Mediterranean Middle East. Likewise the suggestion that James interferes in struggles related to the Jewish War (66–70 C.E.)[17] actually begs the question; unambiguous data pointing in such a direction do not exist. The general scenario presupposed in James for his recipients is thus neither typically Jewish nor specifically Palestinian. The same holds true for the author of this Diaspora letter in an ideal (i.e., fictional) sense. James's "time" has other characteristics.

The absence of "typically Jewish" items is noteworthy on the background of the (as I believe) apparent discussion with Pauline tradition in James.[18] After all, Paul was engaged in a quite controversial debate about Moses, the role of the law, cirumcision, and food regulations. The debate is documented most of all in his epistles to the Galatians and the Romans. The major Jacobean section arguing against Pauline tradition is 2:14–26, as many commentators (I think, rightly) assume.[19] In particular the theme of justification, introduced in 2:21 together with the reference to Gen. 15:6, presupposes a counterposition on the question of faith and works. Now, the argument in 2:14–26 as such would not require such a reference; it could have been finished with verse 21. James has to continue, though, because there are people who (falsely) claim that Paul would proclaim faith without consequences, referring to Abraham and the statement in Genesis 15:6[20] (which is quoted nowhere else in the New Testament but in Rom. 4:3–9; Gal. 3:6 and Jas. 2:23).

There are other sections in James as well which argue against a Pauline tradition, in particular 2:8–12. Of all New Testament texts referring to Leviticus 19:18, only James 2:8 and Romans 13:8–10 (cf. Gal. 5:14) regard the commandment to love your neighbor as yourself (not in combination with Deut. 6:5, the commandment to love God) as the epitome of the law and pose it right before the so-called second table of the Decalogue, beginning with the commandment against adultery (not murder, as, e.g., in Matt. 19:18; Mark 10:19; Luke 18:20). It appears that among James's recipients there were people who had reduced Christian ethics to this one commandment (akin to modern so-called situation ethics). Incidentally, James seems to avoid the term "love" both as a noun and verb wherever possible, except in addressing his recipients as "beloved." The commandment of Leviticus 19:18 was also called "the royal law" and "the law of freedom" apparently (1:25; 2:8, 12). James seems to insist that it will be by this very "much beloved law of yours" that the recipients will be judged (2:12). They think that they keep the whole law, wrongly interpreting Paul's statements in Rom. 13:8f. and Gal. 5:14 ("The entire law is fulfilled in this one word"), by adhering to Lev. 19:18. In 2:10, correctly interpreted, James does not urge that they have to fulfill the entire law, which would make him an advocate of "rigorous nomism," which he has often been accused of. The idea of the "solidarity of all virtues," of the "indivisibility of the law," was common both to Jewish and Hellenistic traditions. James 2:10 has the form of a general statement, different from the dialogue style in the preceding verses. James does not argue, however, that "keeping the law means to keep it totally, for even one violation violates all the commandments." Rather, his emphasis is: "Whoever keeps the whole law, but fails in one point, is guilty of all." The implied condition and consequence are not "If you intend to keep the law, be sure that you fulfill it totally and in all details" (which is the emphasis in Gal. 5:3), but "If you assert that you keep the whole law, be sure that you do not fail even in one detail." His recipients obviously think that they keep the whole law by fulfilling its epitome, as formulated in Leviticus 19:18 and advocated by Paul (as they understood him). James has to tell them that the very assertion "to keep the entire law" necessitates not leaving out anything, as he expounds in 2:11. James wants to correct a misconceived interpretation of what it means to fulfill the law, the misconception having grown on Pauline soil.

To complete the picture, similarities with Pauline elements can be found also in 1:2f. (Rom. 5:3–5; cf. also 1 Pet. 1:6f.); 1:13–15 (relation between desire and death, Rom. 6:23; 7:7ff.); 2:1 (Lord of glory, 1 Cor. 2:8); 2:5 (privileged position of the poor, 1 Cor. 1:26–28); 3:15 (unqualified wisdom, 1 Cor. 2:14). In general, therefore, the situation faced by James is to a large degree shaped by elements originating in a Pauline tradition—however, in such a way that Paul's position became misinterpreted and abused by people who made it an ideology to conceal their own interests, far from what Paul ever intended. Perhaps to some extent such a misinterpretation was rooted in the tradition of the so-called God-fearers (cf. the confession to one God in 2:19), who mistakenly regarded the Pauline gospel as the easier way toward salvation and membership in God's people, rather than the proselyte route. In any case, the situation had become fueled by religio-ideological viewpoints which James has to counter-argue.

To some extent the situation may be compared with the attitude of some people during the Lutheran Reformation; for them it seemed simply easier and cheaper to join the new movement; in addition it promised more freedom. On such a background we might call the movement among James's recipients "early protestantism" (rather than "early catholicism," a term which is sometimes applied to characterize certain developments in that period of the early church; there are also other elements pointing in the indicated direction, such as the emphasis on "the word"). It is no uncommon phenomenon that intentions and key ideas of reformers (like Paul and Luther) are misinterpreted by some who look primarily for their personal or group advantage.

III

The immediate debates which Paul had been fighting through are a matter of the past at the time of James. The general situation is much more comparable with that of Matthew, Luke–Acts, Hebrews, the Pastoral Epistles, i.e., toward the end of the first century, even in the direction of 1 *Clement, Barnabas*, and the *Shepherd of Hermas*, i.e., early second century.[21] Circumcision, laws of purity, etc., are no longer on the Christian agenda. Subsequent issues have to be tackled. It is the phase in the history of early Christianity when various kinds of perilous developments need correction, among them the problem of growing wealth (with some people at least), of mere words rather than actions (cf. Matt. 7:21ff.; Jas. 1:22ff.), of inequality in the church, and (sometimes) of impatience (cf. Jas. 5:7ff.) with regard to the future. Among such elements James does not mention any of the more typically theological deviations, viz., docetism (cf. 1 John 4:2f.; 5:1; 2 John 9), asceticism (1 Tim. 4:2f.; cf. 1 Cor. 7:25ff.; Col. 2:23) and so-called calendar-piety (cf. Gal. 4:10; Col. 2:16f.). James is interested mainly in the practical behavior of the Christians and their relation to the "world."

In particular, Christian leaders receive correction with regard to their use of the "word," in the context of their responsibility within the Christian community, especially as teachers (3:1ff.). He criticizes them for causing quarrels and strife. They are led by their desires to make progress both in daily life and in their ecclesial status,[22] which James deplores. They behave recklessly (cf. 4:1ff.) and import worldly standards into the church, not following true Christian leadership standards which require orientation by "wisdom from above"

(3:13–18), leading to peace and justice. Such people have brought the church into a schizophrenic situation; "with the same tongue we praise the Lord and curse our fellow Christians—this must not be so" (3:9f.). Hence strong warnings and admonitions have to be isued, using the language of old prophetic proclamation (4:7–10; 5:1–6). The church has to face judgment as well; it would be a fatal error to indulge in a premature feeling of being saved. This is exactly the key which also Matthew strikes against a church which forgets "to bring forth fruit" (Matt. 21:33–41).

IV

There are more aspects of life which we do not find mentioned in James's epistle; again, they help us define his situation and intention. First, there is no mention of the state (Rome, empire, Caesar), civil authorities, local administration, taxes, military service, slavery. Just as "Israel" does not occur, so the "nations" (Greeks, barbarians etc.) don't either. Nothing is said about persecutions by the state or evil-minded neighbors. Only "the rich" oppress the believers, dragging them into the courts (2:6). James notes this in a rather by-the-way fashion. He does not expound his statement; his concern in the context (2:1ff.) is to prohibit discrimination, especially against the poor. We gain the impression that, at the time of James, the church was able to develop its life without much hindrance from the official and unofficial instruments of society. Cases like 5:6 (not paying wages to the harvesters) are not typical for an anti-Christian situation, but belong to social injustice in general, and James treats them as such.

Second, James shows no interest in family life, viz, the Christian "house," household codes, the relations between husband and wife or parents and children. On the whole, he depicts a rather masculine world. The address "brethren" could include women; but quite frequently he demonstrates his arguments by referring to a "man" (e.g., 1:12; 3:2). Women and children occur solely as objects of (neglected) social care (1:27; 2:15f.). The only female figure in her own positive right is Rahab of old (2:25), and even here James does not omit the epithet "harlot." The few church leaders mentioned seem to be masculine (3:1f.; 5:14). We receive an overall picture of churches who do not care enough for the poor and needy (including "brethren and sisters" 2:15). There seem to be no real problems from outside (society, state), nor within the "houses," nor problems between the genders (cf. also 2:11b). On the background of contemporary Christian literature (e.g. Ephesians, 1 Peter, the Pastoral Epistles) this is surprising (cf. their statements on the "Christian house" and on relations to the state). Whether or not such problems existed, James does not pick them up; hence they are not a part of his mission.

Third, James only occasionally alludes to internal ecclesial matters. Just twice (3:1; 5:14) he mentions leadership groups, of which the first (teachers) have run into some difficulties. Their number should be kept limited, James urges; this implies an open, unquantified access to that function. James underlines the responsibility of teaching, because we easily make mistakes in speaking. Irresponsible conduct in the realm of the tongue results in all sorts of quarrels and splits and "party-spirit" (3:14, 16) in the church. In any case, James returns to the dangers of the "word" more than once (e.g., 1:19ff.; 4:13ff.). On the other hand, little is said about Christian worship. The two major instances (2:2–4; 2:15f.) are complaints about unsocial behavior, reproaches about empty sacred formulae (2:16; cf. 3:9f.). The same applies to 1:26f., a reference to "void religion," mere "religious correctness." There is nothing in James about charismata and the like (cf. 1 Cor. 12), and even "spirit" is hardly mentioned (in 1:26 it is anthropological; 4:5 is an obscure formulation). In general, then, James is not really dealing with questions of ecclesiology. Life in the churches seems to go its "regular" way, with no particular (spiritual) impetus, but with considerable influx from everyday life. James gives some advice on how to cultivate prayer (5:13ff.). But his main concern which reoccurs in this area is of a socio-ecclesial nature: church leaders cherish their own status and prestige, the church neglects social duties. On top of this misconduct comes the abuse of the "word," instrumentalized as a means of self-excuse and status lifting.

Fourth, the "transcendent world" is hardly in James's scope. Only occasionally does he refer to the "trembling of the demons" (2:19) or the "fleeing of the devil" (4:7). The adjective "demonic" is juxtaposed to "earthly and psychic" (3:15), thus depicting the "world" as dangerous. Such "wisdom" is "not from above"; incidentally, James seems to avoid the counterformulation "wisdom from below"; there is no such wisdom, and "above" has no comparable analog "below." The word *angeloi* in 2:25 means human messengers, not angels. The word *ouranos* in 5:18 (source of rain) should be rendered by "sky" rather than by "heaven." In 5:12 *omnyo* is a traditional religious point of reference ("swear by . . .") which James wants to see ruled out. "Gehenna" in 3:6 simply underscores the dangers of the tongue (the reference as such is disputed in its meaning: is the tongue "set on fire" by hell, or will it be punished in hell-fire?[23]). Neither in 1:13–15 nor in 4:1–3 is James tracing the source of evil back to any transcendent power; rather, evil has its roots in human beings directly. There is no escape into a sphere beyond human responsibility.

V

Summing up our observations, we arrive at a "world" which suffers from its own internal problems. Neither worldly (state, etc.) nor underworldly interferences are registered as considerable menaces; on the contrary, the devil will flee if we resist him (4:7). The absence of public oppression is a fact which can be registered; that of demonic influences is a matter of interpretation. The sociopolitical situation appears to be rather undisturbed and peaceful. Disregard and even exploitation of the poor can be perennial problems, not necessarily typical of the time or of Christian existence as such; some of James's statements reiterate traditional critiques of wealth (5:1–6). Nevertheless, these problems have gained so much weight that James reproaches his churches vehemently. James presupposes that his addressees, at least the majority of them, are neither poor nor rich (2:2ff.); he regards them as able to render social help (2:15f.), albeit collectively by community resources. Some Christians are in the position to conduct extensive commercial voyages (4:13–18), and some (whether they belong to the church or stand only in a [friendly] relation to it, makes no decisive difference to the argument; it is sufficient that James has a word for them) even indulge in luxury and exert grave social injustice (5:1–6). Since Roman society had no "middle class" and the Christians hardly belonged to the *honestiores* (the "upper ten-thousand"),[24] the churches which James is facing were largely composed of people who struggled upward socioeconomically, oriented toward the wealthy and influential (including some patronage framework).[25] James does not mention slaves (even not in 5:4, unlike 1 Pet. 2:18ff.); hence the Christians of his churches were probably freeborn (*ingenui*) or set-free (*liberti*) people. They were eager to make their living and to gain some success. Obviously secular and religious life overlapped and followed values which became detrimental in both areas, as James sees it. Status, honor, and success prevailed as values; social duties toward the poor and needy became disregarded. Competition was carried on inside and outside the church with power and little mercy. Even prayer became abused for private, selfish purposes (4:1–3). Church offices were attained for prestige reasons (3:1, 13ff.), probably also connected with aspects of family status. "Love of the world" prevailed in James's eyes (4:4). His diagnosis hints at an endogenic sickness, not an exogenic one. The problems come from influences inside the persons, not outside. People cannot and must not seek excuses in uncontrollable influences from the divine (1:13); there is no evil from God; rather, "every good gift and present is from above" (1:17). The true problem is the human himself or herself. It may even be that James, in this context, leaves out the area of the genders for similar reasons; evil is not situated in "Eve" (cf. for contrast 1 Tim. 2:13f.; 4:3). The real problem is man's desire (1:14, *epithymia* here used figuratively; 4:1–3). Moreover, the human is cheated by self-deceit. More than once James points out, "Don't deceive yourselves!" (1:16, 22, 26); it's the inner dividedness (*dipsychia*) that creates the basic problems (1:8; 4:1ff., 8). Even prayer and theology are torn into this gorge of self-deceit (2:8ff., 14ff.; 4:1–3). James's mission therefore concentrates on Christian anthropology in its social dimension. His overall intention is noted at the very end of the epistle (5:19f.: to rescue from the way of error and to win people back for truth). It is the "word of truth" that saves us (1:18, 21). The opening and concluding sections of the epistle indicate James's central wish: The recipients should keep on until the work is completed (1:2–4) and the crown of life is received (1:12).[26]

NOTES

1. On this cf. Painter.
2. Arguments in Popkes 2001.
3. Dibelius.
4. Cf. Popkes 1996; Perdue 1981 and 1990; Davids 1988; Frankemölle; Hahn/Müller; Penner; Konradt 1999; Baasland.
5. Cf. Burchard; Konradt 1998; Popkes 2001; Malherbe.
6. Cf. Niebuhr; Verseput; Tsuji.
7. Details in Taatz; Verseput.
8. Tromp, 22.
9. Ibid.
10. Cf. Feldmeier; also J. H. Elliott, *A Home for the Homeless: A Sociological Exegesis of 1 Peter, Its Situation and Strategy*, 2d ed. (Minneapolis, 1990).
11. Popkes 1999.
12. The Job of the Old Testament was not really a figure of patience. Possibly there are connections to the Testament of Job; cf. Hanson; Popkes 2001; Davids 1993.
13. The instances in Matthew, whose Gospel was written after 70 C.E., indicate that no inference can be drawn from James's silence on Jerusalem with regard to dating the epistle after the destruction of town and Temple. A late date of James is based on other evidence.
14. Different opinion: Allison, 165f. on James 1:21, comparing 1 Peter 3:21 and with reference to William Joseph Dalton, *Christ's Proclamation to the Spirits*, AnBib 23 2d ed. (Rome, 1989, 205), and to much older investigations.
15. Cf. Niebuhr.
16. Cf. Laws; Mussner; Johnson, and many other commentaries. "Rain" is not in the text, but is probably meant.
17. Cf. Martin; Townsend.
18. More on this in Popkes 2001.
19. For a different opinion, see, e.g., Johnson, Burchard, Penner.
20. On this see Hahn 1971.
21. The most often quoted evidence is the attestation of the word *dipsychia* (literally "double-souled," 1:8; 4:8).
22. Cf. Kloppenborg.
23. Cf. Bauckham 1998.
24. Alföldy.
25. Cf. Kloppenborg.
26. Cf. Klein, who emphasizes "way" and "goal" as the basic underlying categories in James.
27. Wachob and many others.
28. Cf. Hartin; Klein.

SELECTED BIBLIOGRAPHY

Alföldy, Géza. 1976. "Die römische Gesellschaft—Struktur und Eigenart." *Gymnasium* 83:1–25.

Allison, Dale C., Jr. 2000. "Exegetical Amnesia in James." *ETL* 76:162–66.

Baasland, Ernst. 1988. "Literarische Form, Thematik und geschichtliche Einordnung des Jakobusbriefes." *ANRW* II 25.5:3646–84.

Bauckham, Richard. 1998. "The Tongue Set on Fire by Hell (James 3:6)." Pages 199–231 in idem, *The Fate of the Dead: Studies on the Jewish and Christian Apocalypses*. NovTSup 93. Leiden: Brill.

———. 1999. *James: Wisdom of James, Disciple of Jesus the Sage: NT Readings*. London and New York: Routledge.

Burchard, Christoph. 2000. *Der Jakobusbrief*. HNT 15/I. Tübingen: Mohr (Siebeck).

Davids, Peter H. 1988. "The Epistle of James in Modern Discussion." *ANRW* II 25.5:3621–45.

———. 1993. "The Pseudepigrapha in the Catholic Epistles." Pp. 228–45 in *The Pseudepigrapha and Early Biblical Interpretation*, edited by James H. Charlesworth and Craig A. Evans. JSPSup 14. Sheffield: JSOT Press.

Dibelius, Martin. 1976. *James*. Hermeneia. Philadelphia. Fortress.

Feldmeier, Reinhard. 1992. *Die Christen als Fremde: Die Metapher der Fremde in der antiken Welt, im Urchristentum und im 1. Petrusbrief*. WUNT 64. Tübingen: Mohr (Siebeck).

Frankemölle, Hubert. 1994. *Der Brief des Jakobus*. ÖTK 17/1–2. Gütersloh: Gütersloher Verlagshaus Gerd Mohn; Würzburg: Echter Verlag.

Hahn, Ferdinand. 1971. "Genesis 15,6 im Neuen Testament." Pp. 90–107 in *Probleme biblischer Theologie*, edited by Hans Walter Wolff. FS Gerhard von Rad. Munich: Kaiser.

Hahn, Ferdinand, and Peter Müller. 1998. "Der Jakobusbrief." *ThR* 63:1–73.

Hanson, Anthony Tyrrell. 1983. *The Living Utterances of God: The New Testament Exegesis of the Old*. London: Darton, Longman & Todd.

Hartin, Patrick J. 1996. "Call to Be Perfect through Suffering (James 1:2–4): The Concept of Perfection in the Epistle of James and in the Sermon on the Mount." *Bib* 77:477–92.

Jackson-McCabe, Matt A. 2000. *Logos and Law in the Letter of James: The Law of Nature, the Law of Moses and the Law of Freedom*. NovTSup 100. Leiden: Brill.

Johnson, Luke Timothy. 1995. *The Letter of James: A New Translation with Introduction and Commentary*. AB 37A. New York: Doubleday.

Klein, Martin. 1995. *"Ein vollkommenes Werk": Vollkommenheit, Gesetz und Gericht als theologische Themen des Jakobusbriefes*. BWANT 7/19 = 139. Stuttgart: Kohlhammer.

Kloppenborg, John S. 1998. "Status und Wohltätigkeit bei Paulus und Jakobus." Pp. 127–54 in *Von Jesus zum Christus*, edited by Rudolf Hoppe and Ulrich Busse.

FS Paul Hoffmann. BZNW 93. Berlin: De Gruyter.

Konradt, Matthias. 1998. *Christliche Existenz nach dem Jakobusbrief: Eine Studie zu seiner soteriologischen und ethischen Konzeption*. SUNT 22. Göttingen: Vandenhoeck & Ruprecht.

———. 1999. "Theologie in der "strohernen Epistel": Ein Literaturbericht zu neueren Ansätzen in der Exegese des Jakobusbriefes." *VF* 44:54–78.

Laws, Sophie S. 1980. *A Commentary on the Epistle of James*. BNTC. London: Black.

Malherbe, Abraham J. 1992. "Hellenistic Moralists and the New Testament." *ANRW* II 26.1:267–333.

Martin, Ralph P. 1988. *James*. WBC 48. Waco, Tex..: Word Books.

Mussner, Franz. 1981. *Der Jakobusbrief*. HThK XIII/1. 4th ed. Freiburg: Herder.

Niebuhr, Karl-Wilhelm. 1998. "Der Jakobusbrief im Licht frühjüdischer Diasporabriefe." *NTS* 44:420–43.

Painter, John. 1999. *Just James: The Brother of Jesus in History and Tradition.*. Edinburgh: T. & T. Clark.

Penner, Todd C. 1999. "The Epistle of James in Current Research." *CurBS* 7:257–308.

Perdue, Leo G. 1981. "Paraenesis and the Epistle of James." *ZNW* 72:241–56.

Perdue, Leo G., and John G. Gammie, eds. 1990. *Paraenesis: Act and Form. Semeia 50*. Atlanta: Scholars Press, 1990.

Popkes, Wiard. 1996. *Paränese und Neues Testament*. SBS 164. Stuttgart: Katholisches Bibelwerk..

———. 1999. "James and Scripture: An Exercise in Intertextuality." *NTS* 45:213–29.

———. 2001. *Der Jakobusbrief*. THK 14. Leipzig: Evangelische Verlagsanstalt.

Taatz, Irene. 1991. *Frühjüdische Briefe: Die paulinischen Briefe im Rahmen der offiziellen religiösen Briefe des Frühjudentums*. NTOA 16. Fribourg: Universitätsverlag; Göttingen: Vandenhoeck & Ruprecht.

Townsend, Michael J. 1994. *The Epistle of James*. Epworth Commentaries. London: Epworth.

Tromp, Johannes. 1998. "The Ancient Jewish Diaspora: Some Linguistic and Sociological Observations." Pp. 13–35 in *Strangers and Sojourners: Religious Communities in the Disapora*, edited by Gerrie ter Haar. Leuven: Peeters.

Tsuji, Manabu. 1997. *Glaube zwischen Vollkommenheit und Verweltlichung: Eine Untersuchung zur literarischen Gestalt und zur inhaltlichen Kohärenz des Jakobusbriefes*. WUNT II 93. Tübingen: Mohr (Siebeck).

Verseput, Donald J. 2000. "Genre and Story: The Community Setting of the Epistle of James." *CBQ* 62:96–110.

Wachob, Hiram Wesley. 2000. *The Voice of Jesus in the Social Rhetoric of James*. NTSMS 106. Cambridge: Cambridge University Press.

5

James and Jesus

Richard Bauckham

INTRODUCTION

In the history of interpretation, the Letter of James has often been compared—usually to its disadvantage—with Paul. This has been partly because,
on a superficial reading, one passage in James (2:14–26) seems seriously at
odds with Pauline teaching. In addition, it has been observed that James lacks
the gospel message of salvation by the cross and resurrection of Jesus which is
so central in Paul's writings (as well as in other New Testament works).
Adverse comparison with Paul may well have been one reason why the Letter
of James was rather slow in gaining general acceptance as part of the canon of
the New Testament. It was later expressed very forcefully by Martin Luther.
Modern scholarly study of James has also been overshadowed, until quite
recently, by a strong tendency to read James in the light of Paul, leading not
only to depreciation of James by scholars with strongly Pauline theological
predilections, but also to a serious failure to appreciate the distinctive characteristics and qualities of James's letter in their own right. If we attempt to do
this and in this attempt look for what material within the earliest Christian
writings shows most affinity with the letter of James, we may well conclude
that it is the teaching of Jesus in the Synoptic Gospels which best meets this
criterion and offers the most promising scope for comparative exploration.
That there are striking resemblances between James and the teaching of Jesus
has been noticed often enough, but usually discussion of such resemblances
has adopted a very narrow focus. It has addressed the issue of whether or to
what extent James *alludes* to specific sayings of Jesus known from the Gospels
(the most thorough discussion from this perspective is Deppe 1989). In what
follows we shall attempt to broaden that discussion, and to suggest that the

100

relationship between Jesus' teaching and that of the Letter of James is both deeper and broader than the notion of allusion can illuminate. The author of James, we shall suggest, is a teacher in the tradition of Jewish wisdom instruction, as was Jesus to a notable extent. As a disciple of Jesus, James was deeply informed by the teaching of his master and made it his own, but, as a wisdom teacher in his own right, he reexpressed it and developed it as his own teaching, both profoundly and broadly indebted to Jesus' teaching and also at the same time characteristically his own. His relationship to the teaching of Jesus is not, for the most part, allusive, in the sense that the implied readers are expected to find that specific passages of James recall to their minds specific sayings of Jesus. This may happen, but it is not the main point. Rather James's relationship to the teaching of Jesus is one of creative indebtedness, which makes all of James's teaching a wisdom in the style and tradition of his master Jesus.

This understanding of the author of the letter of James as a Jewish wisdom teacher instructed and inspired by the Jewish sage Jesus does not necessarily require that he have been a personal disciple of Jesus during Jesus' ministry, imbibing the teaching of Jesus from the Master's own lips. He could have been a follower of Jesus who belonged to one of the early Christian communities and learned the teaching of Jesus from the oral traditions of these communities. But it is still worth asking whether the author of James did have a close personal relationship with Jesus before Jesus' death, since this would add a particular interest to our appreciation of his teaching. Two questions arise. First, was the author of the letter that bears his name genuinely James the brother of Jesus, who certainly had some kind of close personal relationship with Jesus? If this question gains an affirmative answer, we can then also ask: Did James relate to his brother Jesus as a disciple during Jesus' ministry? Could his formation as a wisdom teacher in the style and tradition of Jesus have begun among the circle of disciples who listened to and learned Jesus' teaching, memorizing his deliberately memorable sayings and absorbing the distinctive spirit of his interpretation of Jewish faith and practice, in what must have been quite intensive teaching sessions over the course of the two or three years of Jesus' activity as a teacher?

DID JAMES WRITE THE LETTER OF JAMES?

Not so long ago most (though never all) New Testament scholars would have replied with a very confident "no" to this question. But it is noteworthy that recent study in English-speaking scholarship has largely abandoned the once-popular view of the letter: that it is among the later works of the New Testament, of "Hellenistic" (i.e., Diaspora) rather than Palestinian Jewish origin, and that its attribution to James is sheer pseudepigraphal fiction (so Dibelius and Greeven 1975; Laws 1980; Pratscher 1987; and most recently Burchard

2000). Some scholars, for good reasons abandoning this view, have argued that the letter contains teaching coming from the historical James, but that the actual composition of the letter must be attributed to a later editor (see especially Davids 1982; Martin 1988; Painter 1997; Davids 1999; Byrskog 2000, 167–71; and, with more emphasis on the creative contribution of the editor, Walls 1997). But others have abandoned even this degree of distance from actual authorship by James, realizing that if the content can be plausibly attributed to James there is really now no remaining reason not to attribute authorship in the full sense to the historical James (see especially Hengel 1987; Adamson 1989; Johnson 1995; Bauckham 1999).

Authorship in the proper sense would not exclude some assistance in producing the good Greek style of the letter. Even the Jewish historian Josephus, who must have learned Greek in his youth and spoken it quite competently, employed assistants to polish his Greek style, while remaining unequivocally the author of his works. It is difficult to guess what degree of competence in Greek the historical James would have had from his youth, but it is certainly the case that when resident in Jerusalem he had ample opportunity and motives for improving it, as well as easy access to the assistance of native Greek speakers from the Jewish Diaspora resident in Jerusalem and belonging to the early Christian community there.

Though the authenticity of the letter's attribution has been debated, very few scholars have ever supposed that the James to whom it is attributed in its opening sentence is a James other than the brother of Jesus, even though it does not explicitly identify him in this way. Though it might seem paradoxical, the very fact that the name James (Jacob) was common among first-century Jews and borne by several early Christian leaders (see Mark 3:17, 18; 15:40) supports the identification of this James with Jesus' brother James. At least after the early death of James the son of Zebedee (Acts 12:2), James was the one James in the early Christian movement whom people could call simply "James" without risk of misidentification. Paul (Gal. 2:9, 12; 1 Cor. 15:7) and Luke (Acts 12:17; 15:13) both do this. Moreover, the introductory words of the letter (the prescript) do offer some further help in identifying the James in question. The address to the whole of the Israelite Diaspora ("to the twelve tribes in the dispersion") implies that the author writes from the land of Israel, more precisely (in the pre-70 period) from Jerusalem, the religious and national center of the whole Diaspora. When the prescript calls James "a servant of God and of the Lord Jesus Christ," the phrase does not serve to identify him, in distinction from other people called James, but to state his authority for addressing his readers. It functions in the same way as a variety of similar identifications of Paul at the head of his letters do (e.g., Rom. 1:1: "Paul, a servant of Jesus Christ, called to be an apostle"). We have no evidence that the historical James himself made his family kinship to Jesus a basis for his authority as head of the mother church of the Christian movement, and it would therefore be quite consistent with the authenticity of the letter that he does not here call himself brother of the Lord," especially if he knew his brother's own teaching on the irrelevance of such relationships among his disciples (Mark 3:34–35; Luke 11:27–28). His failure to refer to his family relationship with Jesus would not, as some commentators have suggested, be attributable to modesty, a motive which is probably not culturally appropriate in such a context in the ancient world. The point is rather that, not needing to establish his identity (for which "James" sufficed), he did need to indicate his authority, for which "brother of the Lord" was not the appropriate qualification. A pseudepigraphal work fictionally attributed to James would be more likely to call him "the Lord's brother" (the *First Apocalypse of James* from Nag Hammadi has Jesus call him "James, my brother" in its third sentence) or even "the Just" (as the *Second Apocalypse of James* from Nag Hammadi does), though this is not necessarily the case (the *Apocryphon of James* from Nag Hammadi has him call himself merely "James"). The apocryphal (Pseudo-Clementine) letters of Peter and Clement to James address him, respectively, as "lord and bishop of the holy church" and "the lord and bishop of bishops." Though these exalted titles are not untrue to the role the historical James exercised as head of the mother church of the Christian movement, the terminology is not attested in his lifetime. By contrast, "servant of God and of the Lord Jesus Christ" is very plausibly understood as James's own way of stating his authoritative role.

The prescript of the letter presents an "epistolary situation": James writes, from the center of the Jewish world, an encyclical to people throughout the Jewish Diaspora. The reference to all "twelve tribes" need not be merely conventional, nor merely an eschatological hope for the future reconstitution of Israel as a twelve-tribe theocracy. It probably would, in combination with reference to the Diaspora, bring this hope to mind, and the saying of Jesus which promises his disciples, the Twelve, that they will rule the twelve tribes (Matt. 19:28; Luke 23:29–30) shows that such a hope for the restoration of the twelve-tribe theocracy was alive in the Jesus movement. But this does not itself explain the address of the letter of James to the twelve tribes in the Diaspora. There is no reason to doubt that it was genuinely intended to reach members of all twelve tribes. The exiles of the northern tribes of Israel were not at this period "the lost ten tribes," but a well-known part of the Jewish world, still living in the lands of their exile (in northern Mesopotamia and especially Media) and, while the Temple still stood, in touch with Jerusalem. James's encyclical is therefore addressed not just to Jews of the western Diaspora, in the Roman Empire, but also to the eastern Diaspora, in the Parthian Empire. It clearly belongs to a tradition of official letters sent to Jewish communities in the Diaspora from Jewish authorities in Jerusalem, the national and religious center of the Jewish people and the place where God was present with, and accessible to, his people in the Temple (Bauckham 1995, 423–25; Niebuhr 1998). Once the Christian movement spread to Jewish communities outside the land of Israel, as it must have done as soon as pilgrims to Jerusalem heard the message about

Jesus preached there by Christian leaders such as James and, convinced by it, took it back home with them, it would be natural for the mother church to adopt the tradition of encyclicals from Jerusalem to the Diaspora. An example is the letter communicating the so-called apostolic decree (Acts 15:23–29), a halakic ruling made under James's guidance and treated as authoritative for all the Christian communities in the Jewish Diaspora to which it would circulate. The letter of James belongs in this same tradition, though its content, as we shall see, is of a more general nature: a compendium of James's wisdom for the instruction of the Jewish Christian communities. Since the prescript itself refers to "the Lord Jesus Christ" and since the letter is clearly not intended to communicate the Christian message to Jews who know nothing of it or have not already accepted it, it is clear that James intends to address Christian Jews, those who would look to his leadership as authoritative and value his teaching. That he does not make this explicit may well indicate that he regards the Christian movement, not as a sectarian group, but as the beginning of the messianic renewal of the whole of God's people Israel. That he never alludes to the existence of Gentile Christians (and can discuss the law and the relationship of faith and works with no reference to the controversies around these topics that the conversion of Gentiles to the Christian message provoked) may indicate that their numbers were still negligible when the letter was written.

If the letter is correctly attributed to James, the epistolary situation which its prescript projects is entirely plausible and fits well into the historical circumstances of James's leadership of the Jerusalem church as we know them. The burden of proof then surely lies on those who contest its authenticity. In fact, the arguments which used to be deployed against the authenticity of James, especially under the influence of the important commentary by Martin Dibelius (writing in 1921, though the English translation was published in 1975), have lost much of their cogency through more recent developments in our understanding of the first-century Jewish world. The effect of the arguments was that James must have been written in the Diaspora, either by a Diaspora Jew or by a Gentile with close associations with the synagogue, owing to the allegedly Hellenistic character of the letter in language and content. As we have already noted, James is written in quite accomplished Greek with some Greek literary features. Its content is wisdom instructions, supposed by the old arguments against the authenticity of James to be more characteristic of hellenized Judaism in the Diaspora than of Palestine, where a more markedly apocalyptic orientation would be expected. Its interpretation of the law—which makes no reference to "ritual" aspects of the law, such as purity rules and cultic requirements—is supposed to reflect Diaspora Judaism's emphasis on the moral law at the expense of the ritual law, whereas strict observance of the ritual law would be emphasized by a Palestinian Jewish Christian.

All these arguments rely on distinctions between Diaspora Judaism, regarded as hellenized, and Palestinian Judaism, supposed not to be hellenized, which for a variety of reasons have been, since Dibelius wrote, largely disproved (Penner 1996, 75–87). It is now usually stressed that the whole of Jewish culture in this period was to some degree hellenized. The classic case for this made by Martin Hengel may be exaggerated in parts. There were degrees of hellenization, both within Palestine and in the Diaspora, but a distinction between Palestine as such and the Diaspora as such in this respect cannot be maintained. It can no longer be argued that a work shows such proficiency in Greek and such acquaintance with Hellenistic culture that a Palestinian Jew could not have written it. The contrast drawn between wisdom literature in the Diaspora and apocalyptic literature in Palestine should always have been highly dubious. Now that previously unknown wisdom literature has been identified among the texts from Qumran (1Q27, 4Q184, 185, 298, 299–301, 412, 415–18, 420–21, 423, 424, 425, 525), and now that the Palestinian Gospel source Q is widely regarded as basically sapiential in character and Jesus himself increasingly characterized as a Jewish wisdom teacher, few doubt that wisdom instruction is as characteristic of Palestinian Judaism as apocalyptic literature is. As for the allegedly different attitudes to the Torah in Diaspora and Palestinian Judaism, it is clear that most Diaspora Jews took the whole law seriously and, with due allowance for living away from the Temple and outside the land of Israel, observed its "ritual" aspects. No doubt James takes for granted his readers' observance of the whole law, while focusing his attention on its moral demands. There is no reason why a Palestinian Jew should not do this, especially if he were a disciple of Jesus, who also seems to have foregrounded the moral aspects of the Torah without negating others.

A further dimension of the discussion of James has been the way in which the alleged distinctions between Diaspora and Palestinian Judaism, which we have just mentioned, have been related to the so-called "Hellenists" and "Hebrews" within the Jerusalem church (Acts 6:1). The connection is not surprising, since the former were probably Jews of Diaspora origin who had settled in Jerusalem. However, it has been commonly ignored that such Jews would have returned to settle in Jerusalem mainly for reasons of piety, in order to be close to the Temple, and, whatever the attitudes to the Torah prevalent in the Diaspora in general, such returnees are likely to have been more, rather than less, concerned with matters of purity and cult. The terms "Hellenists" and "Hebrews" certainly refer to a linguistic distinction: between Jews whose mother tongue was Greek and Jews whose mother tongue was Aramaic. (This does not mean that the latter could not speak Greek, only that it was not their first language.) Much discussion of James and the Jerusalem church has been distorted by the unfounded assumption that the difference was not just linguistic but corresponded to more liberal and more conservative attitudes to the law, and that James himself was associated with a conservative, rigorist faction in the Jerusalem church. The evidence does not support these popular scholarly positions (see Hill 1992; Bauckham 1995). There were differences of opinion within the Jerusalem church, but it is a mistake to align them with the linguistic differences. Moreover, it is extremely doubtful whether anyone in the Jerusalem church would have questioned that Jewish Christians should continue to observe the whole law. Debates concerned the relationship of Gentile converts to the law, a quite distinct issue (cf. Acts 15; 21:20–25). The only evidence of any value for the view that James was particularly a stickler for strict observance of the "ritual" aspects of the law by Jewish Christians is Galatians 2:12. It is impossible to know whether the "people from James," to whom Paul there refers, actually spoke for James or only claimed his authority. But, even supposing James did, in this context, insist that Jewish Christians should not compromise their observance of the law for the sake of table fellowship with Gentiles, he did so in a context where the question had been raised. This is no reason for thinking that in normal circumstances, where it was taken for granted that Jewish Christians continued to observe the whole law, James would have had any interest in making a point of its ritual aspects. There is no difficulty in supposing that, while taking these entirely for granted, he followed Jesus in regarding the moral aspects of the law as its main point and purpose. Such a position makes good sense of the treatment of the law in the Letter of James, which is addressed to Jewish Christians, who did not question their obligation to the whole law, and does not raise the issue of Gentile converts.

In conclusion, there are no serious arguments to weigh against the plausibility of the epistolary situation indicated by James 1:1. The letter can be read as what it purports to be: an encyclical from James of Jerusalem to the Diaspora.

WAS JAMES A PERSONAL DISCIPLE OF JESUS?

The usual view has been that James, like the other three brothers of Jesus, was not a follower of Jesus during Jesus' ministry, and indeed did not believe in Jesus' mission from God. Since Paul refers to an appearance of the risen Jesus to James (1 Cor. 15:7; there is also a narrative of this appearance in a fragment of the *Gospel of the Hebrews*), it is usually supposed that this must have been the occasion on which James came to believe in Jesus as the Messiah. This view has been challenged by John Painter (1997, 11–41), who argues that the Gospels offer some evidence for and no evidence against the view that James, along with his mother and brothers, were adherents of Jesus throughout his ministry, and also by my own argument (Bauckham 1990, 46–57) that the Gospels offer a variegated picture of Jesus' relationships with his family, from which we could conclude that there was estrangement but also that, at least by the end of his ministry, Jesus' family, probably including James, had joined his movement.

It is John's Gospel which provides both the best evidence that the brothers of Jesus were followers of Jesus during his ministry (2:12) and the evidence, generally considered the best, that they were not (7:5). In 2:12, the brothers of

Jesus are portrayed in company not only with Jesus' mother (as they are also in the Synoptic Gospels) but also as accompanying Jesus and his disciples in the earliest period of Jesus' itinerant ministry. Since John's readers know quite well that Jesus' home town was Nazareth (1:45–46), the journey to and stay in Capernaum must be understood as the beginning of Jesus' itinerant ministry in Galilee, though John's narrative suggests that Jesus' subsequent visit to Jerusalem (2:13–25) marked the formal inauguration of his public ministry. In any case, the natural assumption for readers is that 2:12 puts the brothers of Jesus among the disciples who accompany him from then onward in the narrative.

It is therefore not surprising to find that in 7:1–10 Jesus is in communication with his brothers and it is expected that they should travel to Jerusalem for the feast together, but John also states that the brothers "did not believe in him" (v. 5), because they wanted him to make public proof of his claims in Jerusalem. Whatever we make of this, it is important to notice that this incident occurs, in John's careful chronology of the ministry, eighteen months into the two years (marked by the Passovers of 2:13; 6:4; 11:55) that John allots to Jesus' public ministry. The whole of the Galilean ministry, by John's reckoning, has already taken place (4:43–54; 7:1, which summarizes a period of six months). So John has given us to understand that the brothers of Jesus have been among his followers, at least from time to time, for the greater part of the ministry. Whether or not we think this Johannine chronology of the ministry historically reliable, we must take seriously what it shows to have been John's view of the relationship of Jesus' brothers to him: that they were disciples of Jesus for much of the ministry. In 7:5 it is possible that John means to indicate that from this point onward they are no longer followers of Jesus, like the many disciples who had given up following him some six months earlier (6:66). But even this need not be the sense of the passage. In some sense the brothers do believe in Jesus: they have seen his miracles and have no doubt that he can perform such in Jerusalem. They are rather like those about whom Jesus laments that they will not believe unless they see signs and wonders (4:48), and they want Jesus to make such a display of his supernatural powers that people in general, including no doubt the Jerusalem authorities, will come to believe. In this way, from the evangelist's perspective, they seriously misunderstand Jesus and lack adequate faith in him. But this does not mean that from their own perspective they are not among Jesus' followers. Even about the belief of the twelve, who distinguish themselves from the defectors by believing that he is the Holy One (6:66–69), John is somewhat ambivalent (14:8–10; 16:30–31; but see also 17:8).

John's portrayal of the unbelief of the brothers of Jesus belongs to his quite complex account of belief and unbelief, inadequate and more adequate belief. But the main reason he introduces the brothers, with the attitude to Jesus he condemns as unbelief, at this point in his narrative (7:3–5) is that, as on many other occasions in this Gospel when people misunderstand Jesus, the misunderstanding affords a narrative opportunity for Jesus to clarify his own understanding and intentions (7:6–8). This narrative function is sufficient to explain John's inclusion of this passage about the unbelief of the brothers, and there is no need to resort, as some scholars have done, to the explanation that John was hostile to the Jerusalem church leadership of his time, in which the relatives of Jesus were prominent. In fact, this is wholly implausible in the light of the fact that John names Mary the wife of Clopas among the small group of faithful disciples present at the cross (19:25). She was almost certainly the wife of Jesus' uncle, Joseph's brother Clopas, and the mother of Simeon the son of Clopas, James's successor as head of the church of Jerusalem and the leader of Palestinian Jewish Christianity at the time John wrote (see the full discussion in Bauckham 1992).

Hostility to the Jerusalem church leadership has also been regarded as the reason for the negative treatment of the family of Jesus (in this case including Jesus' mother as well as his brothers and sisters) in the Gospel of Mark (see Mark 3:20–21, 30–35; 6:1–4). But this kind of ecclesiastical polemic is alien to the character of Mark's Gospel. It is much more likely that Mark wishes to portray Jesus as setting the example for his followers, who have to face misunderstanding and opposition from their families and to renounce natural family ties that would hinder their discipleship (1:20; 10:28–30; 13:12). This need not mean that Mark has simply invented the motif of Jesus' estrangement from his family, but it could explain why they appear only in a negative light in Mark's Gospel. As Barton (1994) has shown, Mark's overall redactional purpose in such passages is to relativize natural kinship ties by contrast with the new sociality constituted by discipleship of Jesus. Just how negatively Mark portrays the family of Jesus depends on the interpretation of 3:20–21. Although Painter has made a good case against the most popular recent scholarly view that finds a reference to Jesus' mother and siblings here (1997, 21–28), I still find that view plausible. It sees Mark 3:20–35 as an instance of Mark's so-called "sandwich" technique of narration, which inserts one narrative between the two halves of another (cf. 5:21–43; 6:7–30; 11:12–25; 14:1–11). In this case, the story of the scribes' accusation against Jesus (3:22–30) is inserted within the story of his relatives' misunderstanding of him (3:20–21, 31–35). Those who say that Jesus is "out of his mind" in 3:21 are, then, the family of Jesus who reappear in verse 31. The sandwich technique aligns them in some sense with the scribes, but it does not make them equally culpable, since their motive is implied to be one of concern for Jesus' welfare. But the parallel highlights the two forms of opposition Jesus suffers: misunderstanding from his relatives, slander from his religious opponents. The former recurs in Mark's account of Jesus' visit to Nazareth, where the proverb about the failure of a prophet's own people to honor him, found elsewhere in the Gospel traditions in a shorter form (Luke 4:24; John 4:44; *Gospel of Thomas* 31; *Pap. Oxy.* 132–33), has been expanded, probably by Mark himself, to include Jesus' own family explicitly among those who do not recognize his divine calling. It certainly looks as though Mark's negative references to Jesus' family are largely the effects of his own redaction of the Gospel traditions he knew, but it is surely likely that there was something in those traditions that formed a basis for his development of this motif. Thus Jesus' relationship with his close relatives during his ministry may have been difficult at times, but Mark's Gospel is insufficient basis for supposing that this was true throughout his ministry.

While Matthew retains the Markan picture, but less emphatically (Matt. 12:46–50; 13:54–57), Luke conveys no hint of any rift between Jesus and his family or even of misunderstanding (see Luke 8:19–21; 11:27–28). He does not portray the brothers as disciples of Jesus during the ministry, but on the other hand there is nothing to surprise the reader of Luke's two volumes when they appear, along with Jesus' mother, the twelve and the women disciples, in the small band of Jesus' closest followers after his ascension, in Acts 1:14. Since, in Luke's narrative, the disciples are not said to have returned to Galilee in the meantime, readers are left to assume that the brothers had been among the followers who had traveled with him from Galilee (Luke 23:49), or at least that they had come to Jerusalem for the Passover. Moreover, just as John recalls the presence of Mary the wife of Clopas at the cross, so Luke probably refers to this same Clopas himself, using his Greek name Cleopas (Bauckham 1992), as one of the two disciples who encounter the risen Jesus (24:18). That he names this disciple, and not the other, probably suggests that the name would be known to readers, which would not be surprising if his son were the leader of the Jewish Christian movement in Palestine when Luke wrote. Luke does not need to explain who Cleopas was, any more than he has to tell his readers who James is (Acts 12:17), introducing him into his narrative of the Jerusalem church without even having prepared for this by naming the brothers of Jesus in his Gospel, as the other Synoptic evangelists do. Though we cannot tell from Paul's reference to the resurrection appearance to James (15:7) whether the tradition located it in or near Jerusalem, like the appearance to Cleopas, it certainly coheres with the independent traditions in Luke and John, suggesting that several members of the family of Jesus were with him in Jerusalem on his last visit there and were also among the core of disciples from which the Christian community in Jerusalem grew. We can be reasonably sure that James was already a follower of Jesus before he saw him risen from death, as were all other recipients of resurrection appearances with the exception of Paul, who himself admits the exceptional nature of his case (1 Cor. 15:8).

For our present purposes, the important implication is that, contrary to the usual view, James was among the disciples who accompanied Jesus and learned his teaching, at least for a significant part of Jesus' ministry.

A COMPENDIUM OF JAMES'S WISDOM

James, as we have seen, is a letter. The formal prescript or letter opening (1:1) is sufficient to make it a letter. An ancient letter did not need to have any other generic features specific to the letter in order to make it a letter. In James's case, as in many others, the rest of the text belongs to another literary genre: in this case the genre of wisdom instruction (paraenesis). It is, we shall suggest, a compendium of James's wisdom, instruction not directed to some particular needs or context, but intended as a collection of material from which Jewish Christians, wherever they were, could learn and which they could use as a permanent resource for wise guidance on living life in accordance with the Torah and discipleship of Jesus. In this sense, it is much like the large collection of his wisdom made by the great Jewish sage Jesus ben Sira (in the book known as the Wisdom of Ben Sira or Sirach or Ecclesiasticus) or like the collections of Jesus' sayings found in the Synoptic Gospels, such as the Sermon on the Mount in Matthew. No doubt much of the content of James's letter had been developed by him in his oral teaching, and this is most likely to have been true of the many aphorisms it contains, since these were a literary form developed specifically as a way of encapsulating wisdom in memorable form for oral teaching and learning. But a practiced teacher would likely compose for writing in much the same way as he composed for oral instruction and so there is probably no way of distinguishing the preexisting material in James's letter from what he composed for the collection. If he did compose aphorisms specifically for the written text, he would also have regarded these as destined for oral use among those who read or heard his written work. This is a kind of literature that lives on the boundary between orality and textuality.

How does wisdom teaching differ from other forms of Jewish teaching, such as law, prophecy, or apocalypse? The difference of literary genre here corresponds to a different concept of the kind of teaching the genre is used to convey. Law is the command of God to his covenant people. Prophecy is a message from God to people at a particular juncture in their history. Apocalypse is the communication of revelations of divine mysteries. Wisdom is the teaching of a sage who instructs with the authority of his own experience, observation, insight, and reflection. Typically the sage gives reasons why the behavior he commends should be adopted. Typically he uses analogies and examples from common experience, which help his hearers to see the world in a certain way. He shares with them a perspective on life and the way to live it. But this does not mean his teaching is any less religious in character than that of the other genres. Wisdom was understood as God-given, and "the fear of the Lord" was fundamental to the sage's perspective on the world.

The example of Jewish wisdom instruction which most readers of the Bible know best is the book of Proverbs. So it is important here to appreciate how wisdom changed and developed between Proverbs and the New Testament period. Readers of Proverbs can easily feel themselves to be in a quite different world from that of the law and the prophets. There is no reference to God's saving acts in Israel's history or his revelation of himself to Israel, no reference to law or prophecy. Common human experience and reason are the locus of insight into God's ways and God's world and the proper forms of human behavior. But from the Wisdom of Ben Sira (early second century B.C.E.) onward, this changes. All or most of the books of the Hebrew Bible are by this time authoritative scriptures for all Jewish sages. The law of Moses is understood to embody the same divine wisdom as inspires the sages. Ben Sira's wisdom, though clearly in the tradition of Proverbs, which is its principal scriptural source, also draws freely on the law and the prophets. Other Jewish wisdom texts, such as the Qumran Sapiential Work A and Pseudo-Phocylides, mix precepts drawn from the law with others drawn from the wisdom tradition. Not that the sages propound law as such. Nor do they engage in the kind of legal interpretation that we find in the Qumran text 4QMMT and later in the rabbinic literature. But the law is an important source from which they draw insights which they communicate in sapiential mode.

Wisdom in the later Second Temple period was no longer, even if it had once been, a distinct tradition of thought with a worldview quite different from that found in other types of Jewish literature. Another sign of this is that, after Ben Sira, wisdom literature takes on the eschatological orientation common to nearly all Jewish thought in the later Second Temple period. Ben Sira was the last Jewish sage who had no concept of life after death. Thereafter, as we can see in the Qumran wisdom texts and in the Wisdom of Solomon, wisdom teaches eschatological judgment as a central feature of its perspective on the world. The Qumran texts, which are the Palestinian Jewish wisdom texts closest in date to the New Testament, are very important in decisively demonstrating this point. This by no means destroys the difference between wisdom instruction and apocalyptic literature. Just as wisdom teaching does not propound law, so it does not offer apocalyptic revelations of the eschatological future, as many apocalypses do. These are distinctions of genre and function. But just as later wisdom teaching assumes the authority of the law for Jewish life and bases some of its instruction on the law, so later wisdom teaching views the world in an eschatological perspective and attaches eschatological sanctions to its precepts. Thus, recognizing that James is wisdom instruction does not require us to play down the eschatological element in James, nor, conversely, should we insist that eschatology is the dominant feature of James to which wisdom elements are subordinated. Generically, James is not an apocalypse; it is wisdom instruction. But an eschatological orientation is not therefore anomalous; it is to be expected in wisdom instruction from the first century C.E. From what we have said so far, it should be clear that we should expect James to employ literary forms which belong to the tradition of such works as Proverbs and Ben Sira; to offer sapiential instruction based, among other sources, on the law; and to have an eschatological orientation. These are indeed what we find in James.

It is worth stressing the point that distinctions of literary genre do not, as such, correspond to differing Jewish traditions of thought, religious groups, or "Judaisms." As Qumran shows us so well, people who read wisdom literature also read apocalypses, law, psalms, narratives, and other forms of literature. To classify James as wisdom instruction is not in itself to align it with a particular Judaism. The version of Judaism James propounds must be identified rather by his explicit references to Jesus as Lord and Messiah, and by the very profound way in which, as we shall see, his wisdom is indebted to, resembles, and develops that of Jesus.

Two features of the literary genre of James can be briefly mentioned. In the first place, the most typical literary unit in wisdom instruction is the aphorism, the short, pithy, carefully crafted and therefore also memorable saying, designed to be savored and pondered and thereby to inform life. James has many of these. Indeed the first chapter is almost entirely composed of them. Aphorisms are also scattered throughout the rest of James, and they are especially notable when used to sum up and conclude a topical section of the work (for example, 2:26 is a memorable encapsulation of the conclusion for which the section 2:14–25 has argued). In James, aphorisms play a part in wider literary compositions, but they are nevertheless, like all such aphorisms in wisdom literature, inherently autonomous. Many of them may well have been formulated as independent sayings prior to their incorporation in this compendium, and readers of James can also take them out of their context and ponder and remember them. This is one way in which they could assimilate James's wisdom into life.

Secondly, wisdom instruction does not require or encourage sequential argument throughout or over long stretches of a text. But it need not be a purely haphazard anthology of disparate material. Most of James consists of fairly short topical sections which have sequential structure within themselves. In some cases we can see why one section is placed after another, but by no means always, and it is a mistake to think that coherence in James must be sought in the form of a logical sequence of thought running through the whole text. Essentially, James is a collection of topical sections, preceded by an epitome (chap. 1) which is an anthology of aphorisms, sometimes linked in short sequences of thought through two or three verses, but no more. This epitome is a collection of aphorisms chosen to introduce the main topics that then receive more extended treatment in the rest of the work. The prominence of aphorisms in James should warn us against expecting the kind of coherence we find in the linear development of thought in, for example, a Pauline letter. Coherence in a work of wisdom instruction like James is a matter of consistency of thought rather than literary structure. Aphorisms do not move argument on so much as slow the reader down, inviting pause and reflection. Each section and each aphorism is more or less autonomous and can be read for itself. This is how a compendium of wisdom designed as a resource for living needs to be. Proverbs, the wisdom of Ben Sira, and the Gospel collections of sayings of Jesus are similar.

Wisdom instruction is a genre which is fairly hospitable to different kinds of small literary units. There are many kinds of aphorisms (e.g., admonitions, antithetical statements, beatitudes, similitudes, and short parables) and James has examples of most of them, as does the Synoptic teaching of Jesus. These are the most typical of wisdom forms, but James also has a prophetic judgment oracle (5:1–6), which is not typical of wisdom instruction, and employs examples (e.g., 5:10–11, 17–18) and diatribe style (e.g., 2:18–23), which come from Hellenistic forms of instruction. The relatively open and flexible character of the Jewish tradition of wisdom instruction makes it easily possible for James to incorporate such diverse forms without transgressing the genre.

TRADITION AND CREATIVITY
IN THE WORK OF A WISDOM TEACHER

How does James's wisdom relate to that of the Jewish wisdom tradition, which he knew in its biblical instantiations and probably also in other written forms, and to the wisdom of his master and teacher Jesus? In a longer treatment of this issue (Bauckham 1999), I have suggested that a valuable model can be found in James's distinguished predecessor, the Jewish sage of the second century B.C.E. Jeshua (Jesus) ben Eleazar ben Sira, usually known as Ben Sira. The way in which Ben Sira related to the tradition of Jewish wisdom and especially to the book of Proverbs, for him an authority as Jesus was for James, is very instructive.

He saw himself standing at the end of a long line of wisdom teachers:

> Now I was the last on watch;
> I was like one who gleans after the grape-gatherers;
> by the blessing of the Lord I excelled,
> and like a grape-gatherer I filled my winepress. (33:16–17)

In the initially modest role of gleaner, gathering up, through his study of the Scriptures and other wisdom traditions, what his predecessors had left behind them, Ben Sira made such progress that he succeeded—as gleaners usually do not—in filling a winepress himself, just as his predecessors had done. In other words, from his study of the tradition he was able, by God's blessing, to produce his own wisdom teaching, indebted to the tradition, but very much his own contribution. In a parallel image (24:30–31), he sees his role as a student and teacher of wisdom in the first place as a water channel, irrigating his garden with water channeled from the river of traditional wisdom, but his channel then becomes itself a river and finally a sea.

The scriptural sources of wisdom, not only in what we know as the wisdom literature of the Hebrew Bible, but also in the Torah and the prophets, Ben Sira studied intensively, as he depicts the ideal scribe doing:

> He seeks out the wisdom of all the ancients,
> and is concerned with prophecies;

> he preserves the sayings of the famous
> and penetrates the subtleties of parables. . . .
> If the great Lord is willing,
> he will be filled with the spirit of understanding;
> he will pour forth words of wisdom of his own. (39:1–2, 6)

The role therefore involves passing on the accumulated wisdom of the tradition, but also penetrating its meaning, drawing out its insights, developing it in new ways. Truth is fundamentally what is inherited, but the student who has entered thoroughly into the tradition and himself become a sage (cf. 6:32–37; 18:29), inspired with the divine gift of understanding (cf. 24:33), is a *creative* exponent of the tradition, interpreting it in fresh formulations of his own. What Ben Sira did himself on a grand scale is what he says of the wise person:

> When an intelligent person hears a wise saying,
> he praises it and adds to it. (21:15a)

It is in keeping with this conception of his role as a sage that Ben Sira, despite his enormous indebtedness to the book of Proverbs, never *quotes* a saying (a verse) from it. Only three times does he reproduce word for word as much as half a verse from Proverbs, leaving himself free to develop it creatively (Sir. 1:14a = Prov. 9:10a; Sir. 27:26a = Prov. 26:27a; Sir. 28:8b = Prov. 15:18a). Elsewhere sayings clearly inspired by Proverbs may take over a word or phrase from their source, but, even when they reproduce precisely the idea in the source, they reformulate it in a new way. Sometimes a new saying corresponds in concept quite closely to one in Proverbs without any verbal resemblance. Or a saying of Ben Sira may give a further twist to an idea found in Proverbs. Sometimes a number of different passages in Proverbs or other sources have come together in Ben Sira's study and contributed to a passage indebted to them all. Often a saying from Proverbs or elsewhere provides a theme which Ben Sira develops at greater length (for examples of these relationships, see Bauckham 1999, 77–79). While Proverbs forms the major repository of wisdom on which he draws, other sources are treated in much the same ways.

In summary, since the appropriate response of a sage to a wise saying is to add to it (21:15a), and since a sage's skill is shown in creating apt proverbs (18:29), since the role of a sage is to express *as his own wisdom in his own formulation* the wisdom he has gained from his intensive study of the tradition, Ben Sira transmits and develops the tradition *without simply repeating it*. This reformulation and development of the tradition is, of course, in part contextual. Old wisdom needs to be adapted to new contexts and to be developed in line with fresh developments of thought. But it is important to notice that Ben Sira's avoidance of repetition cannot by any means be fully explained by such contextual adaptation and development. Even where the old wisdom would, in Ben Sira's eyes, have been wholly applicable as it stands, still he reformulates the old wisdom, because it is the role of the sage to make the old wisdom his own and to express it as his own wisdom. Many of the proverbs in Ben Sira seem so traditional we might easily suppose they must have come down to him in the tradition, but in reality they are traditional in content, traditional in style of formulation, but in their actual formulation newly minted by Ben Sira himself.

It follows that in most cases where verbal echoes of his scriptural sources occur, we should probably not regard these as *allusions* to Scripture, in the sense of deliberate intertextual pointers, meant to call the scriptural text to the reader's mind. Only in a very few cases should we identify something like a citation of Scripture intended to be recognized as such (notably 1:14a). Informed readers, students of wisdom like Ben Sira himself, would recognize the profound continuity between scriptural wisdom and his work, but not more so when he happens to pick up words from his source than when he does not.

The analogy with Ben Sira can now help us to appreciate the similar way in which James relates to the wisdom tradition before him, both Jewish wisdom in general and in particular the sayings of Jesus, which to some extent occupy for James the position which Proverbs occupies for Ben Sira, as the major source of his wisdom. It is true that there are in James some formal citations of Scripture (2:8, 11, 23; 4:6; cf. 4:5), but these occur in argumentative sections in which James is establishing a point in debate. In the parts of his letter which are more typical of traditional Jewish wisdom teaching in style he does not quote. Like Ben Sira, James, even at his most traditional, does not repeat; he reformulates.

This perspective puts in a new light the much-discussed question of the relation of James to the sayings of Jesus. That discussion has established beyond question that James knew a tradition of the sayings of Jesus, in oral or written form, and that a few passages of James are certainly related to specific sayings of Jesus known to us from the Synoptic Gospels. Beyond that, however, the discussion has been inconclusive for a reason we can now recognize: it has assumed that, if James is dependent on the sayings of Jesus, he must *allude* to them. This has the effect of making precise verbal correspondence the center of attention, and making the judgment of whether a resemblance is sufficient or striking enough to constitute an allusion very difficult to make convincingly in many cases: one person's verbal allusion is another person's verbal coincidence. It also poses the question of the function of such "allusions," where they are admitted, in a misleading way. Is James appealing to the sayings of Jesus as the authority for his teaching and expecting his allusions therefore to be readily identifiable as such? In that case why does he not explicitly cite Jesus by name?

But in the light of our analogy with Ben Sira, we can see that the evidence fits a much more plausible way of envisaging James's relation to Jesus. James is a sage who has made the wisdom of Jesus his own. He does not repeat it;

he is inspired by it. He creates his own wise sayings, sometimes as equivalents of specific sayings of Jesus, sometimes inspired by several sayings, sometimes encapsulating the theme of many sayings, sometimes based on points of contact between Jesus' sayings and other Jewish wisdom. The creativity and artistry of these sayings are missed when they are treated as allusions to sayings of Jesus. But the indebtedness of James's wisdom to Jesus is much greater than verbal resemblances would show. We shall see that his sayings bear relationships to the teachings of Jesus even when there is not verbal resemblance, that the range of themes his wisdom treats resembles that of Jesus' teaching, and that the way he relates to other traditional Jewish wisdom is guided by his special attentiveness to Jesus' wisdom as his major authoritative norm.

CRAFTING NEW APHORISMS
INDEBTED TO TRADITIONAL SOURCES

Many of commentaries on or studies of James provide lists of resemblances between James and the Synoptic sayings of Jesus (e.g., Davids 1982, 47–48; Hartin 1991, 141–42). Deppe (1989, 231–38) lists 184 parallels that have been suggested by sixty writers on James from 1833 to 1985. Of these, the most that any one individual writer suggests is 65 (Mayor 1897, lxxxiv–vi). Deppe's own very careful and cautious study examines in detail the twenty parallels that he finds cited by at least twenty previous writers. His own conclusion (1989, 219–23) is that there are in James eight "conscious allusions" to Synoptic sayings of Jesus, thus:

Jas. 1:5	Matt. 7:7; Luke 11:9
Jas. 2:5	Matt. 5:3; Luke 6:20b
Jas. 4:2	Matt. 7:7; Luke 11:9
Jas. 4:9	Luke 6:21, 25b
Jas. 4:10	Matt. 23:12; Luke 14:11; 18:14b
Jas. 5:1	Luke 6:24
Jas. 5:2–3a	Matt. 6:19–20; Luke 12:33b
Jas. 5:12	Matt. 5:33–37

But he also concludes that "the primary parallels are those of common theme or subject matter rather than intended allusion or citation" (221). His own list of nine "ethical themes" that "are paralleled emphatically in the Synoptic gospels" is this (from Deppe 1989, 222–23):

joy in tribulation: Jas. 1:2; 5:10–11a   Matt. 5:11–12a; Luke 6:22–23a
faith and doubting: Jas. 1:6   Matt. 21:21; Mark 11:23
exhortations against anger: Jas. 1:19–20   Matt. 5:22

hearing and doing: Jas. 1:22–25   Matt. 7:24–26; Luke 6:46–49; 8:21
faith and action: Jas. 2:14   Matt. 7:21; Luke 6:46
the love commandment: Jas. 2:8   Matt. 22:39; Mark 12:31; Luke 10:27
mercy: Jas. 2:13   Matt. 5:7; 9:13; 12:7; 18:33–35
serving God versus loving the world: Jas. 4:4   Luke 16:13; Matt. 6:24
refraining from judging: Jas. 4:11–12; 5:9   Matt. 7:1; Luke 6:37
those who persevere in trial will receive a blessing: Jas. 1:12; 5:10–11a
    Matt. 5:11–12a; 10:22; Luke 6:22–23a

Deppe's very thorough study (unfortunately not easily accessible and so not
used by most scholars writing subsequently) probably takes this method of
approach to the relationship between James and the Gospels as far as it can be
taken. In the nature of the case, and as is easily seen by comparing the differing results of various scholars, judgments will differ as to what should or
should not count as parallels and as to how the parallels should be classified.
Deppe's judgments may well be contested case by case. But he has probably
shown that "allusion" is not the most helpful category with which to approach
the issue. I myself doubt that even Deppe's eight "conscious allusions" should
all count as such, if "conscious allusions" means that implied readers of James
are expected to recognize these as allusions to sayings of Jesus, or that such
readerly recognition of allusions is part of the literary strategy of the text. In
my view, Deppe's categorization of the material as either "intended allusion"
or thematic parallel distorts the phenomena. The latter category, while it
highlights impressive parallels that cannot truly be called allusions, downplays
the role of specific sayings of Jesus in informing James's own formulations of
the themes. We need to consider the parallels in a way that does not seek
intended allusions but on the other hand does not reduce them merely to thematic parallels.

My suggestion is that we should look instead for the ways in which James,
a wisdom teacher in his own right but one consciously working in the tradition of his master Jesus, has worked creatively with the sayings of Jesus and
the material in the Jewish wisdom tradition. In every case we must respect
both the form of the wisdom sayings he knew and the form of his own wisdom sayings. Precisely how James's aphorisms relate to those of Jesus differs,
as we shall see, from case to case. Since we are proposing to approach the
material from this fresh perspective, we cannot rely on the lists of parallels or
the categorizations of them provided by other scholars. Neither can we do
more than sample the material. In what follows, then, we shall adduce just a
few examples of the way James creates new wisdom sayings indebted to the
sayings of Jesus (two more examples are discussed in Bauckham 1999, 84–85,
88–91). They are chosen with a view to illustrating the variety of kinds of relationship that occur.

We begin with the nearest James comes to actually quoting a saying of
Jesus:

Richard Bauckham

Again, you have heard that it was said to those
of ancient times, "You shall not swear falsely,
but carry out the vows you have made to the
Lord." But I say to you,   Above all, my brothers and sisters,
Do not swear at all,   do not swear
either by heaven, for it is the throne of God,   either by heaven
or by the earth, for it is his footstool,   or by earth
or by Jerusalem, for it is the city of the great or with any other oath,
King.
And do not swear by your head, for you
cannot make one hair white or black.
Let your word be "Yes, Yes" or "No, No";   but let your "Yes" be yes, and your
anything more than this comes from the evil   "No" be no,
one. (Matt. 5:33–37)   so that you may not fall under
                                                  condemnation. (Jas. 5:12)

While it is possible that James 5:12 is closer to the form in which he knew the
saying of Jesus than it is to the only form in which we know it, that in Matthew,
we should certainly not assume that James reproduces verbatim the form of
the saying of Jesus he knew. But it is reasonable to think that here readers
familiar with this saying of Jesus would find an unmistakable allusion to it in
James. In my view, it is the only case in which we can confidently speak of allusion, meaning that reader recognition of an echo of Jesus' teaching belongs to
the literary strategy of the text.

In other cases, by contrast, a relationship is very plausible, but it would be
misleading to speak of allusion. For example:

Ask,   And I tell you,   If any of you lacks wisdom,
                              Ask,   let him ask God who gives
                                                               to all generously and
                                                               ungrudgingly,
and it will be given to you; and it will be given to you;   and it will be given to him.
seek, and you will find;   seek, and you will find;
knock, and it will be opened knock, and it will be opened
to you. . . .   to you. . . .
If you then, who are evil, know If you then, who are evil, know
how to give good gifts to your how to give good gifts to your
children, how much more will   children, how much more will
your Father who is in heaven   the heavenly Father
give good things to those   give the Holy Spirit to those
who ask him! (Matt. 7:7, 11)   who ask him! (Luke 11:9, 13)

                              Have faith in God.
Truly I say to you, if you have Truly I say to you,   But let him ask in faith,
faith and do not doubt, . . .   doubting not at all,
even if you say to this mountain, whoever says to this mountain, for the one who doubts is
"Be taken up and cast into the   "Be taken up and cast into the like a wave of the sea
sea,"   sea," and does not doubt in his driven by the wind and
                                  heart, but believes that what he tossed about.
                                  says will come to pass,   (Jas. 1:5–6)
it will be done.   it will come about for him.

| And whatever you ask in prayer, you will receive, if you have faith. (Matt. 21:21b–22) | Therefore I tell you, whatever you ask in prayer, believe that you receive it, and you will. (Mark 11:22b–24) |

The way in which James in these two verses re-expresses the teaching of Jesus on prayer is very similar to the way in which Ben Sira frequently re-expresses the wisdom of Proverbs. In verse 5 James has taken the first line of Jesus' threefold parallelism and expanded it into a new saying, by (a) specifying what is asked as wisdom, and (b) introducing reference to God's generosity in giving to all. Expansion (b) in effect incorporates into this saying the point which Jesus makes by an *a minore ad majorem* argument in Matthew 7:11//Luke 11:13. Expansion (a) no doubt results from the reflection that if God gives good gifts to those who ask (Matt. 7:11//Luke 11:13), then preeminent among these gifts must be the most needed gift of all: the wisdom from above which enables people to live according to God's will (Jas. 3:17). In this way James is able to connect the saying of Jesus with the wisdom tradition which speaks of wisdom as the gift of God (Prov. 2:6; Sir. 51:17; Wis. 8:21; 9:17; 4Q185 2:11–12) and emphasizes God's generosity in lavishing wisdom on those who love him (Sir. 1:9–10). James's two verses together succeed in expressing very concisely the major elements in Jesus' teaching about prayer. They are not *allusions* to the sayings of Jesus but a *creative re-expression* of the wisdom of Jesus by his disciple the sage James.

A somewhat different example comes in James 2:5b:

| Blessed are the poor in spirit, | Blessed are you poor, | Has not God chosen the poor in the world to be rich in faith |
| for theirs is the kingdom of heaven. (Matt. 5:3) | for yours is the kingdom of God. (Luke 6:20) | and heirs of the kingdom he has promised to those who love him? (Jas. 2:5b) |

James does not quote the Gospel beatitude, but has been inspired by it in composing his own saying. To the thought of the Gospel saying he has added the notion of God's election of the poor and especially the paradox that "the poor in the world" (probably meaning: poor with respect to those material goods which the world considers wealth) are "rich in faith" (i.e., in the sphere of faith), a paradox that brilliantly encapsulates the Jewish tradition of regarding the pious poor as the paradigms of faith, since, in their lack of resources of their own to rely on, they exemplify the utter dependence on God which true faith is. In this case, then, James has drawn both on Jesus' saying and on the kind of Jewish teaching to which Jesus himself was indebted.

Different again is the precise relationship to Jesus' teaching in James 2:13:

| Judge not, that you be not judged. For with the judgment you pronounce you will be judged, | Judge not, and you will not be judged; condemn not, and you will not be condemned; . . . | Judgment will be without mercy to one who has not shown mercy. |

and the measure you give will be the measure you get. (Matt. 7:1–2)	For the measure you give will be the measure you get back. (Luke 6:37a, 38b)	Mercy triumphs over judgment. (Jas. 2:13)

Blessed are the merciful,
for they shall receive mercy.
(Matt. 5:7)

Be merciful, that you may receive mercy. . . . As you judge, so you will be judged. . . . The measure you give will be the measure you get. (Jesus, according to *1 Clem.* 13:2)	Judge not, that you be not judged. . . . Be merciful, that you may receive mercy. . . . The measure you give will be the measure you get back. (Jesus, according to Polycarp, *Phil.* 2:3)

James 2:13 consists of two carefully crafted aphorisms. They do not allude to a specific saying of Jesus, but they put into memorable forms of their own an insight which is very characteristic of the teaching of Jesus (see also Matt. 6:12, 14–15; 18:23–35; Mark 11:25; Luke 11:4). Statements of the same or similar ideas could easily be quoted also from other Jewish literature (Sir. 28:1–4; Prov. 17:5 LXX; 2 *Enoch* 44:3; *b. Šabb.* 151b; *Tg. Neof. Gen.* 38:25), and James will surely have known this thought, not only from the sayings of Jesus, but also from the Jewish traditions from which Jesus himself drew it. But he knew it as a traditional insight which Jesus had made especially his own, and so James in turn has made it his own by coining his own aphoristic expressions of it.

We can also consider two examples which could not conceivably count as allusions, since James does not echo the words or even the image used in the corresponding sayings of Jesus, but in which, once we recognize James's close and creative relationship with Jesus' teaching, we can easily imagine inspiration from the latter. One such example is James 4:4b:

Do you not know that friendship with the world is enmity with God? Therefore whoever wishes to be a friend of the world makes himself an enemy of God.

Compare Luke 16:13 (par. Matt. 6:24):

No servant can serve two masters; for either he will hate the one and love the other, or he will be devoted to the one and despise the other. You cannot serve God and Mammon.

The images used are quite distinct: being a friend to two people, being a servant to two masters. But they are closely parallel: in each case the person cannot love both, but must love one and oppose the other. Devotion to one is incompatible with devotion to the other because each demands an exclusive loyalty. The reference in both cases is the exclusive devotion that God requires of his people, such that devotion to what is opposed to him (the world or Mammon) constitutes idolatry. It looks very much as though James has re-expressed Jesus' thought in a fresh image. Whether or not James's readers would recognize the resemblance is beside the point. Nothing about the effectiveness of James's teaching depends on its being recognized, but when we do see it we gain an insight into the way James's teaching has developed as that of a wise disciple of his wise master Jesus.

A similar case is James 1:23–25:

> If anyone is a hearer of the word and not a doer, he is like a man observing his natural face in a mirror. For he observed himself and went out and immediately forgot what he looked like. But the one who looked into the perfect law, the law of liberty, and remained, being not a hearer who forgets but a doer who acts, that one will be blessed in his doing.

Compare Matthew 7:24–27 (par. Luke 6:47–49):

> Everyone who hears these words of mine and does them will be like a wise man who built his house on the rock; and the rain fell, and the floods came, and the winds blew and beat upon that house, but it did not fall, because it had been founded on the rock. And everyone who hears these words of mine and does not do them will be like a foolish man who built his house on the sand; and the rain fell, and the floods came, and the winds blew and beat upon that house, and it fell; and its fall was great.

In each case there is a pair of short narrative parables, which are so-called "geminate" parables, that is, each of the pair is the mirror opposite of the other. In the passage in James this is not quite explicit, because the second parable has been subsumed into its interpretation ("But the one who looked into . . ."), but the parable in the first two sentences evidently has an implicit twin only partly expressed: If anyone is a doer of the word, he is like a man who looked intently into a mirror and remained and did not forget. It is the opposite of the first parable, just as Jesus' parable of the foolish man is the opposite of his parable of the wise man. The two pairs of parables, Jesus' and James', are quite different stories, but the message they convey is precisely the same. Moreover, they share the same formal structure (one of several different forms of similitude that occur in both James and the sayings of Jesus). (English translations of James usually translate the verbs in the two brief narratives in the present tense, as though they described typical rather than particular events. But this is not at all evident, and it is probably better to read the aorist verbs as telling a particular story, as in the corresponding pair of parables in Matthew.) Again it looks as though James has re-expressed Jesus' teaching in a way he has freshly devised. (The image in James is not as artificial as is sometimes alleged. In the ancient world mirrors were rare and most people were not aware of what they looked like. After a rare glance in a mirror it would be easy to forget what one looked like.)

Finally, in order to show that James's creative debt to authoritative wisdom tradition is not confined to the sayings of Jesus, we can consider a case in which he is similarly dependent on Jewish wisdom other than that of Jesus:

Be quick to hear,
but slow [or: with patience] to answer.
                (Sir. 5:11)
	Let everyone be quick to hear,
	  slow to speak,
	  slow to anger,
	for human anger does not achieve

If you see a man hasty in his words,
know that the fool has hope rather than he.
          (Prov. 29:20 LXX)
	the righteousness of God.
	              (Jas 1:19).

If one gives answer before he hears,
it is his folly and shame.
          (Prov. 18:13)
A wise man will be silent until the right moment.
          (Sir. 20:7a)

Do not be quick to anger,
for anger lodges in the bosom of fools.
          (Eccl. 7:9a)

The one who is slow to anger is better than the mighty.
          (Prov. 16:32a)

We cannot be sure from which of the earlier wisdom sayings James has acquired the insights he expresses in the first half of the verse, but it is clear he has formulated a new aphorism of his own. It succinctly combines the advice previously expressed less concisely and never in a single aphorism. Moreover, his aphorism, despite the remarkable conciseness of its first part, achieves a more precise meaning by associating rash speech with impetuous anger, the two topics which are the subject of distinct aphorisms in previous wisdom. The motive clause in the second half of the verse (most likely formulated originally as an independent aphorism) then gives a reason for the advice without precedent in the tradition. This is a fine example (comparable to many in Ben Sira) of the way the sage, making the wisdom of the tradition his own, expresses it in an apt proverb of his own formulation, not only transmitting but adding to the wisdom of the tradition.

Or as the tradition of the sayings of Jesus itself puts it, in a parable that characterizes James better than any other disciple of Jesus we know: "every scribe who has been trained for the kingdom of heaven is like the master of a household who brings out of his treasure what is new and what is old" (Matt. 13:50).

WISDOM OF JESUS AND WISDOM OF JAMES

We have illustrated the way in which James relates to the tradition of the sayings of Jesus in terms of creative appropriation and re-expression. We must now ask the broader question whether James's teaching as a whole is consonant with the specific character of the teaching of Jesus. Some scholars, such as Witherington (1994), who admit James's debt to the sayings of Jesus, nevertheless question his faithfulness to the distinctive characteristics of Jesus' teaching. According to Witherington, James

> has chosen either to draw on the more conventional parts of the Jesus tradition, or to use the often unconventional teaching of Jesus for some very conventional and traditional purposes, or to remain silent about certain aspects of Jesus' teaching that inculcated a counter order of things. (Witherington 1994, 246)

This judgment depends on a characterization of the wisdom of Jesus as "wisdom of counter-order" contrasted with the "wisdom of order" that characterizes Proverbs and Ben Sira. Instead of an appeal to the authority of traditional wisdom to affirm the conventional values and structures of society, Jesus uses the forms of wisdom speech to question conventional order and to commend a new divine order: the values and structures of the kingdom of God. This characterization of Jesus' wisdom can easily be overdrawn, by focusing too exclusively on the more radically expressed aphorisms in the Jesus tradition and neglecting important continuities in his teaching with much that had gone before. But it does point to something that we must try briefly to characterize more fully in order to adjudicate the question of James's relationship to Jesus' vision of the kingdom of God.

We may begin with one preliminary indication that the wisdom of Jesus does differ significantly from the main tradition of Jewish wisdom instruction and that the wisdom of James can be aligned with that of Jesus in this difference. A remarkable number of features and topics of traditional Jewish wisdom are wholly absent from the wisdom of both Jesus and James. Purely prudential advice on how to behave so as to avoid suffering disadvantage, which appears in traditional wisdom alongside moral instruction, is absent from both Jesus and James. Exhortations not to be idle, to work hard and to earn one's own living, advice about friends, on good and bad wives, upbringing of children and management of daughters, and on the treatment of slaves, are examples of topics prominent in traditional wisdom, but wholly absent from the teaching of both Jesus and James. Discussion of family relationships in general, and discussion of rulers and government, are both rare in the sayings of Jesus and completely absent from James. Neither, it seems, has much to say about how to exercise or to live under the conventional authority structures of society.

By this criterion of topics omitted, James is scarcely any closer to the concerns of the mainstream Jewish wisdom tradition than Jesus is, while the range of topics omitted by each corresponds rather closely. But this purely negative point, striking as it is, does not take us very far in understanding what is distinctive about the teaching of Jesus, or the extent to which James reflects this distinctiveness. The negative point could be complemented by a positive demonstration of the extent to which the themes that do feature in the sayings of Jesus are, for the most part, traditional concerns of the Jewish religious tradition, many found in wisdom instruction, others in the law and the prophets and elsewhere. However, what is needed is an explanation of the way the sayings of Jesus appropriate and develop the tradition, accounting for his total neglect of many themes and his unusual emphasis on, and distinctive development of, others. Only this will enable us reliably to judge whether James has really made his own Jesus' distinctive version of the Jewish religious tradition.

What follows is a brief sketch, in five sections, of the distinctive characteristics and emphases in the Synoptic sayings of Jesus. There is no claim implied that particular themes are unprecedented in Jewish tradition. This is in fact rarely the case. The distinctiveness of Jesus' teaching lies to a large extent in selection and emphasis, focus and development, priorities and concerns. This sets us the difficult and delicate task of determining to what extent the distinctiveness of James's teaching is faithful to this kind of distinctiveness in the teaching of Jesus.

1. Jesus' ethical demands are more radical than those of the Torah, as conventionally interpreted, or of Jewish wisdom instruction. This difference results from taking as seriously as possible the central moral requirements of God's will for his people Israel and pressing their implications as far as possible. From this approach come some of the most distinctive of Jesus' teachings: love for enemies, nonretaliation, prohibition of divorce, prohibition of all oaths. Such teachings represent an extension of a moral demand of the Torah as far as possible or an intensification of such a demand as much as possible. This evidently relates to the extreme character of Jesus' teaching. Hyperbole is employed to bring home the radical demands of God's will. There is no moderation, no compromise, no concern for conventional practicality. As a teaching style this is quite different from the more moderate tone and practical approach of the Jewish sages from Proverbs to Pseudo-Phocylides.

2. Jesus envisages a society under the rule of God which contrasts radically with the hierarchical structures of existing society. All forms of social status are rejected. There are no privileges of fathers over children, since none are to be called father (Matt. 23:9) and disciples are to be brothers and sisters and mothers, but not fathers, to each other (Mark 10:30). There are no privileges of masters over slaves, since the greatest will be the servant of all (Mark 10:44). Those to whom the kingdom paradigmatically belongs are children (Mark 10:14), who had no social status, and the destitute (Luke 6:20), who were at the bottom of the social scale. Others can enter the kingdom only by accept-

ing the same radical lack of status. Jesus privileges the least in order to deprive all others of privilege. This aspect of Jesus' religious vision has some roots in the law and in the prophetic-apocalyptic tradition, and even some contacts with the wisdom tradition's commendations of humility rather than boasting and arrogance, but it is probably the point at which Jesus differs most strikingly from traditional wisdom instruction, which takes for granted the existence of hierarchical structures in society and devotes much attention to proper behavior in the roles they dictate. Jesus' silence on so many of the traditional topics of wisdom instruction stems to a large extent from his concentration on the new, nonhierarchical form of social relationships he commends and initiates.

3. God's eschatological action, in judgment or vindication, is the criterion for judging right or wrong acts, rather than the socially accepted view or the consequences for oneself in the natural course of events. As we have noticed already, this appeal to eschatological sanctions is, by this date, not at all foreign to the wisdom tradition, but Jesus focuses on it to the exclusion of other features of that tradition: the concern for action that enhances one's standing in society and the traditional wisdom appeal to immanent processes of reward and retribution. In this Jesus comes perhaps closer to the prophetic-apocalyptic tradition than wisdom instruction had already done. By his particular use of the traditional themes of eschatological *ius talionis* (e.g., Matt. 7:1–2) and eschatological reversal of status (e.g., Matt. 20:16; Luke 14:11; 16:19–31), Jesus appeals to God's criteria of judgment against conventional attitudes and structures. The eschatological orientation of many of Jesus' sayings is a form of the radical theocentrism which informs all his teaching. It is a form of insistence that God's will and God's values are what ultimately count. It is therefore not inconsistent that Jesus can also argue from God's activity in the created order of nature (Matt 5:45; 6:26–30), in the manner of the wisdom tradition. His conclusions from this run as radically counter to conventional attitudes as do his appeals to God's eschatological action.

4. The understanding of God as compassionate, gracious, and generous takes precedence over God as the dispenser of distributive justice, giving the deserving what they deserve. The latter principle, deeply rooted in the tradition, is not rejected, but Jesus privileges the form of it which promises God's mercy to those who show mercy. The compassion, grace, and generosity of God were already central to the Jewish religious tradition. Jesus is distinctive only in the radical seriousness with which he takes them. Forgiveness for sinners, welcome for outcasts, succor for the sick and the destitute, are God's activity, which should be reflected in the activity of God's people. Assurance of the goodness and generosity of God makes it possible to live with radical trust in his provision, free of anxiety and the quest for security. Jesus' characteristic teaching on prayer—the simple conviction that those who ask receive—stems from his understanding of God as the generous giver of good gifts. Thus Jesus' radical focus on the compassionate and generous nature of

the God of Israel puts certain themes, none of them wholly new, in the center
of the stage, so that they crowd out other matters with which traditional Jewish wisdom had been concerned.

5. Finally, Jesus is concerned with the renewal and reconstitution of Israel
as the people of God. The community of the renewed Israel, of which his disciples are the nucleus, and for which his wisdom instruction is designed, are
those who already live under the rule of God. As such they contrast with the
Gentiles. They are called to be different in the radical seriousness with which
they take God's will, the reflection of the mercy, compassion, and inclusive
love of God in their own activity, their radical trust in God, and the mutual
service and brotherly-sisterliness which replaces hierarchy and status in their
relations with each other. This demanding distinctiveness creates a kind of
dualism in Jesus' religious vision. This is not the exclusivism of the righteous
elect distinguished from the reprobate majority, for the community's role in
the world is to be a city set on a hill, a light to which others will be drawn (Matt.
5:14–16). But it means that as the wisdom of the kingdom of God, Jesus' wisdom instruction is directed to forming and informing a countercultural community, one which differs from the world because it pioneers the life of God's
coming kingdom. Though traditional wisdom had its own dualism of wisdom
and folly, the way to life and the way to death, which Jesus can take up into his
own vision (Matt. 7:13–14, 24–27), it lacked the sense of a prophetic call to
demanding distinctiveness which characterizes Jesus' teaching.

This summary of the distinctive characteristics of the Synoptic sayings of
Jesus will now provide the basis for comparison with James. In five sections
corresponding to the five above, we shall expound those features of James
which correspond to the aspects of Jesus' teaching we have just sketched. Our
concern now is not with James's indebtedness to specific sayings of Jesus, but
with the evidence that James's wisdom has been decisively shaped by the distinctive character and emphases of Jesus.

1. Like the teaching of Jesus, that of James lacks the moderation, practical
compromise, and alignment with social convention that are often characteristic of the Jewish wisdom tradition, focusing rather on the Torah's demand for
perfection, understood as extensively and intensively as possible. Two aspects
of James are especially relevant here. The first is the theme of wholeness or
perfection which is the overarching theme of the letter, conveyed in part by
the *teleios* ("perfect, complete") word group, of which James is fond (1:4, 17,
25; 2:8, 22; 3:2), but also in other ways. Wholeness requires wholehearted and
single-minded loyalty to God (1:8; 4:8), the fulfillment of the whole law
(2:8–12), not only hearing but also doing (1:22–25), not only saying but also
doing (2:16), not only believing but also doing (2:22), consistency in living out
all the qualities of God's grace (1:17; 3:2, 9–10, 17), as well as the wholeness
of a community united by peace rather than divided by ambition (3:14–4:1,
11). Opposed to wholeness is the divided loyalty, the vacillation between loyalty to God and loyalty to the world (4:4), the halfheartedness in devotion to

God, for which James uses the term "double-minded" (1:8; 4:8). So the emphasis on obedience to the whole law, not picking and choosing which commandments to obey (2:8–11; 4:11–12), is far from simply a quantitative demand for obedience to every commandment; it is a requirement to act from the wholehearted love of God which the *Shema'* demands (Deut. 6:5; 11:13; cf. Jas 2:19; 4:12) and to live out all the implications of the love of neighbor (Lev. 19:8; Jas. 2:8–9; 4:12). All this is especially close to the Matthean version of the teaching of Jesus (Matt. 5:19–20, 48; 19:21), but also to Jesus' privileging of the two love commandments (Matt. 22:34–40; Mark 12:28–34; Luke 10:25–37) as the primary interpretive key to the law. The insistence on doing as well as hearing is characteristic of Jesus (Jas. 1:22–25; Matt. 7:21–27; Luke 6:46–49; Matt. 21:28–31; Mark 3:35), as is the impossibility of divided loyalties (Jas. 4:4; Matt. 6:24; Luke 16:13).

Second, James's distinctive concern with speech ethics (1:19, 26; 3:1–12; 4:11–12; 5:9, 12) culminates in what we have seen to be probably the only real *allusion* to a saying of Jesus (5:12; Matt. 5:34–37). This verse, like the Gospel saying it closely resembles, is in effect a demand for total truthfulness in all speech. Oaths, which guarantee the truth of particular statements, imply that other statements are less reliable. They are forbidden here because all speech is to have the truthfulness that oaths require. And since James regards speech as the index of a person's whole moral being, this instruction serves in effect as a requirement of perfection (3:2). Thus, in relation to a topic of special concern in James, he explicitly adopts a dominical teaching which applies to speech ethics Jesus' characteristic pressing of the moral demands of the Torah to their limit.

2. The teaching of James, like that of Jesus, is instruction for a countercultural community, one in which solidarity, especially with the poor, should replace hierarchy and status, along with the competitive ambition and arrogance (3:14, 16; 4:1–2, 16) and the exploitation of the poor (5:1–6) that characterize the dominant society. Hence, whereas traditional Jewish wisdom literature typically addressed an individual as "my son," James addresses the whole community as his brothers and sisters. Fictive kinship relationships of equality and mutuality replace hierarchical ones. The language of shame and honor, the predominant social values to which Ben Sira, for example, often appeals (e.g., Sir. 5:13–6:1, in relation to speech), is absent from James, with one exception (2:6) that itself encapsulates his radical rejection of social status. Behavior which accords special honor to the rich at the expense of the poor is condemned as partiality (2:1–9) and dishonouring of the poor (2:6). This inverts current social attitudes, in the same way as that explicit theme of reversal of status (1:9–11; 4:10) does, both in James and in Jesus' teaching (Matt 20:16; 23:12; Luke 6:20–21, 24–25; 13:30; 14:11; 16:19–31; 18:14). (Such an approach was not entirely without precedent in Jewish wisdom tradition [cf. Prov. 14:21 LXX; Sir. 10:14], but the closest parallels also show that, by contrast, that tradition did not really challenge the existing social order [Sir. 10:30–31]).

James does not require all his readers—most of whom, like most other people, were neither poor nor rich—to become destitute like the poor, though he does expect them to share what little they have with the really poor (2:15–16). What he requires is behavior consistent with God's choice of the poor as heirs of the kingdom (2:5; cf. Matt. 5:3; Luke 6:20). The poor are the paradigm heirs of the kingdom, paradigmatic both in their lack of social status and economic security and in the wholehearted dependence on God in faith that accompanies it. This requires of others a kind of identification with the poor, which appears in James's language of "lowliness" (1:9–10; 4:6, 10), together with that of "boasting" (1:9–10; 3:14; 4:16). This is language of social status. The poor are those who cannot put themselves above anyone else, who cannot take advantage of others, who find their status solely in God's evaluation of them. Others can find salvation only in renunciation of status and social advantage, together with the arrogance before others and before God which status promotes. All must make themselves lowly before the Lord (4:10), which means to put themselves on the same level as the poor, so that none may set themselves above others or take advantage of others.

James's radical rejection of status and the competitive, self-seeking, avaricious, and arrogant ethos that goes with it make it wholly necessary that he reflect none of the wisdom tradition's frequent concern with fitting well into, using advantageously, or even behaving modestly and charitably within, established social structures. In this sense, like Jesus' wisdom, his is a "wisdom of counter-order," and, like Jesus, James surely deserves Witherington's appellation: a "sage from below" (Witherington 1994, 165). However, this terminology is unfortunate with reference to James, because for James wisdom "from below" is that of the existing social order, while true wisdom is "from above" (3:13, 17), that is, from God. It is God who chooses the poor and overturns status (1:9–11; 2:5; 4:10), and so it is the wisdom God gives that opposes privilege and presumption (cf. 4:5–6) in solidarity with the exploited and the murdered (5:4, 6). According to James, not dissimilarly from Jesus, it is not to those who consider themselves "wise and understanding," but practice only the wisdom of the world in their competitive status-seeking (3:13–15), that God gives wisdom from above, but to the lowly and the meek (1:21; 3:17), whom Jesus called "little ones" (Matt. 11:25; Luke 10:21).

3. James writes with the imminent coming of Jesus in view (5:7–8). The judge is already standing at the doors, about to enter (5:9). Not only does eschatological judgment threaten the wealthy oppressors (5:1–5). It is also a reality with which James and his readers must reckon (2:12–13; 3:1; 4:12; 5:8–9, 12), as is the prospect of eschatological reward (1:12; 3:18). As in the teaching of Jesus, God's eschatological judgment is the overriding sanction and motivation for righteous living, to the exclusion of other considerations which often figure in the wisdom tradition. Judgment is the prerogative of God, who alone has the ultimate power to save or to destroy (4:12). In other words, the wisdom of James, like that of Jesus, is wisdom radicalized by escha-

tology and at the same time rendered radically theocentric. Arguably, it is to a large extent the radicalizing of wisdom and Torah by theocentric eschatology that gives the wisdom of Jesus and of James their distinctiveness and commonality. Their "wisdom of counter-order" is not intelligible without the eschatology that informs it.

The countercultural values by which James's readers are called to live are validated by the eschatological belief that they are the values of God's rule which is going to prevail universally. The far-reaching implications of the theme of reversal of status in James, already discussed, depend on the expectation that God's judgment is going to exalt the lowly and bring low the exalted (1:9–11; 4:10). The eschatological *ius talionis* is invoked, much as in Jesus' teaching, in both negative and positive forms (2:13; 3:6, 18). But the effect is not solely reserved for the future. That God has chosen the poor means that their status in his eyes and in those of faith (2:5) is already changed. Honoring the poor is the radical transvaluation of values already incumbent on the Christian community (2:1–9). Peacemaking, contrary to the values of the world, is already sowing the seed of the eschatological harvest of peace (3:18). Endurance (1:3–4, 12; 5:8–11) is not mere waiting for the Parousia, but courageous resistance in living by the values of God's countercultural rule until it comes in power. The eschatological expectation enables this patient resistance, which can wait God's time and not relapse into despairing compromise with the dominant system.

4. The God of James, as of Jesus, is preeminently the giving, generous (1:5, 17–18; 4:6), merciful, and compassionate one (2:13; 5:11). From the conviction that God is the generous giver of all good gifts comes the expectation, shared with Jesus, that those who ask will receive, provided they ask in faith, not with divided loyalties and self-seeking motives (1:5–7; 4:2–3; 5:15–18; cf. Matt. 7:7–11; 21:21–22; Mark 11:22–24; Luke 11:9–13). The attitude envisaged is that total and trusting dependence on God of which the poor provide the paradigm (4:7, 15) and of which the arrogant self-sufficiency of the rich is the opposite (4:13–16). God's reliable goodness is such that he could never be the source of evil (1:13, 17). That God's mercy will be shown in showing mercy to those who themselves have shown mercy to others (2:13), a principle already found in Jewish wisdom tradition (Sir. 28:1–4; Prov. 17:5 LXX), is especially characteristic of Jesus' teaching (Matt. 5:7; 6:12, 14–15; 18:23–35; Mark 11:25). Put otherwise, from the abundant mercy of God flows the abundant mercy shown by his people (3:17), especially to the needy (1:27; 2:15–16), and from the generous giving of God comes the generous giving of God's people to those in need (2:15–16). God's judgment is not to be imitated (4:12; cf. Matt. 7:1–5), but his mercy and generosity are.

5. When James writes to "the twelve tribes in the diaspora" (1:1) he addresses the Jewish Christian communities as the nucleus of the ongoing messianic renewal of the people of Israel and, by evoking the hope of restoration, incorporates them in the messianic program of redemption Jesus initiated

when he appointed twelve apostles. Furthermore, this messianic renewal of Israel has the messianic redemption of the world as its goal. This is clear from 1:18, where those Israelites who have received new birth as children of God are called "a kind of first fruits of his creatures." They are the first sheaf of the eschatological harvest, offered to God in thankful assurance of the full harvest to come. The renewal of Israel is the representative beginning of God's new creation of all things. As such, the Jewish-Christian communities must live with the demandingly distinctive values and lifestyle, reflecting the coming rule of God and at odds with the dominant values of society, as we have already indicated. The requirement of wholehearted devotion to God in a countercultural community entails, as in the teaching of Jesus, a certain sort of dualism.

James's readers can be friends with God (4:4), like Abraham (2:23), or they can be friends with "the world" (4:4), but the choice must be made. The distinction cannot be fudged. The compromise which the "double-minded" (4:8) attempt, dividing their loyalties between God and the world, is in reality not possible. In this sharp contrast the dualism is fundamentally one of value systems. One lives either by God's values or by that dominant value system which James calls "the world" (1:27; 2:5; 4:4; cf. 3:6). "Friendship" (4:4b) has connotations of loyalty and sharing of values. Hence friendship with both God and the world, indicating opposed systems of values to live by, is impossible. We have already noticed how James here teaches exactly what Jesus taught by means of the alternative image of servants and masters (Luke 16:13). James also uses the image of marriage and adultery (4:4a) to the same effect: God's people who compromise with worldly values are like adulterous women, attempting the impossible task of combining marriage to God their husband, who requires exclusive loyalty, and liaison with another partner, the world. This dualism between God and the world appears also in 1:27, where religion that is undefiled in the eyes of God involves keeping oneself unstained by the world. The latter phrase does not imply avoiding contact with outsiders, but refusing to comply with that approach to life which is inconsistent with God's values. That the issue is primarily one of values is very clear in another manifestation of James's dualism: the contrast between two kinds of wisdom (3:15–17), one of which is "earthly" (i.e., of earthly origin rather than coming from heaven), "natural" (i.e., purely human rather than inspired by the divine Spirit) and "demonic" (i.e., associated with the evil spirits who inhabit this earthly realm), while the other is "from above" (i.e., from God; cf. 1:17). The former is characterized by competitive self-seeking (3:14), the latter by the love which respects and seeks the good of others (3:17). As Johnson puts it, James portrays "a community defined and constituted by gift giving and solidarity in the face of a dominant culture defined by envy and acquisitiveness" (1995, 164).

In conclusion, our account of the way James's wisdom corresponds to the major characteristics and points of focus and emphasis which give the Synoptic teaching of Jesus its distinctiveness has included virtually every significant topic and concern in the letter of James. This is not to say that the balance of topics is the same in both cases (in fact, it is not the same in the three Synoptic Gospels, or in putative Gospel sources). James has his own particular concerns, but in the case of the most obvious of the topics he develops at greater length than Jesus—speech ethics—he is very close to what there is in the sayings of Jesus on this topic (Matt. 5:33–37; 12:33–37; Luke 6:43–47; cf. Matt. 15:10–20). Where he appropriates and develops the theme of the evils and control of the tongue as it is found in traditional Jewish wisdom, it is in a way that leaves aside what is unlike the wisdom of Jesus (prudential and self-interested considerations, honor and shame, observation and manners rather than ethics) and develops what is (the tongue's expression of the heart, denunciation of hypocrisy and slander), while he himself contributes the hyperbole, the extremeness, and the exposure to the eschatological judgment of God that especially align James's speech ethics with the general character of Jesus' ethical teaching.

In the tradition of modern New Testament scholarship James has often been considered more Jewish than Christian. In 1894 Adolf Jülicher called it "the least Christian book of the New Testament" (Jülicher 1904 [1st ed. of the German, 1894], 225, quoted in Johnson 1995, 150), a verdict which has been repeated frequently. It rests, of course, on a fundamental mistake: that the more Jewish a work is, the less Christian it can be (and vice versa). Our comparison of James's wisdom teaching with that of Jesus shows that James's relationship to the Jewish religious tradition quite closely parallels Jesus' relationship to it. There is nothing un-Jewish in the teaching either of Jesus or of James. What is distinctive in Jesus' teaching is not merely those particular elements which, so far as our evidence goes, appear to be novel, but rather the characteristic emphases, selection, and configuration of traditional themes, the characteristic ways of developing the tradition, the distinctiveness that emerges in the overall scope and shape of the teaching. This is the kind of distinctiveness which James mirrors, in the way that he appropriates and re-expresses both the teaching of Jesus and other Jewish traditions. The wisdom of Jesus functions for James as the focus and principle guiding his appropriation of other Jewish traditions. His wisdom is the Jewish wisdom of a faithful disciple of Jesus the Jewish sage. Insofar as we can identify the teaching of the Letter of James as "a Judaism" (and it may not be sufficiently comprehensive for this: see below), it is a Judaism that has been very decisively shaped by the teaching of Jesus.

THE LORD JESUS, EXALTED AND COMING

The paucity of references to Jesus Christ in James (only two are indisputable: 1:1; 2:1) has provoked a number of comments on the character of the work. In the first place, it has sometimes in the past been argued that the two references to Jesus (1:1; 2:1) are glosses added to an otherwise purely non-Christian Jewish work. Our discussion of the relationship of James to the tradition of the sayings of Jesus is sufficient to refute this. Second, some have seen this as an argument against the authenticity of the attribution of the letter to James. Would not Jesus' brother, who knew more of Jesus' earthly life than most, have referred to him more? This argument is double-edged. One could also ask: Would not a writer who has adopted the name James as a pseudonym have made much more of it, as commonly happens in pseudepigraphal works? We have already considered why James does not cite sayings of Jesus and attribute them as such. Third, usually as part of the comparison of James with Paul, it is said that James's understanding of Christian faith is markedly nonchristological, in the sense that he does not refer to the salvation-historical christological kerygma: the cross, the resurrection, the exaltation to God's heavenly throne, the future coming in glory. As we shall see, James does refer to the third and fourth of these, and thus presupposes also the second. Moreover, we should not make the mistake of supposing that James's letter is a complete account of Christian faith as he understood it. For example, whether he understood the death of Jesus in sacrificial terms, as was common among Jewish Christians, we simply cannot tell from the letter.

This is really, once again, a matter of literary genre. Wisdom instruction (often known as paraenesis), as we remarked earlier, is a particular literary genre with a corresponding religious function. It would not have been the only kind of Christian literature James or his readers would have known and valued. If we are to compare James with a Pauline letter, we should make the comparison with what is generically comparable in a Pauline letter: ethical instruction (paraenesis). Paul also writes paraenesis somewhat in the style of Jewish wisdom instruction. Romans 12–13 is an extended passage of this type, in which we can check whether it is really the case that Pauline *paraenesis*, specifically, is more christological than James's paraenesis. In the 35 verses of these chapters Paul refers to Jesus Christ only three times (12:5, 11; 13:14) (or only twice if the variant and more difficult reading is preferred in 12:11). This frequency of reference to Christ is not much greater than that of James, who in the space of 107 verses probably refers to Christ seven times (see below). Like James, Paul in these chapters probably echoes the teaching of Jesus, but without identifying it as such (12:14, 17; 13:9), and, again like James, refers to the law and all of its commandments (13:8–10; cf. Jas. 2:8–11). Thus early Christian paraenesis, even in Paul, seems not to have been as christological as critics of James sometimes suppose. James, we might well conclude, is actually as christological as we should expect the kind of Christian literature he writes to be. But if he were genuinely Jesus' brother, would we not expect him to cite his brother's behavior as behavioral example, as 1 Peter 2:21–23 does, and in the way that James himself uses the examples of figures from the Hebrew Bible (5:10–11, 17–18)? In fact, 1 Peter 2:21–23 is exceptional; early Christian paraenesis rarely appeals to the example of the earthly Jesus as a model for behavior. James's failure to do so is thus probably also an aspect of the genre in which he writes.

James only twice uses the name Jesus. He uses it along with the title "Lord" (*kyrios:* 1:1) or "our Lord" (2:1), describing himself as servant to the Lord Jesus as well as to God (1:1). On these two occasions only he also uses the title "Christ," which functions to some degree as a name, identifying the Jesus in question, but has certainly not, for James's Jewish readers, lost its titular meaning: the Messiah. These two references, because they alone use the words "Jesus Christ," are the only two undisputed references to Jesus in James. It should be noted, however, that they are strategically placed. The first is in the prescript, introducing the whole letter and leaving no doubt from the beginning that, even though addressed to the twelve tribes of Israel, not explicitly to the Christians among them, nevertheless this is a Christian letter from a disciple of Jesus the Messiah. The second reference to Jesus Christ (2:1) is equally significantly placed, at the opening of the main body of the text (chaps. 2–5), after the introductory epitome (chap. 1). Thus the significance of these two references is out of proportion to their number. They also show clearly that the Jesus of James is the human Jesus of Nazareth, since he is given that name, but also the exalted Lord. He is the Lord of whom James is a servant and he is the Lord in whom Christians believe. (The "faith" of Jesus Christ in 2:1 has sometimes, as with the same expression in Paul, been taken to be the faith or faithfulness of Jesus himself, the faith the earthly Jesus exercised, but in context this is very improbable, more improbable than the Pauline examples.)

The strategic position of the reference in 2:1 must partly explain the rather elaborate formula: (literally) "our Lord Jesus Christ of glory." The precise function of the last two words (*tes doxes:* "of glory") is not entirely clear, but the phrase is best understood as a combination of the common early Christian formula, "our Lord Jesus Christ," and the rare christological title, "the Lord of glory," found elsewhere as a christological title only in 1 Corinthians 2:8. This phrase is no doubt a Semitism, meaning 'the glorious Lord.' It is used in parts of the Enoch literature as a title for God enthroned in glory, and in close connection with God's throne, God's reign in heaven and in the future, and God's eschatological judgment (*1 Enoch* 22:14; 25:3; 27:3, 5; 40:3; 63:2). It could well be considered a variant of the title "King of glory," used of God in Psalm 24 and in some later Jewish texts (1QM 12:8; 19:1; 4Q427 7:1:13; 4Q510 1:1), no doubt in dependence on Psalm 24. Psalm 24 was certainly read christologically by some early Christians, and may have been so read by James. In any case, whereas the word "Lord" by itself could bear a range of meanings, the title "Lord of glory" suggests participation in God's own sovereignty, portraying Christ as the one who reigns with God in heaven and is coming as Lord and Judge of the world. It makes the same point as the christological use of Psalm 110:1 (portraying the Messiah as the Lord who sits at the right hand of God), which we know to have been current at a very early date in early Christianity. Thus the high christology which seems to be implicit in this unusual christological designation in James seems to be just the kind of high christology that we know to be very early: Jesus is the Lord in the sense that he exercises God's lordship over the world.

Outside of 1:1 and 2:1, James's references to Jesus call him just "the Lord" (*kyrios*), a term which he also uses for God. But there is no doubt that some of these references are to Jesus, since the phrase "the coming (*parousia*) of the Lord," which James has twice (5:7, 8), was in standard early Christian usage as a reference to the future coming of Jesus (cf. 1 Thess. 3:13; 4:15; 5:23; 2 Thess. 2:1), whereas the word *parousia* is never used of God in early Christian usage. In fact, there seem to be seven instances in James, including 1:1 and 2:1, in which "Lord" refers to Jesus (1:1; 2:1; 4:15[?]; 5:7, 8, 14, 15), and seven in which the word refers to God (1:7; 3:9; 4:10; 5:4, 10, 11[2]). Only 4:15 is seriously ambiguous, but most likely refers to God. In the cases of 1:7; 3:9; 4:10 the context makes explicit reference to "God" and shows that "the Lord" has the same reference. In chapter 5, the four references to God as "Lord" (5:4, 10, 11[2]) and the four to "Jesus" as Lord (5:7, 8, 14, 15) are distinguished linguistically (in 5:4, 10, 11, the anarthrous use of *kyrios* after a noun with the article treats the word as a proper name), as well as by the resonances of the Hebrew Bible in the former four cases. To these references to Jesus as "Lord" we can add that he is eschatological "judge" in 5:9, even though the "one lawgiver and judge" of 4:12 must be God. The overlap of terminology, while it may seem confusing to modern readers, is theologically significant. It is not untypical of early Jewish Christianity and it reflects the extent to which the figure of the exalted and coming Jesus was assimilated to God in his sovereignty over the world (cf. Bauckham 1998, 1–42).

Early Christians regularly interpreted as references to the future coming (*parousia*) of Jesus those texts in the Hebrew Bible which say that YHWH (*kyrios* in the Greek version) *will come* in judgment and salvation (e.g., Isa. 40:10 in Rev. 22:12; Isa. 59:20–21 in Rom. 11:26–27; Isa. 66:15–16 in 2 Thess. 1:7–8, 12; Zech. 14:5b in 1 Thess. 3:13; 2 Thess. 1:7; 4:14; cf. 1 Enoch 1:9 in Jude 14–15). Though it seems not to have been noticed by previous scholars, James's parabolic saying about the Parousia in 5:7b contains another instance of this practice in its echo of Hosea 6:3. This shows James to be closely in touch with early Christian christological exegesis of Scripture and the high Christology that it entailed. As the one who shares God's sovereignty from the divine throne and who will come to exercise divine judgment and complete the salvation of God's people, Jesus can be found in the prophecies of YHWH's eschatological coming. (For the comparable Christology in the letter of James's brother Jude, see Bauckham 1990, chap. 6.)

James 4:14–15 refers to the anointing of the sick "in the name of the Lord" and promises that "the Lord will raise [them] up." This reflects the same kind of Christology as Acts 3–4, where Peter heals the lame man in the name of Jesus and treats this as evidence that Jesus, risen from the dead, is living and powerful (Acts 3:6, 16; 4:9–12). The expectation is that, just as Jesus had healed the sick during his ministry, so he continues to do in his activity as the exalted Lord. In James's phrase "the Lord will raise him up" there may even be implicit reference to the healing activity of the earthly Jesus (cf. Mark 1:31; 5:41) as model for the expectation of his healing work in the present. In that case James in his letter refers not only to the teaching but also to the miracles of Jesus in his ministry, though in both cases only indirectly.

Finally, we may notice that the "beautiful name" invoked over Christians according to James 2:7 is most likely the name of Jesus invoked in baptism. But it corresponds to a usage in the Hebrew Bible and later Jewish literature, according to which God's ownership of his own people Israel is indicated by referring to them as those "over whom the name of YHWH has been invoked" (e.g., Deut. 28:10; 2 Chron. 7:14; Dan. 9:19). This treatment of the name Jesus as equivalent to the divine name of the God of Israel is of a piece with the considerable influence of Joel 2:32 ("everyone who calls on the name of YHWH shall be saved"), understood christologically, in early Christian usage (Acts 2:21, 38, where it is connected with baptism in the name of Jesus; Acts 9:14, 21; 22:16; Rom. 10:13; 2 Tim. 2:22). Once again the implicit Christology is high. For many reasons adduced in recent scholarship we must abandon the notion that a properly divine Christology developed only as the Christian movement spread outside its early Jewish Palestinian context. Even though the Christology of the letter of James is largely "submerged Christology" (Witherington 1998, 201), taken for granted rather than the subject of deliberate exposition, it fits the picture of a high Christology at a very early stage that is emerging from other studies (cf. Bauckham 1998). We may now assert quite confidently that the self-consciously low Christology of the later Jewish Christian sect known as the Ebionites does not, as has sometimes been asserted, go back to James and his circle in the early Jerusalem church.

BIBLIOGRAPHY

Adamson, J. B. 1989. *James: The Man and His Message*. Grand Rapids: Eerdmans.

Barton, S. C. 1994. *Discipleship and Family Ties in Mark and Matthew*. SNTSMS 80. Cambridge: Cambridge University Press.

Bauckham, R. 1990. *Jude and the Relatives of Jesus in the Early Church*. Edinburgh: T. & T. Clark.

———. 1992. "Mary of Clopas (John 19:25)." Pages 231–55 in *Women in the Biblical Tradition*, edited by G. J. Brooke. Lewiston, N.Y.: Edwin Mellen Press.

———. 1995. "James and the Jerusalem Church." Pages 415–80 in *The Book of Acts in Its Palestinian Setting*, edited by R. Bauckham. Carlisle: Paternoster; Grand Rapids: Eerdmans.

———. 1998. *God Crucified: Monotheism and Christology in the New Testament*. Exeter: Paternoster; Grand Rapids: Eerdmans.

———. 1999. *James: Wisdom of James, Disciple of Jesus the Sage*. New Testament Readings. London and New York: Routledge, 1999.

Burchard, C. 2000. *Der Jakobusbrief*. HNT 15/1. Tübingen: Mohr (Siebeck).

Byrskog, S. 2000. *Story as History—History as Story: The Gospel Tradition in the Context of Ancient Oral History*. WUNT 123. Tübingen: Mohr (Siebeck).

Davids, P. H. 1982. *The Epistle of James*. NIGTC. Exeter: Paternoster.

———. 1999. "Palestinian Traditions in the Epistle of James. Pages 35–57 in *James the Just and Christian Origins*, edited by B. Chilton and C. A. Evans. NovTSup 98. Leiden: Brill.

Deppe, D. B. 1989. *The Sayings of Jesus in the Epistle of James*. Dissertation, Free University of Amsterdam, 1989. Privately published; Chelsea, Mich.: Bookcrafters.

Dibelius, M., and H. Greeven. 1975. *James*. Translated by M. A. Williams. Hermeneia. Philadelphia: Fortress.

Hartin, P. J. 1991. *James and the Q Sayings of Jesus*. JSNTSup 47. Sheffield: Sheffield Academic Press.

Hengel. M. 1987. "Der Jakobusbrief als antipaulinische Polemik." Pages 248–78 in *Tradition and Interpretation in the New Testament*, edited by G. F. Hawthorne and O. Betz. E. E. Ellis FS. Grand Rapids: Eerdmans.

Hill, C. C. 1992. *Hellenists and Hebrews: Reappraising Divisions within the Earliest Church*. Minneapolis: Fortress.

Johnson, L. T. 1995. *The Letter of James*. AB 37A. New York: Doubleday.

Jülicher, A. 1904. *An Introduction to the New Testament*. Translated by J. P. Ward. New York: Putnam.

Laws, S. 1980. *A Commentary on the Epistle of James*. BNTC. London: A. & C. Black.

Martin, R. P. 1988. *James*. WBC 48. Waco, Tex.: Word.

Mayor, J. B. 1987. *The Epistle of St. James*. 2d ed., London: Macmillan.

Niebuhr, K.-W. 1998. "Der Jakobusbrief im Licht frühjüdischer Diasporabriefe," *NTS* 44:420–43.

Painter, J. 1997. *Just James: The Brother of Jesus in History and Tradition.* Studies on Personalities of the New Testament. Columbia: University of South Carolina Press.

Penner, T. C. 1996. *The Epistle of James and Eschatology: Re-reading an Ancient Christian Letter.* JSNTSS 121. Sheffield: Sheffield Academic Press.

Pratscher, W. 1987. *Der Herrenbruder Jakobus und die Jakobustradition.* FRLANT 139. Göttingen: Vandenhoeck & Ruprecht.

Wall, R. W. 1997. *Community of the Wise: The Letter of James.* New Testament in Context. Valley Forge, Pa.: Trinity Press International.

Witherington, B. 1994. *Jesus the Sage: The Pilgrimage of Wisdom.* Edinburgh: T. & T. Clark.

———. 1998. *The Many Faces of the Christ.* New York: Crossroad.

6

James in Relation to Peter, Paul, and the Remembrance of Jesus

Bruce Chilton

INTRODUCTION

Any evaluation of James is fraught with the basic difficulty that his perspective and personality are not represented directly within the New Testament. A case can be made for the argument that the Epistle of James represents something of both, but if so, it does so indirectly. In that source, as in the book of Acts and in Hegisippus and Eusebius, James is taken up within the theological perspective of the work as a whole, so that it is difficult to sort him out from his hagiography. Even the reference in Josephus is far from straightforward. It is a positive assessment of James, but in the interests of a negative assessment of the high priest who had James put to death.

Although this problem of the quality and perspectives of the sources can never be wholly overcome (absent a fresh discovery), there is a way of getting at James's own orientation and influence. That is through his relationships with people and perspectives that are well characterized in the sources. Our purpose here is to locate James in respect of Peter, Paul, and those who framed the Gospel traditions, and then to offer a conclusion in regard to his status and position with the primitive church (that is, the church prior to any conscious separation from Second Temple Judaism).

PETER: BAPTISM INTO JESUS' NAME

The remarkable and early agreement that Jews and non-Jews could be included in the same movement by baptism established a radical principle of inclusion. This is reflected in the book of Acts, an indirect but powerful witness to the character of Petrine Christianity. Peter's conviction, signaled by the story of his visit to the house of Cornelius, a Roman centurion, was that God's Spirit flowed from the risen Jesus, not only upon his original followers, but to any believers, circumcised or not, who would be immersed (that is, baptized, following a practice which Judaism followed in cases of Jews and Gentiles) in his name (Acts 10).

Even at Pentecost, the Spirit in Acts is portrayed as descending on the twelve apostles (including the newly chosen Matthias), and they speak God's praises in the various languages of those assembled from the four points of the compass for that summer feast of harvest, both Jews and proselytes (Acts 2:1–12). The mention of proselytes (2:11) and the stress that those gathered came from "every nation under heaven" (2:5) clearly point ahead to the inclusion of non-Jews by means of baptism within Acts. Peter's explanation of the descent of the Spirit explicitly does that. He quotes from the prophet Joel (3:1–5 in the Septuagint), "And it will be in the last days, says God, that I will pour out from my Spirit upon all flesh." "All flesh," not only historic Israel, is to receive of God's Spirit: in other words, what happens at that Pentecost is less a social marker of inclusion than it is the fulfillment of a prophetic, eschatological promise of the universality of Spirit.

Now we are in a position to see why it was natural within the Petrine circle to speak of immersion "into the name of Jesus": this is not idiomatic Greek, but more probably reflects the Aramaic *leshun* (or Hebrew *leshem*). The Mishnah (Zeb. 4:6) refers to those "for the sake of" whom (or: that for the sake of which) a given sacrifice is offered: that cultic usage was inspired by the environment of Pentecost. Those who entered into a fresh relationship to God by means of the Holy Spirit were themselves a kind of "first fruits" (the offering of Pentecost) and found their identity in relation to Christ and Spirit as "first fruits" (so Rom. 8:23; 11:16; 16:5; 1 Cor. 15:20, 23; 16:15; Jas. 1:18; Rev. 14:4). The wide range of that usage, which attests the influence of the Petrine theology, reflects the deeply Pentecostal character of primitive Christianity. Access to the covenant by means of the Spirit meant that they entered sacrificially "into the name" (*eis to onoma*) of Jesus in baptism. Similarly, within the Petrine circle, Eucharist was celebrated in covenantal terms, when one broke bread and shared the cup "into the remembrance of" Jesus (*eis ten anamnesin*; Luke 22:19; 1 Cor. 11:24–25), a phrase associated with covenantal sacrifice (see Lev. 2:2, 9, 16; 5:12; 6:8; 24:7; Num. 5:26). Both baptism and Eucharist are sacrificial in the Petrine understanding, and both intimately involve the Spirit of God.

When Peter is speaking in the house of Cornelius in Acts 10, the Spirit falls upon those who are listening, and those there with Peter who were circumcised were astounded "that the gift of the Holy Spirit has been poured even upon the nations" (10:44–45). The choice of the verb "to pour" is no coincidence: it is resonant with the quotation of Joel in Acts 2:17. Indeed, those in Cornelius's house praise God "in tongues" (10:46) in a manner reminiscent of the apostles' prophecy at Pentecost, and Peter directs that they be baptized "in the name of Christ Jesus" (10:47–48). That is just the direction Peter gave earlier to his sympathetic hearers at Pentecost (2:37–38). Probably in the case of his speech at Pentecost, and more definitely in the case of his speech in the house of Cornelius, Peter's directions were in Greek, and we should understand that immersion is not in any general sense and that "Jesus" (*Iesous*) has entered the Greek language. Christian baptism, immersion into the name of Jesus with reception of the Holy Spirit, was developed within the practice of the circle of Peter. Lucidity of speech, as Paul would later insist in 1 Corinthians 14, was taken to be a mark of the Spirit's presence.

In aggregate, the two passages from Acts do not suggest any real dispute as to whether the gift of the Spirit followed or preceded baptism into Jesus' name. The point is rather that belief in and baptism into him is connected directly with the outpouring of God's Spirit. The apparent disruption of the usual model in Acts 10 is intended to call attention to the artificiality (from the point of view of the emergent Petrine theology) of attempting to withhold baptism from those who believe (as Peter actually says in 10:47). Two questions immediately arise at this point. First, why would it have been so natural for Peter to have extended baptism to non-Jews on the basis of the outpouring of Spirit, when he was still sensitive to the scruples of Judaism? (And Paul, a contemporary witness, records that sensitivity; see Gal. 2:11–14.) Second, where did Peter understand the new infusion of Spirit to have derived from?

As it happens, those two questions have a single answer. The source of the Spirit is Jesus as raised from the dead. In Peter's speech at Pentecost, Jesus, having been exalted to the right hand of God, receives the promise of the Holy Spirit from the Father and pours it out on his followers (2:33). The Spirit that is poured out, then, comes directly from the majesty of God, from his rule over creation as a whole. This is the Spirit as it hovered over the waters at the beginning of creation (Gen. 1:1), and not as limited to Israel. Because the Spirit is of God, who creates people in the divine image, its presence marks God's own activity, in which all those who follow Jesus are to be included. Jesus' own program had involved proclaiming God's kingdom on the authority of his possession of God's Spirit (see Matt. 12:28; Luke 11:20). Now, as a consequence of the resurrection, Jesus had poured out that same Spirit upon those who would follow him. Baptism in the Spirit (see Acts 1:4–5) and baptism into the name of Jesus were one and the same thing for that reason. That was why believing that Jesus was God's son and calling upon his name were the occasions on which the Spirit was to be received. In the new environment of God's Spirit which the resurrection signaled, baptism was indeed, as Matthew 28:19 indicates, an activity and an experience which involved the Father (the source of one's identity), the Son (the agent of one's identity), and the Holy Spirit (the medium of one's identity).

The influence of Peter's stance is attested by the agreement of James, and teachers such as Barnabas and Paul, that circumcision should not be made a requirement for Christians. Deep though this agreement was, it also brought about the greatest and most enduring controversies within the early church. Although Peter, James, and Barnabas agreed that circumcision could not be demanded of non-Jews who received baptism, there were strong factions which did not concur who are styled as Christian Pharisees (see Acts 11:1–18; 15:1–5). They had weighty arguments on their side, above all the covenant of circumcision (Gen. 17:9–14) that, on a plain reading of the text, brooks no exceptions. They were obviously a considerable contingent within primitive Christianity, and the requirement of circumcision was honored at least until the second century. Even among those teachers—the most influential, in the end—who extended baptism to non-Jews without requiring circumcision, disagreements arose.

ANTIOCH: THE DISPUTE
AMONG PAUL, PETER, AND JAMES

The best-attested argument occurred at Antioch, where non-Jews had begun to eat together with Jews in the context of the Christian practice of Eucharist and other common meals. Paul's version of events, written in his letter to the Galatians around 53 C.E., is the best available (see Gal. 2:11–21). At Antioch, Jews and non-Jews who had been baptized joined in meals of fellowship together. According to Paul, Peter fell in with the practice and Barnabas apparently tolerated it. Barnabas, a Levite from Cyprus, was a prominent, loyal recruit in Jerusalem, who enjoyed the trust of the apostles and mediated relations between them and Paul.

Paul's policy of including Gentiles with Jews in meals, as well as in baptism, needed the support of authorities, such as Peter and Barnabas, in order to prevail against the natural conservatism of those for whom such inclusion seemed a betrayal of the purity of Israel. It was when representatives of James arrived, James who was the brother of Jesus and the preeminent figure in the church in Jerusalem, that this natural conservatism reasserted itself. Peter "separated himself," along with the rest of the Jews, and even Barnabas (Gal. 2:12, 13). Jews and Gentiles again maintained distinct fellowship at meals, and Paul accuses the leadership of his own movement of hypocrisy (Gal. 2:13).

The radical quality of Paul's position needs to be appreciated. He was isolated from every other Christian Jew (by his own account in Gal. 2:11–13: James, Peter, Barnabas, and "the rest of the Jews"). His isolation required that he develop an alternative view of authority in order to justify his own practice. Within Galatians, Paul quickly articulates the distinctive approach to Scripture as authoritative which characterizes his writings as a whole. His invention of the dialectic between grace and law, between Israel as defined by faith and Israel after the flesh, became a founding principle in the intellectual evolution of Christianity in its formative period. But the Pauline character of that evolution was by no means predictable at the time Paul himself wrote, and Paulinism can become an obstacle to historical study, insofar as it prevents us from imagining other forms of theological commitment to Jesus, such as that of James.

The confrontation at Antioch that Paul recounts to his audience in Galatia did not turn out happily for him at the time. His explanation of his own point of view is triumphant and ringing only in retrospect. Indeed, by the time he recollects his argument for the benefit of the Galatians (to whom he writes some four years after this confrontation), he seems so confident that one might overlook the fact that he was the loser in the battle with the representatives of James. It was he, not they, who left the area of Antioch (so Acts 15:22–41).

THE ADJUDICATION OF JAMES

The position of James is not represented, as is Paul's, by a writing of the thinker himself. But the book of Acts does clearly reflect his perspective in regard to both circumcision and the issue of purity (Acts 15), the two principal matters of concern in Galatians. The account in Acts 15 is romanticized; one sees much less of the tension and controversy which Paul attests. But once allowance has been made for the tendency in Acts to portray the ancient church as a body at harmonious unity, the nature and force of James's position become clear.

The two issues in dispute, circumcision and purity, are dealt with in Acts 15 as if they were the agenda of a single meeting of leaders in Jerusalem. (Paul in Galatians 2 more accurately describes the meeting he had with the leaders as distinct from a later decision to return to the question of purity.) The first item on the agenda is settled by having Peter declare that, since God gave his Holy Spirit to Gentiles who believed, no attempt should be made to add requirements such as circumcision to them (Acts 15:6–11). Believers who are named as Pharisees insist that "it is necessary both to circumcise them and to command them to keep the law of Moses" (15:5). That sets the stage for conflict, not only with Paul and Barnabas, but with Peter. And it is Peter who, in the midst of great controversy, rehearses what happened in the house of Cornelius, which he has just done a few chapters previously (see Acts 11:1–18; 15:7–11). Peter comes to what is not only a Pauline expression, but, more particularly, to an expression of the Pauline school, that "through the grace of the Lord Jesus we believe to be saved, in the manner they also shall be" (Acts 15:11, see Eph. 2:8). For that reason, it seems natural for the reference to Barnabas and Paul to follow (15:12). (That order of names is no coincidence: after all, Barnabas is much better known and appreciated in Jerusalem than Paul.) Paul could scarcely have said it better himself; and that is consistent with the version of Paulinism represented in Acts.

The second item on the agenda is settled on James's authority, not Peter's, and the outcome is not in line with Paul's thought. James first confirms the position of Peter, but he states the position in a very different way: "Symeon has related how God first visited the Gentiles, to take a people in his name"

(Acts 15:14). James's perspective here is not that all who believe are Israel (the Pauline definition), but that *in addition* to Israel God has established a people in his name. How the new people are to be regarded in relation to Israel is a question that is implicit in the statement, and James goes on to answer it. James develops the relationship between those taken from the Gentiles and Israel in two ways. The first method is the use of Scripture, while the second is a requirement of purity. The logic of them both inevitably involves a rejection of Paul's position (along the lines laid out in Galatians 2).

The use of Scripture, like the argument itself, is quite unlike Paul's. James claims that "with this [that is, his statement of Peter's position] the words of the prophets agree, just as it is written" (Acts 15:15), and he goes on to cite from the book of Amos. The passage cited will concern us in a moment; the form of James's interpretation is an immediate indication of a substantial difference from Paul. As James has it, there is actual agreement between Symeon and the words of the prophets, as two people might agree: nowhere else in the New Testament in the verb *symphoneo* used in respect of Scripture. The continuity of Christian experience with Scripture is marked as a greater concern than within Paul's interpretation, and James expects that continuity to be verbal, a matter of agreement with the prophets' words, not merely with possible ways of looking at what they mean.

The citation from Amos (9:11–12, from the version of the Septuagint, the Bible of Luke–Acts) comports well with James's concern that the position of the church agree with the principal vocabulary of the prophets (Acts 15:16–17):

> After this I will come back and restore the tent [or: hut] of David which has fallen, and rebuild its ruins and set it up anew, that the rest of men may seek the Lord, and all the Gentiles upon whom my name is called. . . .

In the argument of James as represented here, what the belief of Gentiles achieves is, not the redefinition of Israel (as in Paul's thought), but the restoration of the house of David. The argument is possible because a Davidic genealogy of Jesus—and therefore of his brother James—is assumed.

The account of James's preaching in the Temple given by Hegesippus (quoted in Eusebius, *H.E.* 2.23) represents Jesus as the son of man who is to come from heaven to judge the world. Those who agree cry out, "Hosanna to the Son of David!" Hegesippus shows that James's view of his brother came to be that he was related to David (as was the family generally) and was also a heavenly figure who was coming to judge the world. When Acts and Hegesippus are taken together, they indicate that James contended Jesus was restoring the house of David because he was the agent of final judgment (the "son of man" of Dan. 7:13), and was being accepted as such by Gentiles with his Davidic pedigree.

But in James's view, Gentiles remain Gentiles; they are not to be identified with Israel. His position was not anti-Pauline (at least not at first). His focus was on Jesus' role as the ultimate arbiter within the Davidic line, and there was never any question in his mind but that the Temple was the natural place to worship God and acknowledge Jesus. Embracing the Temple as central meant for James, as it meant for everyone associated with worship there, maintaining the purity which it was understood that God required in his house. Purity involved excluding Gentiles from the interior courts of the Temple, where Israel was involved in sacrifice. The line of demarcation between Israel and non-Israel was no invention within the circle of James, but a natural result of seeing Jesus as the triumphant branch of the house of David.

Gentile belief in Jesus was therefore in James's understanding a vindication of his Davidic triumph, but it did not involve an absolute change in the status of Gentiles vis-à-vis Israel. That characterization of the Gentiles, developed by means of the reference to Amos, enables James to proceed to his requirement of their recognition of purity. He first states that "I determine not to trouble those of the Gentiles who turn to God" (15:19), as if he were simply repeating the policy of Peter in regard to circumcision. (The implicit authority of that "I" contrasts sharply with the usual portrayal in Acts of apostolic decision as communal.) But he then continues that his determination is also "to write to them to abstain from the pollutions of the idols, and from fornication, and from what is strangled, and from blood" (15:20).

The rules set out by James tend naturally to separate believing Gentiles from their ambient environment. They are to refrain from feasts in honor of the gods and from foods sacrificed to idols in the course of being butchered and sold. (The notional devotion of animals in the market to one god or another was a common practice in the Hellenistic world.) They are to observe stricter limits than usual on the type of sexual activity they might engage in, and with whom. (Gross promiscuity need not be at issue here; marriage with cousins is also included within the likely area of concern. That was fashionable in the Hellenistic world, and proscribed in the book of Leviticus [see chap. 18 and 20:17–21]). They are to avoid the flesh of animals that had been strangled instead of bled, and they are not to consume blood itself. The proscription of blood, of course, was basic within Judaism. And strangling an animal (as distinct from cutting its throat) increased the availability of blood in the meat. Such strictures are consistent with James's initial observation, that God had taken a people from the Gentiles (15:14); they were to be similar to Israel and supportive of Israel in their distinction from the Hellenistic world at large.

The motive behind the rules is not separation as such, however. James links them to the fact that the Mosaic legislation regarding purity is well and widely known (15:21):

> For Moses from early generations has had those preaching him city by city, being read in the synagogues every Sabbath.

Because the law is well known, James insists that believers, even Gentile believers, are not to live in flagrant violation of what Moses enjoined. In the words of Amos, they are to behave as "all the Gentiles upon whom my name is called." As a result of James's insistence, the meeting in Jerusalem decides to send envoys and a letter to Antioch, in order to require Gentiles to honor the prohibitions set out by James (Acts 15:22–35).

The same chapter of Leviticus that commands, "love your neighbor as yourself" (19:18), also forbids blood to be eaten (19:26) and fornication (19:29; see also 18:6–30). The canonical (but secondhand) Letter of James calls the commandment of love "the royal law" (Jas. 2:8), acknowledging that Jesus had accorded it privilege by citing it and the commandment to love God as the two greatest commandments (see Mark 12:28–32). In Acts James himself, while accepting that Gentiles cannot be required to keep the whole law, insists that they should acknowledge it, by observing basic requirements concerning fornication and blood and idolatry.

It is of interest that Leviticus forbids the eating of blood by sojourners as well as Israelites, and associates that prohibition with how animals are to be killed for the purpose of eating (17:10–16). Moreover, a principle of exclusivity in sacrifice is trenchantly maintained: anyone, whether of Israel or a sojourner dwelling among them, who offers a sacrifice which is not brought to the Lord's honor in the Temple is to be cut off from the people (17:8–9). In other words, the prohibitions of James, involving sacrifice, fornication, strangled meat produce, and blood, all derive easily from the very context in Leviticus from which the commandment to love is derived. They are elementary and involve interest in what Gentiles as well as Israelites do.

James's prohibitions as presented in Acts are designed to show that believing Gentiles honor the law which is commonly read, without actually changing their status as Gentiles. Thereby, the tent of David is erected again, in the midst of Gentiles who show their awareness of the restoration by means of their respect for the Torah. The interpretation attributed to James involves an application of Davidic vocabulary to Jesus, as is consistent with the claim of Jesus' family to Davidic ancestry. The transfer of Davidic promises to Jesus is accomplished within an acceptance of the terms of reference of the Scripture generally: to embrace David is to embrace Moses. There is no trace in James's interpretation of the Pauline gambit, setting one biblical principle (justification in the manner of Abraham) against another (obedience in the manner of Moses). Where Paul divided the Scripture against itself in order to maintain the integrity of a single fellowship of Jews and Gentiles, James insisted upon the integrity of Scripture, even at the cost of separating Christians from one another. In both cases, the interpretation of Scripture was also—at the same moment as the sacred text was apprehended—a matter of social policy.

Amos 9:11 was also cited at Qumran. In one citation (in 4Q174 3:10–13, a florilegium), the image of the restoration of the hut of David is associated with the promise to David in 2 Samuel 7:13–14 and with the Davidic "branch" (cf.

Isa. 11:1–10), all taken in a messianic sense. Given the expectation of a son of David as messianic king (see *Psalms of Solomon* 17:21–43), such an application of the passage in Amos, whether at Qumran or by James, is hardly strange. On the other hand, it is striking that the passage in Amos—particularly, "the fallen hut of David"—is applied in the *Damascus Document* (CD 7:15–17), not to a messianic figure, but to the law which is restored. Now the book of Amos itself makes Judah's contempt for the Torah the pivotal issue (Amos 2:4) and calls for a program of seeking the Lord and his ways (Amos 5:6–15), so it is perhaps not surprising that "the seeker of the law" is predicted to restore it in the *Damascus Document*. Still, CD 7:15–20 directly refers to the "books of the Torah" as "the huts of the king," interpreted by means of the "fallen hut of David." Evidently, there is a precise correspondence between the strength of the messiah and the establishment of the Torah, as is further suggested by the association with the seeker of the law *not only here*, in the *Damascus Document*, but also in the Florilegium. A contextual reading of the two passages demonstrates a dual focus, on messiah and Torah in each case, such that they stand in a complementary relationship. The possibility of Essene influence on James's interpretation of Amos as presented in Acts 15 may not be discounted.

JAMES AND THE NAZIRITE VOW

The ideal of Christian devotion that James has in mind is represented in Acts 21. There, Paul and his companions arrive in Jerusalem and are confronted by James and the elders' report to them that Paul's reputation in Jerusalem is that he tells Jews in the Diaspora to forsake Moses, and especially to stop circumcising their children (Acts 21:17–21). Paul is then told to take on the expense of four men who had taken a vow, entering the Temple with them to offer sacrifice (Acts 21:22–26).

The nature of the vow seems quite clear. It will be fulfilled when the men shave their heads (so Acts 21:24). We are evidently dealing with a Nazirite vow. As set out in Numbers 6, a Nazirite was to let his hair and beard grow for the time of his vow, abstain completely from grapes, and avoid approaching any dead body. At the close of the period of the vow, he was to shave his head, and offer his hair in proximity to the altar (so Num. 6:18). The end of this time of being holy, the LORD's property, is marked by enabling the Nazirite to drink wine again (6:20).

Just these practices of holy abstinence are attributed by Hegesippus to James. The additional notice, that he avoided oil, is consistent with the especial concern for purity among Nazirites. They were to avoid any contact with death (Num. 6:6–12), and the avoidance of all uncleanness—which is incompatible with sanctity—follows naturally. The avoidance of oil is also attributed by Josephus to the Essenes (*J.W.* 2.123), and the reason seems plain: oil, as a fluid pressed from fruit and water in small vessels, was considered to absorb impurity to such an extent that extreme care in its preparation was vital (see Josephus, *J.W.* 2.590–94; Lev. 11:34, 38; *M. Menaḥ* 8:3–5 and the whole of Makhshirin). Absent complete assurance, abstinence was a wise policy. James's vegetarianism also comports with a concern to avoid contact with any kind of corpse. Finally, Hegesippus makes the odd assertion that James could actually enter the sanctuary. That seems exaggerated to the point of implausibility, but his acceptance of a Nazirite regime, such as Acts 21 explicitly associates him with, would account for such a remembrance of him, because Nazirites were to be presented in the vicinity of the sanctuary (Num. 6:18–20).

As it turned out, James's advice proved disastrous for Paul. Paul's entry into the Temple caused a riot, because it was supposed he was bringing non-Jews in. As a result, he was arrested by a Roman officer (Acts 21:27–28:21), and so began the long legal contention which resulted ultimately in his death. The extent to which James might have anticipated such a result cannot be known, but it does seem obvious that his commitment to a Nazirite ideology caused him to ignore the political dangers that threatened the movement of which he was the nearest thing to the head.

JAMES'S CONCERN FOR THE TEMPLE
AS REFLECTED IN THE SYNOPTIC TRADITION

The particular concern of James for practice in the Temple has left its mark on teaching attributed to Jesus. In Mark 7:15, Jesus set down a radical principle of purity:

> There is nothing outside a person, entering in, that can defile,
> but what comes out of a person is what defiles a person.

That principle establishes that those in Galilean Israel were to be accepted as pure, so that fellowship at meals with them, as was characteristic in Jesus' movement from the beginning, was possible. Their usual customs of purity, together with their generosity in sharing and their willingness to receive and accept forgiveness, readied them to celebrate the fellowship of the kingdom of God. His program was not as suited to Nazirites as it was to those his opponents called "tax agents and sinners"; to them Jesus seemed a drunk and a glutton (see Matt. 11:19; Luke 7:34).

But within this same chapter of Mark, in which Jesus' Galilean principle is clearly stated, a syllogism is developed to attack a particular practice in the Temple (Mark 7:6–13):

> But he said to them,
> > Duly Isaiah prophesied about you frauds, as it is written,
> > "This people honors me with lips,

But their heart is far distant from me.
In vain they worship me,
teaching men's commandments as doctrines."

Leaving the commandment of God, you adhere to men's tradition.

And he was saying to them,
Duly you annul the commandment of God,
so that you establish your tradition. For Moses said,
"Honor your father and your mother,"
and,
"Let the one who curses father or mother die the death."
But you say, If a person says to father or mother, "Whatever you
were owed from me is Qorban [that is, gift]," you no longer let him
do anything for father or mother, voiding the word of God by your
tradition. And you do many such things.

Two features of this argument are striking. It assumes familiarity with the vow of *qorbana* (as it is called in Aramaic), which does indeed mean "gift." One could, in effect, shelter one's use of property by dedicating it to the Temple at one's death, continuing to use it during one's life. Mishnah envisages a man saying, "Qorban be any benefit my wife gets from me, for she stole my purse" (Ned. 3:2). The simple complaint about the practice in vv. 11–12 may indeed reflect Jesus' position, since his objection to commercial arrangements involving worship is well attested. But that only focuses our attention all the more on the syllogistic nature of the argument, which is unlike what we elsewhere find attributed to Jesus.

The argument as a whole is framed in Mark 7:6–7 by means of a reference to the book of Isaiah (29:13): the people claim to honor God, but their heart is as far from him as their vain worship, rooted in human commandments. That statement is then related to the custom of *qorban*, which is said to invalidate the plain sense of Moses' prescription to honor parents (compare Exod. 20:2; 21:17; Lev. 20:9; Deut. 5:16). By reading Isaiah through the lens of the commandment, it is shown that this prophet's words are fulfilled much as Amos's are in Acts 15. In both cases, direct correspondence with prophecy is claimed, and the prophets' continuity with Moses is invoked as a principle. The simple and inevitable conclusion is that the tradition violates the command of God (see Mark 7:8–9, 13).

The logic of the syllogism is not complicated, and it can easily be structured in a different way (as happens in Matt. 15:3–9). The association of similar Scriptures is reminiscent of the rabbinic rule of interpretation, that a principle expressed in a text may be related to another text, without identity of wording between the two passages. But the scriptural syllogism by no means requires the invocation of any such formal principle. The fundamental argument is that the Law and the Prophets are antithetical to the practice of authorities in the Temple.

The rhetoric of the syllogism turns on the necessity of honoring Moses, as in the interpretation attributed to James in Acts 15 (see Acts 15:21). Moreover, the principle inherent here is that Scripture is actually implemented in the case of Jesus' movement. Finally, the centrality of the Temple as a settled institution is manifest throughout. All this attests to the influence of James, and to the development in Mark 7 of a rhetoric within his circle which focused on the actual fulfillment of Scripture's meaning in the focal concern with purity and sanctity in the Temple.

JAMES'S EUCHARIST PASSOVER

Recent scholarship has rightly seen that the identification of the Last Supper with Passover is theologically motivated. The Gospels correctly report that the authorities had every reason to deal with Jesus *before* the crowds of Passover arrived (Matt. 26:1–5; Mark 14:1–2; Luke 22:1–2). Jesus' final meals would therefore have taken place near the paschal season, but not during the feast. That would explain why the most basic elements of the Seder—lamb, unleavened bread, bitter herbs (see Exod. 12:8)—are notable in the narratives only for their absence. Jesus might well have expressed a desire to eat the Passover, such as Luke 22:15 attributes to him, but if so, that desire remained unfulfilled.

For all that, there is no question of any ambiguity in Matt. 26:17–20; Mark 14:12–17; Luke 22:7–14: the pericope which prefaces the meal explicitly and emphatically presents the Last Supper as paschal. Whatever the sense of the meal originally, there is no doubt a theological investment in the Synoptics as great as Paul's (see 2 Cor. 5:17) in presenting the meal in that light, just as the Johannine timing of Jesus' death when the paschal lambs were normally slain accomplishes a similar aim (John 19:36 with Exod. 12:46). But where Paul is content to make that link in purely theological terms, the Synoptics and John in their different ways insist upon a calendrical correspondence (albeit without being able completely to agree) between Passover and the Last Supper. The degree of concern to link the entire complex of material related to the death of Jesus with Passover is so great throughout the sources, that certainty regarding the actual course of events is unattainable. It is clear that the calendar of the early church has vitiated the historical value of all the extant documents.

When the Synoptic pericopae specify the timing of the Last Supper, its identification as a Seder appears problematic. Matt. 26:17; Mark 14:12; Luke 22:7 insist that Jesus' instructions to prepare to celebrate the feast in the city were given on the first day of unleavened bread, when the paschal lamb was to be slain. By any reckoning, that must be regarded as short notice, in that the lamb was to be selected on the tenth day of the month, for slaughter on the fourteenth day of the month (Exod. 12:3–6). Whatever arrangements needed to be made therefore required several days prior to the feast in strictly cultic terms. The exigencies of accommodation in Jerusalem—which is commonly recognized to have had an infrastructure grossly inadequate for the number of its pilgrims—would no doubt have required even more notice. The paradox, then, is that the only pericope to insist upon a paschal chronology (see Matt. 26:19; Mark 14:16; Luke 22:13), with the unequivocal reference to the meal as the Passover, does not make good sense in the light of that chronology.

The strain which the pericope places upon plausibility emerges in another, more technical consideration. Commentators have observed that the reference to "the first day of the unleavened bread" in Mark 14:12 and Matt. 26:17 is odd, since that would presumably be Nisan 15. But the lambs were slain on Nisan 14, so that they could be eaten on the evening which marked the beginning of Nisan 15 (see *Pesaḥ*. 1:1 in the Mishnah). Luke's Gospel appears both to recognize and to clean up the difficulty, by referring to "the day of the unleavened bread, in which it was necessary to sacrifice the Passover" (22:7). But with or without the Lukan explanation, a pericope which otherwise makes good sense of the considerable preparations involved in keeping Passover in Jerusalem then betrays its own credibility by confining the action to a short and ill-defined period of time. If the substance of the story seems plausible, its paschal chronology appears schematic at best.

The Synoptic Gospels nonetheless proceed with the chronology invoked by the pericope. The tensions involved with the narrative of Jesus' meal—which is neither explicitly nor implicitly paschal—are evident, but they would have become less striking, the greater the distance from the actual practices of Passover. The most severe tension is confronted in Luke, where the originally unfulfilled desire of 22:15 is now expressed in the setting of a Seder. Luke 22:16 puts 22:15 into a new key, by framing its meaning to accord with that of verse 18 (cf. Matt. 26:29; Mark 14:25), as if Jesus were swearing an oath not to eat or drink of Passover until the fulfillment of the kingdom. But the Lukan gambit is only successful if Jesus is supposed in the meal recounted by the narrative to be drinking fulfilled wine or eating fulfilled Passover in the kingdom of God. Luke provides a window into the considerable adjustments of meaning which were consequent upon transforming Jesus' meal from a surrogate of sacrifice enacted near (but before) Passover into a Seder in a strict sense.

What purpose is served by the strict identification of the Last Supper as a Seder in Matthew 26:17–20; Mark 14:12–17; Luke 22:7–14? Several changes in the understanding of the meal are effected by a single shift of liturgical setting, however implausible its precise chronology in historical terms. First, of course, the meal becomes a unique occasion within the ritual year: it is a paschal supper, and only that. Second, it is possible to keep the Passover only because Jesus makes specific preparations in or near Jerusalem (see Matt. 26:18, 19; Mark 14:13–16; Luke 22:8–13), where it is assumed he is acquainted with at least one householder sufficiently sympathetic with his position to permit him to use a space for the celebration. The intentionality of Jesus' timing of the Last Supper as a Seder is underlined by the narrative.

None of the Synoptics makes mention of the paschal lamb or its sacrifice, although they may be assumed to have been a part of the preparations which are envisaged, once the identification with the Seder was accepted. In any case, from the moment of Jesus' arrival (Matt. 26:20; Mark 14:17; Luke 22:14), there is no express reference to the Passover, except in Luke 22:15, 16, as part of a statement that Jesus will eat and drink of the paschal celebration only in the kingdom. Moreover, there is no reference to any of the constituent elements of a Seder: the roasted lamb with unleavened bread and bitter herbs (Exod. 12:8). They are all left to be inferred, on the strength of the context created by Matthew 26:17–20; Mark 14:12–17; Luke 22:7–14.

The mention of singing in Matthew 26:30; Mark 14:26 is sometimes taken as evidence of a paschal setting, and it may belong to the presentation of the meal as a Seder. In order to construe the singing in that way, however, it must be assumed that the Hallel, a sung version of some form of Psalms 113–118, is at issue; even on that assumption, the Hallel was not uniquely paschal, but amounted to a festal song which might be used on several occasions. Whether or not the mention of singing is of a piece with the vignette concerning preparations for Passover, it adds nothing to the introductory setting which is the principal instrument of the paschal presentation. That presentation makes the last meal of Jesus into a Passover, truly repeatable only once a year, and then only with the sympathetic cooperation of other Jews of sufficient wealth to provide the conditions necessary for the celebration.

By a stroke of artificial context, then, the meal is more tightly linked to the liturgical year than it ever had been before, and its only possible occasion is in Jerusalem. The dominical meals as practiced by Peter and Paul were repeatable anywhere and frequently, as Jesus' meals had been. The present transformation of what is now a last Passover could only truly be enacted, to use the Rabbinic phrase, "between the evenings" (during the twilight of passage from one day to the next within the calendar of Judaism) of 14 and 15 Nisan, and in the vicinity of the Temple, where the paschal lambs were slain. If Jesus' "Last Supper" were understood as strictly paschal, its reenactment would be limited in three ways. Temporally, it would only take place at Passover; geographically, the only appropriate venue would be Jerusalem; socially, participants would need to be circumcised (see Exod. 12:48).

The last limitation appears the most dramatic, given the increasing importance of non-Jewish Christians during the course of the first century and later. By fully identifying Jesus' meal and Passover, the circle of potential participants in Eucharist excluded the uncircumcised and was limited to those who were Jews or who accepted circumcision, since circumcision was an explicit requirement for males who took part in a Seder (according to Exod. 12:48–49).

Once Jesus' movement reached Gentiles, the matter of their participation in such a paschal supper would become problematic. Before we proceed to investigate a paschal limitation in the understanding of who might participate in Eucharist, we need to consider whether difficulties of the sort which might be caused by such a paschal policy in fact arose.

Problems accommodating Eucharist and Passover were in fact a feature of the early church. A strict association of the meal and Passover lies at the heart of the Quartodeciman controversy. Eusebius provides the fullest account of the controversy, as it erupted toward the end of the second century (*H.E.* 5.23–24). The consequence of the policy of ending the fast prior to Easter on 14 Nisan was that the day of the resurrection would often be other than Sunday, and such a practice conflicted with apostolic tradition. But such was the tenacity of Quartodeciman practice, Eusebius reports, that councils were convened in Palestine, Rome, Pontus, Gaul, Osrhoene, and Corinth (5.23).

Eusebius's claim of a cheerfully unanimous rejection of Quartodecimanism is dubious, especially in the light of his own premise, that the controversy persisted in Asia. Polycrates is designated as the leader of bishops there in insisting upon the antiquity of their practice (5.24). Eusebius proceeds to cite Polycrates' position in some detail, he says on documentary evidence. Polycrates claims that keeping the day is connected to the rising of the luminaries to meet the coming Lord, and the gathering of the saints. Some of the saints are enumerated, including Philip, John, Polycarp, and Melito; it is furthermore claimed that they all kept "the day of the fourteenth of Passover according to the gospel," as does Polycrates himself in the tradition of his kin.

Several features of Polycrates' apology invite our immediate attention, in that the strict association of Passover and Jesus' last meal, such as is achieved in Matthew 26:17–20; Mark 14:12–17; Luke 22:7–14, would largely account for his position. The observance is indeed Quartodeciman, and in this attachment to the fourteenth day of the month it is paschal in a calendrical sense. The calendrical observation is linked to the position of the luminaries, much as Passover was to be observed on the basis of the coincidence of a full moon and the vernal equinox. The practice is said to derive from the gospel; a continuous tradition from the apostles allegedly derives from that evangelical mandate; the tradition is kept alive, not only in Asia, but in precisely those churches in which the Judaic environment is attested in Acts and/or the Pauline letters.

The Quartodecimans do not provide the cause for the association with Passover, only the assertion that it is correct (indeed, that it is both evangelical and apostolic). Eusebius would have us believe that the controversy is simply a matter of when the fast ends and the feasting begins, and that may have been the case by his time (at least in his own mind). But the heat of the controversy is such as to suggest that the identification of Jesus' Last Supper and Passover carried with it far more profound implications. Melito of Sardis, for example, dwells in his paschal homily on the correspondence between Jesus and the lamb of Passover in a manner which shows why by his time the entire language of paschal sacrifice had been appropriated by Christians. The evident affinity between the Quartodecimans and Jewish practice serves to confirm that, at an earlier stage, identifying Eucharist with Passover and limiting participation within it to circumcised believers were tendencies which went together.

The letter to the Galatians mentions some of the elements cited here as observances, practices, and beliefs which are to be avoided. Paul warns his readers against their observation of days, months, seasons, and years and connects those practices to serving the "elements" of nature (4:8–11). The question of the meaning of the term (*stoicheion*) as employed by Paul is not entirely settled, but it is the same word which clearly means "luminaries" in Eusebius's citation of Polycrates' position. Paul is also upset that "another gospel" should be competing with his among the Galatians (1:6–12; 2:7); he is nearly scathing in his reference to the apostolic authority of others in chapter 2 (vv. 6, 9, 11–14); he attacks those who would impose Judaic customs upon non-Jews in the name of Christ (2:14–21; 5:1–12; cf. 1:13, 14), and Peter in particular (2:11–14); he identifies that threat with Cephas and James's followers in Antioch, who are said to have influenced Barnabas and "the other Jews" (2:11–13). In aggregate, Paul is opposing practices involving the observation of a calendar, practices which themselves claim evangelical and apostolic warrant, rooted in Christian Judaism.

The fundamental dispute in which Paul was engaged, and which would take up his attention for years after the particular argument which he relates, was far more profound than the simple question of dating Easter. His charge is that Cephas, Barnabas, and "the rest of the Jews" were unduly influenced by unnamed followers of James, with the result that they ceased to eat with the Gentiles, and separated from them (2:11–13). Quartodecimanism was a dispute regarding when to end the fast prior to the celebration of baptism and Eucharist within the Christian institution of the paschal mysteries. The archaic tradition from which it derived was based upon the custom among Christian Jews of keeping Passover and recollecting Jesus' last eucharistic meal, a custom which by the definition of Exodus 12:43–49 would exclude the uncircumcised. Circumcision is, of course, just the line of demarcation which Paul in Galatians wishes to eradicate (cf. 2:3–5, 7–9, 12; 5:2, 3, 6, 11, 12; 6:13, 15).

An extension of the Torah to the "Last Supper," as to a paschal meal, would carry with it the consequence that "no uncircumcised person shall eat of it" (Exod. 12:48). Insofar as eucharistic meals were modeled on Jesus' final meal, exclusive fellowship would prevail then, as well, for two reasons. First, ordinary considerations of purity would make separation from non-Jews natural for Jews (as in Gal. 2:11–13). Second, even those who might permit

exceptional social intercourse with non-Jews could not circumvent the strictures of the Seder. The exclusionary policy of James, as reflected in Galatians 2 and Acts 15, finds its narrative rationale in Matthew 26:17–20; Mark
14:12–17; Luke 22:7–14: only the circumcised celebrated the last Seder, and
even then only at Passover, as part of the ritual of the Temple (the only place
where paschal lambs could be slain).

This policy of associating Eucharist and Passover would accord with a
deliberate attempt to avoid confrontation with the authorities of the Temple,
as well as with an insistence upon the Judaic identity of the new movement and
upon Jerusalem as its center. The narrowing of eucharistic celebration to the
practice of Passover would be consistent, then, with James's policy in regard
to purity, Gentiles, and the Torah. Moreover, his standing within the church,
along with the supportive authority of "prophets" such as Judas and Silas (Acts
15:30–35), would explain why the Synoptics are so emphatically stamped with
a paschal interpretation of Jesus' meal.

The reach of the Jacobean circle, from the group in Jerusalem to envoys
such as Judas Barsabbas and Silas in Antioch, helps to explain the development
of tradition associated with James. Matthew 26:17–20; Mark 14:12–17; and
Luke 22:7–14 represent a frustrating mixture of plausible and implausible
material. Incidental references to the preparation of a Passover in Jerusalem
seem to reflect local knowledge. The disciples know that Jesus will celebrate
Passover, they have only to ask where, and Jesus instructs them how to go
about making the contact necessary to complete preparations. It is only the
strictly chronological insistence that all those preparations were accomplished
on the fourteenth day of Nisan, and that the Last Supper itself was a Seder,
which strains credibility. The Jacobean tradition began by associating Jesus'
final meal with the Passover for which he wanted to prepare (but which he did
not observe). In the midst of conflict concerning the meaning of and appropriate participation in Eucharist, involving prophetic teachers such as Judas
Barsabbas and Silas, the cycle of tradition hardened into a chronological identification of that supper with the Seder.

The Jacobean source, as derived through Judas Barsabbas and Silas,
needed to take account of paschal practice in the Diaspora. Even prior to
70 C.E., all the Jews of Antioch were scarcely in a position to acquire lambs
which had been slaughtered in the Temple. The only other options were
(1) to revert to the domestic conception of the paschal meal (as in Exod.
12) against the provisions of Deuteronomy 16:5–7, or (2) to suppress the
consumption of the lamb itself, as in later, rabbinic practice. The Jacobean
source, absent an explicit mention of the lamb, could proceed on the tacit
understanding that, within its community, the paschal lamb was either
eaten (in the vicinity of Jerusalem, and elsewhere by a special cultic and
commercial arrangement) or it was not (further afield). The device would
particularly come into its own after the destruction of the Temple in 70
C.E. and its demolition in 135 C.E., from which points, from the perspec-

tive of sacrifice, Jerusalem itself entered the Diaspora. The burden of the pericope is that Jesus joined with the "twelve" specifically, the signature group of the Jacobean source (cf. Mark 4:10–12), for a commemoration of Passover, and that he followed the appropriate customs. The meal was therefore marked definitively—both before and after 70 C.E.—as a Last Supper and a paschal meal.

CONCLUSION: JAMES, NAZIRITE AND BISHOP

The stance of James as concerns purity, the Temple, and Eucharist, as well as his interpretation of Scripture, comports well with Hegesippus's description of his particular practices. The evidence in aggregate suggests that James understood his brother as providing an access to God through the Temple, such that Israel could and should offer God the Nazirites with their vows so as to achieve the sanctity and inherit the blessing promised by Moses in Numbers 6.

It has been argued by other scholars that Jesus himself adhered to such a position, but that seems to me inconsistent with his usual practice of fellowship at meals. The reference in the *Gospel of the Hebrews* to the risen Lord giving the linen (*sindona*) to the servant of the high priest before his appearance to James, evokes a powerful theme in the Jacobean view of the resurrection: raised from the dead, Jesus—as the son of man—offers an access to the sanctuary which no one else can. Just as Jesus healed the servant of the high priest when he was wounded during his arrest (see Luke 22:50–51), so he presents him with the cultic linen after his resurrection. Both the removal of the physical defect and the provision of the garment amount to an enabling of the figure to conduct acceptable sacrifice. Such an emphasis on the acceptability of worship in the Temple was obviously crucial within the circle of James. As a consequence, Hegesippus relates, James wore only linen, ordinarily the high priest's unique garment on the Day of Atonement (Lev. 16:4), but also a more generally priestly (see Lev. 6:3, for example) and angelic (see Dan. 10:5, for example) garment. Linen was an expression of the linkage between Jesus as the son of man in heaven and the Sanctuary as God's throne on earth (cf. Mark 14:51 in relation to Mark 16:5).

Indeed, my suggestion that James was a Nazirite, and saw his brother's movement as focused on producing more Nazirites, enables us to address an old and as yet unsolved problem of research. Jesus, bearing a common name, is sometimes referred to as "of Nazareth" in the Gospels, and that reflects how he was specified in his own time. There is no doubt but that a geographical reference is involved (see John 1:45–46). But more is going on here. Actually, Jesus is rarely called "of Nazareth" or "from Nazareth," although he was probably known to come from there. He is usually called "Nazoraean" or "Nazarene." Why the adjective, and why the uncertainty in

spelling? The Septuagint shows us that there were many different transliterations of "Nazirite": that reflects uncertainty as to how to convey the term
in Greek. (That uncertainty is not in the least surprising, since even the
Mishnah refers to differing pronunciations [see *Nazir* 1:1].) Some of the
variants are in fact very close to what we find used to describe Jesus in the
Gospels.

In the Gospel according to Mark, the first usage is in the mouth of a demon,
who says to Jesus (Mark 1:24):

> We have nothing for you, Nazarene Jesus!
> Have you come to destroy us?
> I know who you are—the holy one of God!

In this usage, "Nazarene" in the first line clearly parallels "the holy one of
God" in the last line. The demon knows Jesus' true identity, but those in the
synagogue where the exorcism occurs do not. And they do not hear the
demons, because Jesus silences them (so Mark 1:25). This is part of the well-
known theme of the "Messianic secret" in Mark.

For James and those who were associated with him, Jesus' true identity was
his status as a Nazirite. The demons saw what others did not, and after the resurrection the knowledge of the holy one of God could be openly acknowledged and practiced by means of the Nazirite vow. That practice could include
men, women, and slaves, in accordance with the Mishnah (*Nazir* 9:1). In the
Christian movement, the custom was apparently widespread. In Acts 18:18, it
is said that even Paul "had his head shorn in Cenchreae, because he had a vow."
Such vows in regard to hair alone were held in Mishnah to equate to a Nazirite
vow (*Nazir* 1:1), so that, whatever Paul thought of his vow from his own perspective, many would have seen him as falling in with the program of James,
the brother of Jesus. Under the influence of James, they might have said, even
Paul was concerned with getting it right.

Just as the observation of how Amos is interpreted in Acts 15 helps us to
characterize the theology of James and his circle, so Amos proves to be a key
to James's Nazirite practice. Within the same section of Amos which blames
Judah and Israel for ignoring the Torah, a particular example is given (Amos
2:11–12):

> I raised up some of your sons as prophets, and some of your young
> men as Nazirites. . . . But you caused the Nazirites to drink wine, and
> you commanded the prophets, saying, "Do not prophesy."

James took the "hut of David" to be symbolic of the Torah (see Acts 15:16;
Amos 9:11), and his practice of the Nazirite vow is a metonym for the Torah.
In both cases, the book of Amos actuates his understanding.

The content of his understanding cannot be compared in detail to the theology of the Essenes, although a comparison of the manner of interpretation involved is instructive. As in the case of the *Damascus Document*, James in Acts claims that his community guards the understanding which restores the Torah, and he does so with recourse to Amos. Reference in general terms has frequently been made to the technique of *pesher* from Qumran as an antecedent of biblical interpretation within the New Testament. But the precise similarity between James and the *Damascus Document*, that the community in its present teaching is held directly to actuate the biblical image, makes such a reference far more helpful and exact here.

Comparing James to an Essene document does not make him an Essene. As far as I am aware, nothing in the scrolls found near the Dead Sea imagines that the inclusion of uncircumcised non-Jews as being a people God takes for himself amounts to the restoration of the house of David. The social constitution James was engaged with seems quite unlike anything the Covenanters of Qumran were willing to countenance.

The similarity with Essene interpretation remains, however, that James in his cultic emphasis developed an immediately halakic understanding of the Scripture, in which the prophetic books, properly interpreted in the life of the community, realized the sense of the Torah. That was a distinctive perspective, and not only in contrast to Paul's. If we turn back to the example of Mark 7, the difference between the halakic syllogism of Mark 7:6–13 and the demand for inner purity in Mark 7:17–23 is manifest. Still more striking is the variance from the claim that Jesus here transcends the entire question of purity in the normal understanding (Mark 7:1–5, 19). James's Nazirite focus brought with it a natural recourse to the prophetic corpus as establishing a restorative halakah.

James's status as Jesus' brother and therefore as head of the Christian congregation in Jerusalem, his dedication to worship in the Temple in Jerusalem, and his exercise of authority on the basis of a precise citation of the Scriptures of Israel are commonly acknowledged. To that we now have to add his status as a Nazirite and a further element: Eusebius on several occasions refers to James as having been the first bishop of Jerusalem, and once cites a source of the second century to do so (see Eusebius, *H.E.* 2.1, 23; 7.19; in the first passage referring to Clement's *Hypotyposes*). James died in the year 62 C.E., so that his example had been there to influence the emerging model of episcopal hierarchy within the church attested within the Pastoral Epistles for some three decades before the Pastoral Epistles themselves were written. James was clearly a local leader, who made decisions on the basis of Scripture, and the exercise of his authority—owing to his familial relationship—brought with it a personal link to Jesus himself which was reinforced by his own martyrdom. The personal model of James as bishop was evidently sufficient to elevate that office above other possible contenders for what was to be the predominant authority within the church by the end of the first century.

There is, no doubt, a degree of anachronism in Eusebius's portrait of James's episcopal authority. He conceived of it as being a "throne" (see *H.E.* 2.1, 23; 7:19) in the manner of the image of dominant power which only the fourth century saw fully achieved, and he imagines a formal election as being involved. In fact, if one sees the episcopate as an entirely Hellenistic invention within the life of the church, it is easy enough to dismiss the entire reference to James as bishop. But that would be a hasty judgment. Eusebius's reference is persistent, and grounded in an identification of James's office from the second century. Moreover, if Eusebius helps us correctly to identify that office (for all his own anachronism), then we can explain the key shift in the hierarchy of the church during the first century, from apostolate to episcopate.

Still, the objection remains that the Greek word *episcopos* (a secular, managerial title) is an odd designation for James—or for any Aramaic speaker—to bear. In just this regard, a suggestion made many years ago by Joachim Jeremias turns out to be helpful. Jeremias fastened his attention on the office of the *mebaqqer* at Qumran (see Jeremias, 260–62). That term in fact means "overseer," just as *episcopos* does, and the *mebaqqer* was charged to do many of the same things that an *episcopos* was to do: he was to teach the Torah (even to priests) as well as the particular traditions of the community, to administer discipline, and to see to the distribution of wealth (see *Damascus Document* 13:1–19; 14:3–22). As Jeremias points out, comparisons are made between the *mebaqqer* and a father and a shepherd (*Damascus Document* 13:9); he does not mention, but the point is worth making, that Christ himself is said to be an *episkopos*, to care as a shepherd does in bringing us to God (so 1 Peter [2:25], a letter, like the Pastorals, written around 90 C.E.). Divine care and the institution of the overseer appear to have been linked in both Essene theology and primitive Christianity.

The connection as Jeremias attempted to make it was vitiated by his surmise that the community at Qumran somehow represented the Pharisaic ethos. In fact, the Essenes pursued their own system of purity, ethics, and initiation, followed their own calendar, and withdrew into their own communities, either within cities or in isolated sites such as Qumran. There they awaited a coming apocalyptic war, when they, as "the sons of light," would triumph over "the sons of darkness": not only the Gentiles, but anyone not of their vision (see the *War Scroll* and the *Community Rule*). The culmination of those efforts was to be complete control of Jerusalem and the Temple, where worship would be offered according to their revelation, the correct understanding of the law of Moses (cf. *Damascus Document* 5:17–6:11).

Now James is quite unlike the Essenes in his acceptance (however qualified) of uncircumcised followers of his brother, as well as in his fellowship in Jerusalem with a group centered on the Temple, and not associated with Qumran. Yet his devotion to the Temple involved tension with the administration there (tension severe enough ultimately to bring about his death), and he appears to have had recourse to an interpretation of Scripture which may be compared to the Essenes'. For all that his practice and encouragement of the Nazirite vow in the Temple of his time also distinguished him from the Covenanters of Qumran, his prominence among Jesus' disciples in Jerusalem earned him the respect which at Qumran would have been accorded a *mebaqqer*.

BIBLIOGRAPHY

Bernheim, Pierre-Antoine Bernheim. 1997. *James, the Brother of Jesus.* Translated by J. Bowden. London: SCM.

Bokser, Baruch M., 1984. *The Origins of the Seder: The Passover Rite and Early Rabbinic Judaism.* Berkeley: University of California Press.

Chilton, Bruce. 1994. *A Feast of Meanings. Eucharistic Theologies from Jesus through Johannine Circles.* NTSup 72. Leiden: Brill.

Chilton, Bruce, and Craig A. Evans. 1994. "Jesus and Israel's Scriptures." Pages 281–335 in *Studying the Historical Jesus: Evaluations of the State of Current Research.* New Testament Tools and Studies 19. Leiden: Brill.

Davids, Peter H. 1989. *James.* NIBC. Peabody, Mass.: Hendrickson.

Dibelius, Martin. 1984. *Der Brief des Jakobus.* Göttingen: Vandenhoeck & Ruprecht.

Eisenman, Robert. 1996. *James the Brother of Jesus: The Key to Unlocking the Secrets of Early Christianity and the Dead Sea Scrolls.* New York: Viking.

Falk, Zeev W. 1996. "Notes and Observations on Talmudic Vows," *Harvard Theological Review* 59:309–12.

Hartman, Lars. 1997. *"Into the Name of the Lord Jesus": Baptism in the Early Church.* Studies of the New Testament and Its World. Edinburgh: T. & T. Clark.

Jeremias, Joachim. *Jerusalem in the Time of Jesus: An Investigation into Economic and Social Conditions during the New Testament Period.* Translated by F. H. and C. H. Cave. London: SCM, 1969.

Léon-Dufour, Xavier. *Le partage du pain eucharistique selon le Nouveau Testament.* Paris: Editions du Seuil.

Painter, John. 1997. *Just James: The Brother of Jesus in History and Tradition.* Studies on Personalities of the New Testament. Columbia: University of South Carolina Press.

Pratscher, Wilhelm. 1987. *Der Herrenbruder Jakobus und die Jakobustradition.* FRLANT 139. Göttingen: Vandenhoeck & Ruprecht.

7

Comparing Judaisms: Qumranic, Rabbinic, and Jacobean Judaisms Compared

Craig A. Evans

COMPARING JUDAISMS

Before one can compare various expressions of Judaism, or "Judaisms," definition is required. What is "Judaic," or what qualifies as a "Judaism"? In the present volume Jacob Neusner enumerates four essential elements or traits:

1. the privileging of ancient Israelite Scripture;
2. the identification of that community with the "Israel" of which Scripture speaks;
3. the insistence upon the priority of that system over all competing accounts of an "Israel" in context;
4. the certainty that all who adhere to that community, and live by that system of practice and proposition, constitute "Israelites."

The traits identified by Neusner are apropos. The expressions of Judaism encountered in the Qumran scrolls, in rabbinic literature, and in James exhibit these elements and so provide us with sufficient common ground that meaningful comparison may be made. By way of introduction, let us review the presence of these traits in the expressions of Jewish faith found in the communities of Qumran, the Rabbis, and James.

1. Privileging of ancient Israelite Scripture

The Judaisms of Qumran, James, and the Rabbis do indeed privilege ancient Israelite Scripture. There are hundreds of quotations and thousands of allusions to Scripture in the non-Bible scrolls from Qumran. Indeed, nearly one fourth of the scrolls are Bible. The most important doctrines are anchored in Scripture. Scripture clarifies history, explains the present, and foretells the future. Without it, the Community of the Renewed Covenant could not have existed. Although different in its expressions and emphases, rabbinic literature is every bit as dependent upon ancient Israelite Scripture for guidance and instruction. Every law ultimately derives from Scripture. Without it, Rabbinic Judaism could not explain itself and could not carry on as a living faith.

Although the evidence is less overwhelming in the case of Jacobean Judaism—perhaps simply because we lack sufficient documentation—there are reasons to believe that Scripture was just as central to its self-understanding, beliefs, and practices. To be sure, there are few explicit quotations of Scripture in the letter attributed to James. Important passages from Moses are cited, as well as a few passages from the wisdom texts. But there can be no doubt that the ancient Scripture of Israel undergirds the faith and practice of the Jacobean community. Indeed, the author of the Letter of James assumes that keeping the "whole law" is right and that failure to keep one part of it is be guilty of breaking all of it (Jas. 2:10–11).

2. Identification with the "Israel" of Scripture

Qumran clearly understood itself as the righteous of Israel, those who obeyed the law and honored the covenant. Indeed, they considered themselves the men of the new, or renewed, Covenant. Similarly, rabbinic Judaism saw itself in continuity with historic, biblical Israel, expressing this conviction in part by portraying Israel's greatest figures of the past as rabbis and teachers of the Law. Jacobean Christianity, at least as we may infer it from the letter of James, speaks of itself as constituting the "twelve tribes which are in the Diaspora" (Jas. 1:1). The epithet "twelve tribes" is unmistakably Jewish and scriptural (cf. Gen. 49:28; Exod. 24:4; 28:21; 39:14; Ezek. 47:13; Sir. 44:23). The Dispersion or Diaspora is of course a Jewish designation of Israel scattered among the nations (cf. Tob. 3:4; Jdt. 5:19; 2 Macc. 1:27; *Pss. Sol.* 8:28; 9:2), a designation owing to biblical language, especially as expressed in the Greek Bible (cf. Deut. 28:25; 30:4; Isa. 49:6; Ps. 146[147]:2; Neh. 1:9; Dan. 12:2). In James we find several references to "brothers" or "my brothers" (1:2; 2:1, 14; 3:1, 10, 12; 4:11; 5:7, 9, 10, 12, 19), which reflect Jewish idiom (*m. Yad.* 4:3; cf. Acts 9:17; 21:20; 22:13; Rom. 16:23; 1 Cor. 1:1; 2 Cor. 1:1; Phlm. 7, 20). Jacobean identification with Israel's heritage is also seen in the frequent appeal to biblical characters (e.g., Abraham [2:21, 23]; Rahab [2:25]; Job [5:11]; Elijah [5:17]; or simply "the prophets who spoke in the name of the Lord" and were an example of "suffering and patience" [5:10]).

3. Priority of the community's system
over all competing accounts of an "Israel"

This priority is seen in the Judaisms of Qumran, the Rabbis, and the Jacobean Christian community. It often expresses itself as criticism of other groups, groups that in various ways are thought of as wayward, even apostate. The sharpest and most categorical expressions are found in the literature of Qumran. Those who do not repent and accept the halakic teachings of the Community of the Renewed Covenant will be condemned in the day of judgment. Less severe are the teachings of the Rabbis (cf. *m. Sanh.* 10:1: "All Israelites have a share in the world to come"; though this teaching goes on to say that those who deny the resurrection and the divine inspiration of the Torah "have no share in the world to come"). The views of Jacobean Christianity are not as explicit, but in the Letter of James an ethical criterion is plainly expressed: Faith not backed up by works of love is worthless (Jas. 2:14–17); visiting orphans and widows in their distress is "religion that is pure and undefiled before God" (1:17). The Jacobean author of this letter (perhaps James himself) apparently distinguishes his community from other Jewish (and Jewish Christian?) communities which do not in his view practice "true religion."

4. All who adhere to that community
and live by its practice
and proposition constitute "Israelites"

Neusner's fourth trait rightly recognizes the positive side to the third trait and the logical consequence of the first two traits. Faithful adherence to the laws and statutes of the Renewed Covenant, as taught by the Teacher of Righteousness and his successors, was the presupposition of the Qumran community. The men of Qumran were the true Israelites (in contrast to the "builders of the shoddy wall" or the "wicked priests" or the "men of mockery," and so forth). For the Rabbis, those who constitute true Israel vary somewhat. Those who study Torah and obey it are certainly true Israelites; they will enter the life to come. But sometimes the view seems to be that all circumcised Israelites will enter life (or all who observe the Sabbath). Jacobean Christianity, at least as it is expressed in the Letter of James, focuses on ethics as the prime indicator of the purity of one's religion. Care for orphans and widows, fairness to laborers, and forbearance toward one another are marks of "true religion." When the wanderer is brought back to the truth of these things, his soul will be saved from death (Jas. 5:19–20).

In view of the significant overlaps briefly summarized above, comparison of Qumranic, Rabbinic, and Jacobean Judaisms appears to be fully justified. It is also difficult, and given the limits imposed on the present essay, it will have to be quite selective.

QUMRANIC, RABBINIC,
AND JACOBEAN JUDAISMS COMPARED

Comparing the Judaisms of Qumran, the Rabbis, and the Jacobean community proves instructive. In these three self-conscious movements we have an important cross section of Torah-observant Jewry from late antiquity. Of the three the Judaism of Qumran is oldest, though before it passed from the scene Jacobean Judaism had taken hold and would make important contributions to what would eventually emerge as Christianity. But even as Jacobean Judaism was being eclipsed by Christianity, rabbinic Judaism had begun to grow from the roots of the tradition of the sages and to react to the upheaval that followed Israel's war with Rome. Thus these three expressions of Judaism overlap in time and place and, more importantly, share the essential elements that made up Torah-observant Judaisms in this period of time.

The Judaisms of Qumran, the Rabbis, and the Jacobean community overlap significantly in all four of these elements, thus making meaningful comparison possible, even necessary. But there are important points of difference, at least as can be inferred from sources that probably only give us part of the whole picture. This is especially true in the case of Qumran and the Jacobean community. Both expressions of Judaism were marginalized and we cannot be sure that we are now in possession of the whole of their respective systems of thought. We have no "Mishnah," as it were, for Qumran or the community of James. In the case of the former, we come close with the Damascus Covenant and the Rule of the Community, but in the case of the community of James, we only have the Letter of James, whose authorship and provenance are uncertain, a limited narrative and report in the book of Acts, which is both selective and very probably tendentious, and a few late, at times legendary traditions in later Christian writers, such as Eusebius. We may have a report of the death of James in Josephus, but not all agree that this passage in its original form actually concerned the brother of Jesus. Thus, whereas we have a substantial body of literature, especially in the Mishnah and the Tosefta, from which we may infer the Judaism of the Rabbis, and a myriad of scrolls, many which are fragmentary, from which we may infer the Judaism of Qumran, we have a comparatively meager data base from which we may infer the Judaism of Jacobean Judaism/Christianity. Nevertheless, we have adequate materials whereby meaningful comparison of several important elements may be made, even if quite tentatively.

Four of these common elements will be treated in this essay: (1) Ethics, Piety, and Wisdom; (2) Scripture; (3) Election and Covenant; and (4) Kingdom of God. The first element concerns the practice of one's faith and constitutes what may be regarded as the "public" component of one's religion. The second element concerns the authoritive and sacred point of reference forming the basis upon which theology and lifestyle may be developed. The third element concerns membership and community, especially in relation to

God. The fourth element concerns teleology, looking for meaning and antic-ipating the fulfillment of God's purposes for humanity.

1. Ethics, piety, and wisdom

In matters of ethics and piety the Qumranic and Jacobean Judaisms overlap at many points. James speaks of a "religion that is pure and undefiled before God" (1:27). This concern coheres with similar language found in some of the sectarian scrolls from Qumran, where there is much concern with separating the pure from the impure (esp. 1QS 5:1–3; 7:24–25; 8:21–24; 9:9). Portions of these passages should be cited: "This is the rule for the men of the Yahad who volunteer to repent from all evil and to hold fast to all that He, by His good will, has commanded. They are to separate from the congregation of perverse men" (1QS 5:1–2). However, with regard to apostates:

> Any covenant member of the Yahad (Community) of Holiness (they who walk blamelessly as He commanded) who transgresses even one commandment from the Law of Moses intentionally or deviously is to be expelled from the Council of the Yahad, never to return. Further, none of the holy men is to do business with that man or advise him on any matter whatsoever. But if the sinner transgressed unintentionally, then he is to be separated from the pure food, and from the Council. . . . (1QS 8:21–24)

The antithesis between pure and impure also finds expression in spiritual dualism. James enjoins the faithful to "resist the devil and he will flee from you. Draw near to God and he will draw near to you. Cleanse your hands, you sinners, and purify your hearts, you men of double mind" (4:7–8). In the Rule of the Renewed Community we find a similar perspective:

> For only through the spirit pervading God's true society can there be atonement for a man's ways, all of his iniquities; thus only can he gaze upon the light of life and so be joined to His truth by His holy spirit, purified from all iniquity. Through an upright and humble attitude his sin may be covered, and by humbling himself before all God's laws his flesh can be made clean. Only thus can he really receive the purifying waters and be purged by the cleansing flow. (1QS 3:6–9)

The well-known passage of the warring spirits should also be considered (cf. 1QS 3:13–4:26). Cognate is the distinction between the spirits of pride and humility (cf. Jas. 4:6–10; 1QS 4:9–11; 11:1).

Social responsibility, especially the care for the orphan, widow, and needy, is emphasized in the Qumran and Jacobean communities (Jas. 1:27; 2:14–16; CD 6:16, 21; 14:14). All of the commandments of Moses are to be observed (Jas. 2:10–11; 1QS 8:22); community discipline is to be enforced (Jas. 5:19–29;

1QS 5:24–25; 6:1). In both traditions Abraham is regarded as a "friend of God" because he obeyed God (Jas. 2:23; CD 3:2). Finally, certain social graces are enjoined: speaking in anger is forbidden (Jas. 1:19; 1QS 7:2); so also foolish speech (Jas. 1:26; 1QS 7:9).

There are many parallels between Jacobean Judaism and Rabbinic Judaism. As already mentioned, the letter of James speaks of "religion pure and undefiled" (Jas. 1:27) and of cleansed hands and purified hearts (Jas. 4:8). Rabbinic Judaism carefully works through all aspects of purity. The purity of which James speaks is primarily ethical, but the ceremonial purity to which the Rabbis devote so much attention is ultimately ethical in nature also. For to live in purity is to embrace a "religion pure and undefiled."

The Rabbis urged disciples to take upon themselves the "yoke of the kingdom" ('*Abot* 3:5). Indeed, obeying Torah gives one "kingship and dominion" ('*Abot* 6:1). This language is consistent with the declaration in James that Torah is a "royal Law" (Jas. 2:8). According to James, the Torah is the "law of liberty" (Jas. 1:25; 2:12). So also in '*Abot*: "There is no freeman except him that occupies himself in the study of the Law" ('*Abot* 6:2). The Rabbis and the community of James view God and humanity in the same way: Human beings have been created in the image of God ('*Abot* 3:15; Jas. 3:9); God is humanity's Creator and Judge ('*Abot* 2:21; 4:22; Jas. 4:12); yet God is a merciful Judge ('*Abot* 3:16; Jas. 2:13). One who obeys the Torah is a "friend of God" ('*Abot* 6:1; Jas. 2:23; 4:4).

At many points Jacobean and Rabbinic Judaisms share common language and piety. In both Abraham is called "our father" ('*Abot* 5:2, 19; Jas. 2:21). Specific acts of piety and religious devotion are common to each: respect for the divine Name ('*Abot* 4:4; 5:9; Jas. 2:7); praying with integrity ('*Abot* 2:13; Jas. 4:3); practice consistent with profession of faith ('*Abot* 1:2, 15; 2:12; 3:10, 18; 4:5; 5:14; 6:5; Jas. 2:14–26); fair judgment ('*Abot* 1:6; 2:5; 4:5; Jas. 2:4); avoiding perjury ('*Abot* 1:9; 4:7–8; Jas. 5:12); giving alms ('*Abot* 5:13; Jas. 2:16); avoiding jealousy and greed ('*Abot* 4:21; Jas. 3:16); and avoiding envy ('*Abot* 2:9, 11; 5:19; Jas. 4:1–5).

There are several points of overlap between Qumranic, Rabbinic, and Jacobean Judaisms that bear the distinct stamp of wisdom tradition: wisdom and understanding are understood to be of divine origin (CD 2:3; *Gen. Rab.* 17.5 [on Gen. 2:21]: "the wisdom from above is Torah"; cf. '*Abot* 3:18; Jas. 3:13–17: "wisdom from above is first pure"); wisdom and folly are contrasted (1QS 4:18, 24; '*Abot* 3:18; 5:7; Jas. 3:13–16); slowness to anger is enjoined (Jas. 1:19; '*Abot* 4:1); the pious are to be swift to hear, slow to speak (Jas. 1:9; '*Abot* 5:7, 12); they are to be circumspect in speech (Jas. 1:19, 26; 3:1–12; '*Abot* 1:5, 9, 11, 17; 3:14); and should know that forgiveness of sins is available to the humble (Jas. 4:6–10; 5:16; 1QS 3:8–9).

A popular theme in Jewish wisdom tradition is the danger of the human tongue. Many warnings are found in Proverbs (e.g., 6:2, 17; 10:18–19, 31–32; 12:13, 18–19; 13:3; 14:3; 18:6–8, 13, 20–21). According to James:

So also the tongue is a small member, yet it boasts of great exploits. How great a forest is set ablaze by a small fire! And the tongue is a fire. The tongue is placed among our members as a world of iniquity; it stains the whole body, sets on fire the cycle of nature, and is itself set on fire by hell. For every kind of beast and bird, of reptile and sea creature, can be tamed and has been tamed by humankind, but no one can tame the tongue—a restless evil, full of deadly poison. (Jas. 3:5–8)

According to two sages in late antiquity:

Beware then of useless grumbling, and keep your tongue from slander; because no secret word is without result, and a lying mouth destroys the soul. (Wis. 1:11)

Honor and dishonor come from speaking, and the tongue of mortals may be their downfall. (Sir. 5:13)

A person may make a slip without intending it. Who has not sinned with his tongue? (Sir. 19:16)

Happy is the one who does not sin with the tongue, and the one who has not served an inferior. (Sir. 25:8b)

The blow of a whip raises a welt, but a blow of the tongue crushes the bones. Many have fallen by the edge of the sword, but not as many as have fallen because of the tongue. (Sir. 28:17–18)

(He who masters the tongue) will not be burned in its flame. (Sir. 28:22)

A few scrolls from Qumran offer similar advice:

In my mouth shall be heard neither foolishness nor sinful deceit; neither fraud nor lies shall be discovered between my lips. Rather, the fruits of holiness will be upon my tongue—abominations will not be found thereon. For thanksgiving shall I open my mouth, the righteousness of God shall my tongue recount always. Human rebellion, made full by sin, as vain I shall purge from my lips; Impure and crafty design I shall expunge from my mind. Counseled by wisdom, I shall recount knowledge. (1QS 10:21–24)

[Blessed is he who . . .] with a clean heart and does not slander with his tongue. Blessed are those who hold fast to its statutes and do not hold fast . . . (4Q525 2 ii 1)

Answer correctly in the midst of princes and do not [. . .] with your lips. Be very careful of causing offense with your tongue[. . .] lest you be entrapped by your lips [and ens]nared together with [your . . .] (4Q525 14 ii 25–27)

[. . .] Your [. . .] and You have made my mouth like a burning sword, my tongue You have unbound to speak holy words, and You put [on my lips] a chain lest they babble of the deeds of the man whose utterances are corrupt. My feet You have strengthened [. . .] by Your power You have sustained my right hand, and You have sent me[. . .] against evil[. . .] [. . . impure thoughts] You have kept from me, and put a pure heart in their place. You have kept the evil impulse from me[. . .] (4Q436 1 i 7–10)

Rabbi Eleazar is remembered to have said in the name of Rabbi Yose ben Zimra:

Greater is [learning in] the Law than priesthood or kingship; for kingship is acquired by thirty excellences and the priesthood by twenty-four; but [learning in] the Law by forty-eight. And these are they: by study, by the hearing of the ear, by the ordering of the lips, by the understanding of the heart . . . (*'Abot* 6:6)

The tongue is set between two cheeks, while a water-channel passes beneath it [i.e. saliva glands] . . . yet see how many conflagrations it has caused! (*Lev. Rab.* 16:4 [on Lev. 14:2])

R. Ḥama b. Hanina said: What is the remedy for slanderers? If he be a scholar, let him engage in the Torah, as it is said: The healing for a tongue is the tree of life, and "tongue" here means the evil tongue, as it is said: "Their tongue is a sharpened arrow," and "tree [of life]" means only the Torah, as it is said: She is a tree of life, to them that lay hold upon her. But if he be an ignorant person, let him become humble, as it is said: But perverseness therein is a wound to the spirit. R. Aha b. R. Hanina said: If he has slandered already, there is no remedy for him, for King David, in his holy spirit, has cut him off already, as it is said: May the Lord cut off all flattering lips, the tongue that speaketh great [proud] things! Nevertheless, what shall be his remedy so that he may not come to [utter] evil speech? If he be a scholar, let him engage in the Torah, and if he be an ignorant person, let him humble himself, as it is said: "But perverseness therein is a wound to the spirit." (*b. 'Arak.* 15b)

Mar the son of Rabina on concluding his prayer added the following: My God, keep my tongue from evil and my lips from speaking guile. May my soul be silent to them that curse me and may my soul be as the dust to all. (*b. Ber.* 17a)

2. Scripture

As has already been mentioned, the Judaisms of Qumran, the Rabbis, and the community of James recognized the authority of the Scripture of Israel and believed that obedience to it was requisite for salvation. It was not enough to know the Law; it was necessary to "do" it. It was not enough to believe certain things; it was necessary to live them.

Josephus calls the Essenes *Essēnoi* (*Ant.* 18.1.5 §18–22). Philo calls the Essenes *Essaioi* and thinks this name is derived from *hosiotēs*, which means "holiness" (*Omn. prob. lib. sit* 75). However, elsewhere Philo relates the Essenes to the mysterious Therapeutae of Egypt, whose Greek name *therapeutai* means "healers" or "ministers" (*Contemplative Life* 2). The first etymology has led some to think the Aramaic word *ḥasêaʿ* ("pious ones") underlies the term, while the second etymology has led some to think the Aramaic word *ʾasêaʾ* ("healers") underlies the term. But both of these suggestions remain doubtful, primarily because the proposed Aramaic words are unattested in the literature of the time. The most likely etymology derives from the verb *ʿāśāh* ("to do").

The Qumran community distinguished themselves from other Jews by claiming to be "those who do the Torah" (*ʿôśê hatôrāh*, 1QpHab 8:1) and "men of the truth who do the Torah" (*ʿôśê hatôrāh*, 1QpHab 7:10–11). In 1QpHab 12:4–5 the community describe themselves as the "poor ones" who are "the simple of Judah, doer(s) of the Torah" (*ʿôśê hatôrāh*). In 4Q185 3 i 3 we have a fragment with a reference to "doing the words of the covenant" (*ʿôśēh dibrê berit*). One should note also 4QpPsᵃ which speaks of the "doers of his will" (*ʿôśê raṣônô*, 1–10 ii 5) and, very importantly, of the "doers of Torah who are in the council of the community" (*ʿôśê hatôrāh*, 1–10 ii 15). It is probable, therefore, that the members of Qumran called themselves the "doers" of the covenant, or of the will of God, or of the word of God, and so forth. From these texts one may conclude that the Greek name "Essene" is a transliteration of the Hebrew participle "doing." It is the Hebrew "doers" (*ʿôśê*) that the Greek transliterations attested in Josephus, Philo, and other writers attempt to express.

To "do the Torah" is of course biblical parlance, especially as it is expressed in Deuteronomy. The Israelite is to "learn to fear the LORD his God, by keeping all the words of this law [*kāl-dibrê hatôrāh*] and these statutes, and doing [*laʿaśotām*] them" (Deut. 17:19). Several other parallel texts may be cited:

"Cursed be he who does not confirm the words of this law by doing them." And all the people shall say, "Amen." (Deut. 27:26)

If you are not careful to do all the words of this law which are written in this book, that you may fear this glorious and awful name, the LORD your God. (Deut. 28:58)

The secret things belong to the LORD our God; but the things that are revealed belong to us and to our children for ever, that we may do all the words of this law. (Deut. 29:29)

Assemble the people, men, women, and little ones, and the sojourner within your towns, that they may hear and learn to fear the LORD your God, and be careful to do all the words of this law. (Deut. 31:12)

> Lay to heart all the words which I enjoin upon you this day, that you
> may command them to your children, that they may be careful to do
> all the words of this law. (Deut. 32:46)

The people of the New Covenant at Qumran understood themselves as heed-
ing the commands of Deuteronomy. Even if the rest of Israel remains back-
slidden and apostate, they of Qumran will "do the words of the law."

Although not as emphatic as the Essenes, the Rabbis also speak of doing
Torah. "Great is the Torah, for it gives life to them that do it [*le'ôśehā*] both in
this world and in the world to come" (*'Abot* 6:7). Linking the doing of Torah
with life in the world to come proves to be another important point of agreement between Qumran, the Rabbis, and early Christianity. This point will be
taken up shortly.

In the Letter of James Jacobean believers are admonished to "be doers of
the word, and not hearers only, deceiving" themselves. "For if any one is
hearer of the word and not a doer, he is like a man who observes his natural
face in a mirror . . . and at once forgets what he was like" (Jas. 1:22–23). Not
only does James's exhortation to be "doers of the word" parallel exactly the
Essenes' claims to be "doers of the word" (*'ôśê hadābār* = *poiētai Logou*), the
contrast between doing and hearing invites comparison with an interesting
rabbinic tradition in which a similar contrast is developed:

> Rabbi Eleazar said: When Israel gave precedence to "we will do"
> [*ne'eśāh*] over "we will listen" [*nišemaʿ*], a heavenly voice went forth
> and exclaimed to them, Who revealed to my children this secret,
> which is employed by the ministering angels, as it is written, "Bless the
> Lord, you angels of his: You mighty in strength, who fulfill his word,
> who listen to the voice of his word" (Ps. 103:20)—first they do and
> then they listen?
>
> Rabbi Ḥama son of Rabbi Hanina said: What is meant by "As the
> apple tree among the trees of the wood, [so is my beloved among the
> sons]" (Song 2:3)? Why were the Israelites compared to an apple tree?
> To teach you: just as the fruit of the apple tree precedes its leaves, so
> did the Israelites give precedence to "we will do" over "we will listen."
> (*b. Šabb.* 88a)

Overlooking the faulty horticulture, Ḥama's analogy is nevertheless apt and
seems to offer a genuine parallel to the earlier Jacobean parenesis.

Jacobean Judaism insists on the priority of doing over hearing, which means
that one's faith must translate into "works" (*ma'eśe* = *erga*). Because Abraham
offered up his son Isaac, he demonstrated his faith through his works and so
"it was reckoned to him as righteousness" (Jas 2:21–24, citing Gen. 15:6). It is
in this sense that "the scripture was fulfilled" (Jas. 2:23). So goes the logic of
Ḥama's exegesis: They that "do," as well as "listen," are they that "fulfill his
word" (citing Ps. 103:20).

Yet further overlap between the Judaisms of Qumran, the Rabbis, and the community of James is seen their agreement that to "do the Law" is to inherit life. According to the Damascus Covenant:

> But when those of them who were left held firm to the command-ments of God he established his covenant with Israel forever, revealing to them hidden things, in which all Israel had erred: his holy sabbaths, his glorious festivals, his righteous laws, his reliable ways. The desires of his will, "which a person shall do and so have life in them," he opened up to them . . . those who hold firm to it shall receive everlasting life and all the glory of Adam will be theirs. (CD 3:12–16, 20)

The words "which a person shall do and so have life in them" are taken from Leviticus 18:5: "You shall therefore keep my statutes and my ordinances, which a person shall do and so have life in them: I am the LORD." In context, Leviticus 18:5 promises life to Israel in the land of Israel, that is, in this world, if the nation remains faithful to the covenant. But exegesis in late antiquity understood this passage to promise life in the world to come as well. According to the author of the Damascus Covenant, "those who hold firm to it [i.e., the Covenant] shall receive everlasting life" (CD 3:20).

Jesus, the brother of James, evidently understood Leviticus 18:5 in the same way:

> And behold, an expert in Torah stood up to put him to the test, say-ing, "Teacher, what shall I do to inherit eternal life?" He said to him, "What is written in the law? How do you read?" And he answered, "You shall love the Lord your God with all your heart, and with all your soul, and with all your strength, and with all your mind; and your neighbor as yourself." And he said to him, "You have answered right; do this, and you will live." (Luke 10:25–28)

Jesus finds the legal expert's answer fully satisfactory and so tells him, "Do this, and you will live" (Luke 10:28), alluding to Leviticus 18:5. But the man had asked Jesus' opinion concerning what he must to to inherit eternal life—not life in this world. Jesus' understanding, in all probability shared by the legal expert, is that Leviticus 18:5 pertained to life in the world to come, as well as to life in this world. We see this in rabbinic exegesis:

> "You shall observe my ordinances and my laws, which if a person prac-tices them [he will live]" (Lev. 18:5). This formulation of the matter serves to make keeping and doing into laws, and keeping and doing into rules. "Shall live": in the World to Come. And should you wish to claim that the reference is to this world, is not the fact that in the end one dies? Lo, how am I to explain "shall live"? It is with reference

to the World to Come. "I the Lord am your God": faithful to pay a reward. (*Sipra Lev.* §193 [*Aharé Mot* §8])

Whoever breaks down a fence set up by the sages will eventually suffer penalties, as it is said: "Whoever breaks through a fence, a serpent will bite him" (Eccl. 10:8). But [Ben Dama] had been bitten by a serpent! [The meaning is] a serpent will not bite him in the world to come. What could he have quoted [as proof]? "Which if a man do, he shall live by them" (Lev. 18:5). "He shall live by them," that is, not die by them. (*Eccl. Rab.* 1:8 §3)

"One male goat for a sin offering" (Num. 7:16) alludes to the proselytes who would embrace Judaism in the future and to those who were present on that occasion, indicating that they were all worthy [to study] the Torah, as may be inferred from the text, "My ordinances, which if a man do, he shall live by them" (Lev. 18:5). It does not say "priests" or "Levites" or "Israelites," but "a person." This teaches that even an idolater who becomes a proselyte and studies the Torah is like a high priest. (*Num. Rab.* 13:15–16 [on Num. 7:16]; cf. *Midr. Ps.* 1:18 [on Ps. 1:3])

We also see it in the Aramaic paraphrases of Leviticus 18:5:

You shall observe my ordinances and (my) laws, which if a person practices them, he will live through them in eternal life. (Onqelos)

You shall observe my ordinances and my laws, which if a person practices them, he will live through them in eternal life, and his portion shall be with the righteous. (Pseudo-Jonathan)

And we see it in the Aramaic paraphrases of Ezek. 20:11, 13, 21.

The Rabbis reason that because we die, and yet Leviticus 18:5 promises life, then the life promised must be life in the world to come. So powerful is this promise of life, or better, so powerful is the Torah, that if obeyed—by anyone, even an idolater—it confers life. Accordingly, he who studies and obeys Torah "is like a high priest."

Although the Letter of James makes no mention of Leviticus 18:5, and does not make an explicit link between Torah and life, an implicit link seems probable. We see this in 1:2–18, in which the author encourages his readers to endure trials and to remain faithful. Those who do "will receive the crown of life which God has promised to those who love him" (Jas. 1:12). It is presupposed here that the "perfect law, the law (or Torah) of liberty" has been obeyed (by the "doers of the word" in vv. 22–23) and that the result is life.

The paradigmatic function of Genesis 15:6 in all three expressions of Judaism considered in this essay is also instructive for comparison. In the earliest rabbinic traditions Genesis 15:6 ("And he [Abraham] believed the LORD; and he reckoned it to him as righteousness") underscores the importance of the faith of the great patriarch. Two pertinent and related traditions are found in the Mekilta:

> Shemayah says: (God says:) "The faith with which their father Abraham believed in me is deserving that I should divide the sea for them." For it is said: "And he believed the LORD" (Gen. 15:6). Abtalyon says: (God says:) "The faith with which they believed in me is deserving that I should divide the sea for them." For it is said: "And the people believed" (Exod. 4:31). (*Mek.* on Exod. 14:15 [*Beshallah* §4])

> So also you find that our father Abraham inherited both this world and the world to come only as a reward for the faith with which he believed, as it is said: "And he believed the LORD" (Gen. 15:6). And so also you find that Israel was redeemed from Egypt only as a reward for the faith with which they believed, as it is said: "And the people believed" (Exod 4:31). And thus it says: "The LORD preserves the faithful" (Ps. 31:24). He keeps in remembrance the faith of the fathers. (*Mek.* on Exod. 14:26–31 [*Beshallah* §7])

The emphasis on faith approximates Paul's argument in Romans and Galatians, although the apostle underscores the principle of Abraham's faith as example, not as merit. But Paul's opponent, or at least someone who holds to a very similar view and who argues for justification on the basis of works of the Torah, seems finally to have come to light in the much talked about 4QMMT, the manifesto that instructs readers in "some of the works of the Torah" (*miqṣat ma'ese ha-tôrah* = [*tina*] *erga nomou*).

> Now, we have written to you some of the works of the Torah, those which we determined would be beneficial for you and your people, because we have seen [that] you possess insight and knowledge of the Torah. Understand all these things and beseech him to set your counsel straight and so keep you away from evil thoughts and the counsel of Belial. Then you shall rejoice at the end time when you find the essence of our words to be true. And it will be "reckoned to" you "as righteousness," in that you have done ['*aśot*] what is right and good before him, to your own benefit and to that of Israel. (4Q398 14–17 ii 2–8)

The author's "reckoned to" you "as righteousness" probably alludes to Psalm 106:30–31:

> Then Phinehas stood up and interposed, and the plague was stayed. And that has been reckoned to him as righteousness from generation to generation for ever.

The psalm alludes to the deed of Phinehas in checking the apostasy to the Baal of Peor (cf. Num. 25:1–13). The author of 4QMMT appeals to the language of reckoning and righteousness, but in reference to Phinehas, not Abraham. What Phinehas did was "right and good" before God and it was to the benefit of Israel. Just as the hero of old was reckoned righteous, so too will be the Israelites of Qumran, if they follow in his example and do what is right and good in reforming, even purging a wayward and corrupt priesthood.

Paul also appeals to Scripture's language of being reckoned righteous, but on the basis of faith not works. Hence his appeal to Gen. 15:6, which speaks of Abraham who "believed" God. Nevertheless, the Letter of James is able to appeal to the same passage and find a teaching that approximates the view of the author of 4QMMT. True, Abraham "believed" God and "it was reckoned to him as righteousness." But this faith was seen as an act, or good work, in his willingness to offer up his son Isaac. Thus, Genesis 15 is interpreted in the light of Genesis 22, just as Paul himself interprets the significance of Genesis 17 (the circumcision of Abraham) in the light of his earlier faith in God recounted in Genesis 15 (cf. Romans 4).

3. Election and covenant

The word "covenant" (*berith*) occurs more than 200 times in the Dead Sea Scrolls. At least five times it is qualified as the "new covenant" (CD 6:19; 8:21; 19:33; 20:12; 1QpHab 2:3); and this number grows if the verb "renew" is taken into account (e.g., 1QSb 3:26; 5:5, 21; 1Q34bis 3 ii 6). Of course, many times the "covenant" to which reference is made is the "new" one of Qumran, even if the adjective is not used. The most important of the sectarian writings are the Damascus Document and the Community Rule, in which *berith* occurs some 90 times (including their respective fragments in caves 4, 5, and 6). Fifteen more occurrences are found in the supplements 1QSa and 1QSb. Moreover, *berith* is found some 26 times in 1QHodayot[a], 13 times in the War Scroll, and 9 or 10 times in the Pesharim. Also *berith* figures prominently, though less often, in Liturgical Prayers (1Q34), Apocryphal Lamentations B (4Q501), Words of the Luminaries[a] (4Q504), and the Temple Scroll[a] (11Q19). These numbers indicate how significant the theme of covenant was to the men of the Community, the Yahad. Indeed, one recently published conference volume is appropriately entitled the "Community of the Renewed Covenant." Not only are all of these texts sectarian compositions, they represent the major literary works of the sect, laying down rules for membership, conduct, worship, and interpretation.

Israel's ancient covenant, and here it is primarily the Sinai Covenant that is in view, and its renewal constitute the Qumran community's very *raison d'être*. Interest in the Covenant, in obeying it as perfectly as possible, provides the *rationale* for the formation of the community, the *guidance* for community development, and the *hermeneutic* for interpretation of the Scriptures.

The distinctive feature of covenant theology at Qumran was its eschatological and prophetic perspective. Although the "new" or "renewed" covenant at Qumran was in reality the original covenant God established with Israel at Sinai, it nevertheless does represent a new stage in God's dealings with his people. Having rebelled against God and having suffered decline, Israel was in need of awakening and restoration. To that end, God stirred up the spirit of the Teacher of Righteousness, through whom covenant renewal may take place. This renewal was predicted in Scripture (obviously so in Jer. 31:31, less obviously elsewhere in Scripture, where it required pesher exegesis to find it) and was fulfilled in the ministry of the Teacher and his faithful following, the Yahad.

Herein lies an important agreement with early Christianity, for it too emphasized the fulfillment of the "new covenant," an idea probably rooted in Jesus' words at his last meal with his disciples (cf. Jer. 31:31 in Matt. 26:28; Luke 22:20; 1 Cor. 11:25). Jesus probably anticipated the renewal of Israel's covenant, not a replacement of it. But in some Christian circles the new covenant implied not *renewal* of the original covenant, but a *break* with it. We see this clearly in Hebrews 8, where after quoting Jer. 31:31–34 the author asserts: "In speaking of a new covenant he treats the first as obsolete [*pepalaiōken*]. And what is becoming obsolete [*palaioumenon*] and growing old [*gēraskon*] is ready to vanish away" (Heb. 8:13; cf. 9:15; 12:24).

Not surprisingly, the rabbinic understanding of the covenant is closer to that of Qumran than to Jesus and his earliest following. Continuity is clearly presupposed. However, there is little interest in speculating about the "new" covenant of Jeremiah 31 (in fact, Jer. 31:31 is almost never cited in rabbinic literature). Here is where rabbinic Judaism differs noticeably from the Judaisms of Qumran and James.

The antecedents of rabbinic Judaism are found in the wisdom of the sage Jesus ben Sira: e.g., Sir. 17:11–12 ("allotted to them the law of life. He established with them an eternal covenant"); 24:23 ("All this is the book of the covenant of the Most High God, the law which Moses commanded us"; 28:7 ("remember the covenant of the Most High"); 39:8 (the well-studied scribe "will glory in the law of the Lord's covenant"); 42:1–2 ("Do not be ashamed . . . of the law of the Most High and his covenant"); 45:5 ("the law of life and knowledge, to teach Jacob the covenant"), 7 ("He made an everlasting covenant with [Aaron]").

That the covenant of the fathers could not be taken for granted is seen in the struggle against Hellenism in the Maccabean period, important traces of which are found in 1 Maccabees: e.g., 1 Macc. 1:15 ("they removed the marks of circumcision, and abandoned the holy covenant. They joined the Gentiles and sold themselves to do evil"), 1:57 ("book of the covenant"), 2:20 ("covenant of our fathers"), 2:27 ("zealous for the law and supports the covenant"), 2:50 ("show zeal for the law, and give your lives for the covenant of our fathers"). Other Jewish texts from late antiquity include *Pss. Sol.* 10:5; *T. Mos.* 1:9; 3:9; 11:17; 12:13; 4 Ezra 4:23; 7:24.

Early rabbinic references to the covenant include the following:

On account of your love, O Lord our God, with which you have loved Israel your people, and in your pity with which you, our King, have pitied the sons of your covenant [benê bᵉrîthka], you have given us, O Lord our God, this great and holy sabbath in love. (t. Ber. 3:7)

Be watchful in the study of the Torah and know what answer to give to the unbeliever [lit. Epicurean], and let not one word in the Torah be forgotten by you, and know before whom you toil and who is the Master of your Covenant [ba'al bᵉrîthka] ('Abot R. Nat. 17:8).

Why the covenant was made with Israel and not with other peoples is explained:

Another interpretation: "And he said: The Lord came from Sinai" (Deut. 33:2). When God revealed himself to give the Torah to Israel, he revealed himself not only to Israel but to all the nations. He went first to the children of Esau and asked them, "Will you accept the Torah?" They replied, "What is written in it?" He said to them, "You shall not murder" (Exod. 20:13). They replied that this is the very essence of these people, and that their forefather was a murderer, as it is said, "But the hands are the hands of Esau" (Gen. 27:22), and "By your sword shall you live" (Gen. 27:40). He then went to the Ammonites and the Moabites and asked them, "Will you accept the Torah?" They replied, "What is written in it?" He said, "You shall not commit adultery" (Exod. 20:13). They replied that adultery is their very essence, as it is said, "Thus were both the daughters of Lot with child by their father" (Gen. 19:36). He went next to the Ishmaelites and asked them, "Will you accept the Torah?" They replied, "What is written in it?" He said, "You shall not steal" (Exod. 20:13). They replied that theft is their very essence and that their forefather was a thief, as it is said, "And he shall be a wild ass of a man" (Gen. 16:12). And thus it was with every other nation. He asked them all, "Will you accept the Torah?," as it is said, "All the kings of the earth shall give you thanks, O Lord, for they have heard the words of your mouth" (Ps. 138:4). . . . So also Israel accepted the Torah, with all of its explanations and details, as well as the seven commandments which the children of Noah had not been able to observe and had cast off. (Sipre Deut. §343 [on Deut. 33:2])

Election is not earned by keeping the Torah; the former is the presupposition for the giving of the latter. God acted first to save Israel from slavery in Egypt and death in the wilderness. Having proven his love and fidelity, God now invites Israel to enter into a covenant relationship with him (Mek. on Exod. 20:2 [Baḥodeš §5]):

Why were the Ten Commandments not said at the beginning of the Torah? They give a parable. To what may this be compared? To the following: A king who entered a province said to the people: "May I rule over you?" But the people said to him: "Have you done anything good for us that you should rule over us?" What did he do then? He built the city wall for them, he brought in the water supply for them, and he fought their battles. Then when he said to them: "May I rule over you?" They said to him: "Yes, yes." So it is with God. He brought the Israelites out of Egypt, divided the sea for them, sent down manna for them, brought up the well for them, brought the quails for them. He fought for them the battle with Amalek. Then he said to them: "May I rule over you?" And they said to him: "Yes, yes."

Another illustrative passage is found in *Sipra Lev.* §194 (on Lev. 18:1–30). It is not formally introduced as a parable, but its fictive conversation between God and the wilderness generation is parable-like. In all probability this material is related to the above parable:

The Lord spoke to Moses saying, "Speak to the sons of Israel and say to them: I am the Lord your God" [Lev. 18:1–2]. Rabbi Simeon ben Yohai says, "This is in line with what is said elsewhere: 'I am the Lord your God (who brought you out of the land of Egypt, out of the house of bondage)' [Exod. 20:2]. 'Am I the Lord, whose sovereignty [lit. kingdom] you took upon yourself in Egypt?' They said to him, 'Yes, yes.' 'Indeed you have accepted my dominion [lit. my kingdom]. They accepted my decrees: "You will have no other gods before" [Exod. 20:3].' That is what is said here: 'I am the Lord your God,' meaning, 'Am I the one whose dominion [lit. kingdom] you accepted at Sinai?' They said to him, 'Yes, yes.' 'Indeed you have accepted my dominion [lit. my kingdom].' They accepted my decrees: 'You shall not copy the practices of the land of Egypt where you dwelt, or of the land of Canaan to which I am taking you; nor shall you follow their laws' [Lev. 18:3]."

Faith also plays an important role, as seen in an important passage from the Mekilta (on Exod. 14:31 [*Beshallah* §6]):

"And they believed in the Lord and in his servant Moses" (Exod 14:31). If you say they believed in Moses, is it not implied by *qal vahomer* that they believed in God? But this is to teach you that having faith in the shepherd of Israel is the same as having faith in him who spoke and the world came into being. In like manner you must interpret: "And the people spoke against God, and against Moses" (Num. 21:5). If you say they spoke against God, is it not implied by *qal vahomer* that they spoke against Moses? But this is to teach you that speaking against the shepherd of Israel is like speaking against him who spoke and the world came into being.

Great indeed is faith before him who spoke and the world came into being. For as a reward for the faith with which Israel believed in God, the Holy Spirit rested on them and they uttered the song; as it is said: "And they believed in the Lord . . . Then sang Moses and the children of Israel" (Exod. 14:3; 15:1). Rabbi Nehemiah says: Whence can you prove that whosoever accepts even one single commandment with true faith is deserving of having the Holy Spirit rest upon him? We find this to have been the case with our fathers. For as a reward for the faith with which they believed, they were considered worthy of having the Holy Spirit rest upon them, so that they could utter the song, as it is said: "And they believed in the Lord . . . Then sang Moses and the children of Israel" (Exod. 14:3; 15:1). And so also you find that our father Abraham inherited both this world and the world beyond only as a reward for the faith with which he believed, as it is said: "And he believed in the Lord," etc. (Gen. 15:6). And so also you find that Israel was redeemed from Egypt only as a reward for the faith with which they believed, as it is said: "And the people believed" (Exod. 4:31). And thus it says: "The Lord preserves the faithful" (Ps. 31:24). He keeps in remembrance the faith of the fathers. (Lauterbach 1.252–53)

The point is that the children of Israel believed in God and so were delivered (or "saved"). But faith must be worked out in obedience. That is, to "keep faith" with God, one must keep his commandments. The grace of God is clearly understood as the presupposition of the election of Israel, as reflected in the various covenants, especially those of circumcision and Sinai. In principle, the theology of election presupposed here coheres with what the Jacobean community affirms in James 2: Genuine faith expresses itself in obedience and good works.

4. Kingdom of God

The covenanters of Qumran regarded themselves as the "poor" (CD 19:9; 1QH 10:34; 1QM 14:7 ["poor in spirit"]; 4Q434 1 ii 2), who have been marginalized. Although plotted against by the wicked of Jerusalem's Temple establishment (4QpPs[a] 1–10 ii 13–20), they nevertheless look forward to inheriting the kingdom of God.

Hope of a "kingdom of God" is expressed in the War Scroll: "And to the God of Israel shall be the kingdom, and by the saints of his people will he display might" (1QM 6:6); and "You, O God, resplendent in the glory of your kingdom" (1QM 12:7). The reference to "his kingdom" in 1QH 11 i 4–7 should probably be understood in the same way. 4Q491, which is related in some way to the War Scroll, says: "And [the kingdo]m shall be for God and the salvatio[n] for His people . . ." (11 ii 17).

In the Rule of Blessing the following is said of the High Priest: "May you serve in the Temple of the kingdom" (1QSb 4:25–26). This is the prayer of blessing for the priest who will serve when Israel is restored and the Messiah takes his place. The last column of 1QSb blesses this figure as well. Part of the blessing says: "And he shall renew for him the covenant of the community, so as to establish the kingdom of His people forever" (1QSb 5:21). The passage goes on to quote parts of Isaiah 11 and apply them to the awaited Messiah. (See also 4Q286 7 i 5, which speaks of God supporting "your kingdom in the midst of . . ." The singular suffix probably refers to the anticipated Messiah.)

No texts more than the Songs of the Sabbath have extolled the glory of the kingdom of heaven. We find more than twenty references to the celestial kingdom in these fragmentary scrolls. Although in no one instance do we have the exact phrase "kingdom of God," it is nevertheless about the kingdom of God that these texts speak. The pronouns appear in the second and third persons: "[Your] lofty kingdom" (4Q400 1 ii 1); "His lofty kingdom" (4Q403 1 i 8; 1 i 14; 4Q405 3 ii 4; MasŠŠ 2:20); "the beauty of Your kingdom" (4Q400 1 ii 3); "the praiseworthiness of Your kingdom among the holiest of the h[oly ones]" (4Q400 1 ii 3; 2 1; 4Q401 14 i 7); "and they declare His kingdom" (4Q400 2:3); "the heavens of Your glor[ious] kingdom" (4Q401 14 i 6); "[in all] the heavens of His kingdom" (4Q400 2:3–4); "[who pr]aise His glorious kingdom" (4Q403 1 i 25); "in the splendor of praise is the glory of His kingdom" (4Q403 1 i 32); "the praises of all the gods together with the splendor of all His kingdom" (4Q403 1 i 32–33); "And the tabernacle of highest loftiness, the glory of His kingdom" (4Q403 1 ii 10); "a seat like the throne of His kingdom" (4Q405 20–22 ii 2); "the kingdom . . . glorious seats of the chariot thrones" (4Q405 20–22 ii 4); "the throne of His glorious kingdom" (4Q405 23 i 3); "the chiefs of the realm of the holy ones of the King of holiness in all the heights of the sanctuaries of His glorious kingdom" (4Q405 23 ii 11–12); and "the glorious kingdom of the King of all the g[ods]" (4Q405 24:3) are among the best-preserved texts that speak of the divine kingdom.

The datum best attested and best remembered to have been uttered by Jesus is that the kingdom of God has come (cf. Mark 1:14–15). Like Qumran, Jesus also believed that the "poor in spirit" would inherit the kingdom of God (cf. Matt. 5:3). Jesus' idea that the poor would inherit the kingdom of God was a major component of his proclamation of "good news" and very probably derives in large measure from Isa. 61:1–2 (cf. Matt. 11:6 = Luke 7:22; 4:18–19).

It is to this tradition that Jacobean Judaism is indebted, when we read in the Letter of James: "Listen, my beloved brethren. Has not God chosen those who are poor in the world to be rich in faith and heirs of the kingdom which he has promised to those who love him?" (Jas. 2:5). The exhortation to "ask in faith, with no doubting" (2:6) recalls the similar exhortation of Jesus (cf. Matt. 7:7–11 = Luke 11:9–13).

The Rabbis too expressed ideas about the kingdom of God. There are some 325 Tannaitic parables, more than half of which feature a king, who almost always represents God. Many of these parables resemble in theme and in details the parables of Jesus. Among these we have the parable of the Forgiving King (b. Roš Haš. 17b; attributed to Rabbi Yose the priest, ca. 90–100 C.E.; cf. Matt. 5:23–24; 18:21–35), the parable of the King's Wise and Foolish Servants (b. Šabb. 153a; cf. Eccl. Rab. 9:8 §1; Midr. Prov. 16:11; attributed to Rabbi Yoḥanan ben Zakkai, ca. 70–80 C.E.; cf. Matt. 24:45–51; Luke 17:7–10), the parable of the King's Banquet Guests (*Sem.* 8:10; attributed to Rabbi Meir, ca. 150 C.E.; cf. Matt. 22:1–10; Luke 14:15–24), the parable of the King's Steward (*'Abot R. Nat.* A 14.6; attributed to Rabbi Eleazar ben Arak, ca. 90 C.E.; cf. Matt. 25:14–30 = Luke 19:12–27), and that of the King's Two Administrators (*Mek.* on Exod. 20:2 [*Baḥodeš* §5]; attributed to Rabbi Simon ben Eleazar, ca. 170 C.E.; cf. Matt. 25:21 = Luke 19:17). Other parables could be mentioned, but these are among the most illustrative.

More than one half of Jesus' parables speak of the "kingdom of God," which Jesus seemed to have understood in terms of God's powerful presence. Although the rabbinic parables usually speak of God as king and Jesus' parables speak of the kingdom of God, I believe these expressions are closely related and merit comparison.

Years ago T. W. Manson noted that in a few rabbinic passages "kingdom" sometimes means God's dominion, the meaning that the term seems to have in Jesus' parables. The parable cited above (in *Mek.* on Exod. 20:2 [*Baḥodeš* §5]) supports this suggestion. The king (who is God, of course), asks the people: "May I rule over you?" Impressed by his mighty, salvific works, the Israelites reply, "Yes, yes." In the parable found in *Sipra Lev.* §194 (on Lev. 18:1–30), the use of the word kingdom (*malkût*) closely approximates the meaning of kingdom in the proclamation of Jesus: "'I am the Lord your God,' meaning, 'Am I the one whose dominion [lit. kingdom] you accepted at Sinai?' They said to him, 'Yes, yes.' 'Indeed you have have accepted my dominion [lit. kingdom].'" Jacob Neusner has rightly translated *malkût* in both instances "dominion."

The two rabbinic parables are quite instructive. The second coheres with the first one, in which God rules over Israel as a king. The second passage understands the acceptance of Torah as acceptance of God's royal sovereignty. In my judgment this idea of God as exercising dominion approximates Jesus' proclamation of the kingdom of God, a concept presupposed by Jacobean Christianity and closely approximating the understanding of the Judaism of Qumran.

Comparisons in the four areas surveyed above amply illustrate the significant overlap in theology and practice in the Judaisms of Qumran, the Rabbis, and the Jacobean community. But extensive overlap does not justify speaking of these Judaisms as though they are merely three versions of the same religion. There are also significant systemic differences and distinctions that should be recognized. The next section will touch on these differences.

THE ESSENCE OF QUMRANIC, RABBINIC, AND JACOBEAN JUDAISMS

Before concluding, it will be instructive to state the essence, or native features, of Qumranic, Rabbinic, and Jacobean Judaisms. A few points of difference have been mentioned in the above comparisons, but here it will be useful to underscore the differences when the essence of each Judaism is described and compared. These remarks will be brief.

The most obvious feature of the Judaism expressed in the sectarian scrolls of Qumran is the emphasis on covenant renewal and cultic restoration. Qumran's expectation and hope of renewal are heavily colored by an understanding of Israel's religious history that is reminiscent of the Deuteronomistic tradition. According to this perspective, Israel is viewed as having repeatedly abandoned the Law and violated the covenant. The nation's apostasy has reached its nadir in recent years (initially in reference to the Hasmonean high priests, later in reference to the ruling priests of the Herodian and Roman period). But God who is faithful to his promises has raised up a righteous priest and teacher through whom Israel's covenant has been restored. Although initially rejected, the teaching and hopes of the sectarian teacher will be vindicated. Israel will be purged, the righteous will be exalted, the true priesthood will be restored, the wicked and guilty will be judged.

The essence of the Judaism of Qumran is thus covenant renewal, tightly linked to a vigorous eschatological expectation. Although a "Messiah of Israel" is anticipated, Qumran's Judaism is not really messianic (at least, not in the sense that Christianity is messianic). A royal Messiah is anticipated, to be sure, but he is neither the center of the eschatological drama, nor its occasion. The goal, the *telos*, of Qumran's eschatology is the cultic renewal of Israel. The pragmata and the calendar of the Temple of Jerusalem will finally be observed as God had intended them to be observed from the beginning. This faithful observance will lead to a time of unprecedented national righteousness and blessing.

In rabbinic Judaism, eschatology and messianism have receded. This is not to say that they have no place; indeed they do. But the heart of the Judaism of the framers of the Mishnah and its complementary supplement the Tosefta concerns faithful obedience to Torah, its careful study, and the preservation of tradition felt to be edifying and in keeping with God's will. For the Rabbis the covenant continues. The written Torah was given at Sinai; but so was the oral Torah, which faithful students of Scripture are obliged to unpack, digest, commit to memory, and pass on.

The emphasis on Torah and its study has influenced messianism. We see this in the idea that the Messiah will come as a scholar, able to answer all remaining questions of the interpretation of Torah. But we also see it in the cautious and reserved nature of the messianism of the Rabbis. The bitter lessons of Simon ben Kosibah, the so-called "son of the star," and his messianic predecessors in the various wars and insurrections of 115 C.E., 66–74 C.E., and 4 B.C.E. have not been forgotten. Yes, Messiah will some day make his appearance, "in the world to come," but not any day soon. For now, one's duty is to obey the Law, to practice charity, and to make disciples.

The essence of Christianity is clearly messianic, a messianism focused on Jesus the brother of James. Christians believe that the prophecies and promises of Scripture have been fulfilled in the life, death, and resurrection of Jesus. All that remains is his triumphant return and the consummation of the kingdom of God.

How much overlap there is between Pauline and Gentile Christianity and the Judaism of the Jacobean community is difficult to determine. The essence of the Judaism of the epistle of James is similar to the Judaism of the prerabbinic period, the Judaism of Jesus ben Sirach, for example. The Judaism of James is marked by paraenesis and wisdom. Yet, if the patristic traditions about the person James are anything to go on, messianism was an essential component of Jacobean Judaism as well. We should recall that according to Eusebius, who draws on Hegesippus, James taught that "Jesus was the Messiah" (*H.E.* 2.23.8–9). Eusebius says that it was James's evangelistic efforts that ultimately led to controversy and death (2.23.10–18).

In sum, we could say that if we drew three circles to represent the Judaisms of Qumran, the Rabbis, and James, the circles would overlap. But the centers of these circles, centers which represent the essence of the respective Judaisms, would not. We would have three overlapping circles, but three distinct, separate centers. The Judaism of Qumran is focused on the renewal of the covenant, with great emphasis on cultic reform. The Judaism of the Rabbis is focused on studying and obeying the Torah, the key to life in this world and in the world to come. The Judaism of James is focused on faith and piety centered on Messiah Jesus.

CONCLUSION

Although not wishing to minimize the differences of the Judaisms of Qumran, the Rabbis, and the Jacobean community, one cannot help but be struck by the extent of systemic agreement. Piety, practice, authority, heritage, sense of the rule of God—in all of these things we find significant overlap. The extremism of Qumran would no doubt have been unpalatable to most Rabbis, while the messianic focus of early Christianity (even if not so emphatic in Jacobean circles) would have been viewed as insufficiently oriented to the Temple and to purity, as far as both Qumran and rabbinic Judaisms would have been concerned.

Yet for all their differences, these expressions of Judaism have much in common. The major differences can be explained as due in large part to the circumstances in which foundational beliefs were worked out. Qumranic Judaism was formed in the context of serious disagreements with Hasmonean rule and the consequent encroachment of Greco-Roman cultural influence and political pressure. The covenanters of Qumran awaited the appearance of the royal Messiah, who along with the anointed priest, would restore the cultus and the nation. But the awaited Messiah did not make his appearance. Jacobean

Judaism believed that the Messiah had appeared and that the restoration of cultus and nation was under way. Rabbinic Judaism developed in the aftermath of two, possibly three, failed messianic revolutions (i.e., 66–74 C.E., 115 C.E., and 132–135 C.E.). And, unlike Jacobean Judaism, which arose in a brief span of time, the rabbinic Judaism of the Mishna developed over the course of some two centuries, with definitive shaping taking place in the generations following the defeat of Simon ben Kosiba. Thus, Israel's history and the experiences of the Jewish people go a long way in explaining distinctive features of the Judaisms of Qumran, James, and the Rabbis.

Of the three expressions of Judaism, it is not surprising that it was the rabbinic expression that survived. For of the three, rabbinic Judaism was not time bound and therefore vulnerable to the vicissitudes of history. Of the expressions of Christianity, it is not surprising that the Pauline variety, with its emphasis on evangelizing the nations, eclipsed the Jacobean. Although Jacobean Judaism/Christianity did not die out suddenly, as did the Judaism of Qumran and the Judaisms of other smaller, lesser-known messianic and restorative movements, it too would eventually disappear (ca. fourth century). Nevertheless, Jacobean Judaism/Christianity has left behind footprints whose careful study throws the diversity of Judaisms and Christianities in late antiquity into a sharper and clearer light.

Epilogue

Bruce Chilton

The findings and suggestions of each of the essays in this volume are too clear to require summary, and differences of opinion obviously remain. But perhaps it would be helpful to set out the structure of the knowledge we have acquired regarding James.

Initially, we understand the entire religious system of James as Judaic, and Professor Neusner has specified the contours of any such system, with reference to the Scriptures of Israel and the identification of the practicing community with Israel. In his magisterial survey of the relevant literary and historical evidence, Professor Painter demonstrates that James was a revered leader of primitive Christianity, and he explains how his leadership is reflected in the sources.

A sequence of three articles, by Professors Davids, Popkes, and Bauckham, sets out three different but overlapping positions in regard to the Epistle of James. In Peter Davids's reconstruction, the letter is posthumous, but only just, in that it was produced in the confused conditions between the death of James and the destruction of the Temple. Wiard Popkes, while stressing the Judaic setting of the epistle, envisions an environment well after the destruction of the Temple, and construes the message of the literary James in terms of the social responsibility demanded of Christian congregations. Richard Bauckham's approach, by contrast, is to characterize the epistle in terms of a deep affinity with the Jesus tradition, developed along the lines of Israelite Wisdom. All of these stances, for all that divides them, take up the Judaic orientation of the epistle as a matter of course, and demonstrate how richly rewarding that perspective is.

My own approach is to seek guidance in the study of James from sources other than the epistle attributed to him, and my characterization of James in relation to other Christian leaders of his time particularly highlights the practical influence of Jesus' brother, in his encouragement of the completion of Nazirite vows in the Temple and in his reputation in Jerusalem as a *mebaqqer* or bishop. Finally, Professor Evans ties a tight bow around the exposition of the volume, by demonstrating that the Judaism of James is directly comparable to other Judaisms of the period (and thereafter).

The intellectual movement of our inquiry involved three levels of progress. From the assessment of James's theology, as a Judaic and Christian thinker (in the essays by Professors Neusner and Painter), we moved to James's moving appeal to his hearers in the epistle attributed to him (in the contributions of Professors Davids, Popkes, and Bauckham), and from there to the practical outworking of James's Christian Judaism in relation to other Christianities (my angle of approach) and other Judaisms (Professor Evans's perspective). In typifying the theological stance of James, its emotional and ethical resonance, and its pragmatic enactment, we may fairly claim to have mapped the religious system of a formative leader of primitive Christianity.

Important differences of opinion have been a part of our investigation, and these are by no means masked in this volume. We have agreed to differ over whether James was the full brother of Jesus, whether he was a prominent disciple during Jesus' lifetime, and whether the Epistle of James or sources such as Acts and Josephus should be accorded precedence in characterizing James. Obviously, such issues are more than incidental, and schools of thought in the field of apologetic theology (including some New Testament scholarship) define themselves by means of hard-and-fast answers to these questions. But I see no virtue in pretending to more certainty than the evidence to hand permits our inquiry to attain. One of the great advances of the Consultation on James, in my experience, has been the communal discipline of listening to and engaging lines of analysis which may seem unlikely from the outset—and which may prove to be so in the end. But provided a reading engages the evidence and opens its inferences to testing, it enriches our analytic capacity. Robert Price's review of the contributions of Robert Eisenman (which have been the occasion of sometimes intemperate controversy elsewhere) is a case in point.

Although the pretense of certainty is no virtue, the postmodern habit of leaving the ends of all discussion untied is no real advance either. Even where we differ, we commend the scholarly judgments advanced here and the bodies of work on which they are based. And those differences serve to emphasize our considerable degree of consensus. James the Just was, in the time between Jesus' resurrection and his own death, the most prominent and widely respected leader in Christendom. His theology, and its corollaries of emotion and practice, were grounded in the Scriptures of Israel and in the conviction that his brother, risen from the dead and installed in divine glory, offered both Israel and the nations the prospect of justice when he arrived to judge the earth (Jas. 5:7–8).

Appendix

Eisenman's Gospel of James the Just

A Review

Robert M. Price

Robert Eisenman, *James, the Brother of Jesus: The Key to Unlocking the Secrets of Early Christianity and the Dead Sea Scrolls*. Viking Penguin, 1997, xxxvi + 1074 pp., $39.95. ISBN 0-670-86932-5.

PRE-HISTORIC CHRISTIANITY

In his recent publications *The Dead Sea Scrolls Uncovered* (with Michael Wise) and *The Dead Sea Scrolls and the First Christians*, Robert Eisenman of the Institute for the Study of Judeo-Christian Origins and the Institute for Higher Critical Studies has been threatening/promising to redraw the map of Christian origins and now, by God, he has done it. The breadth and detail of Eisenman's investigation are breathtaking, as are its implications. In *James, the Brother of Jesus* he tells the long-lost tale of formative "prehistoric" Christianity as it emerged from the crucible of revolutionary Palestine and from the internecine hostilities between Pauline and Ebionite Christianities. I call it "pre-historic" because Eisenman reconstructs the events lying before and beneath our canonical histories of early Christianity. His enterprise is in this sense akin to that of Burton L. Mack, that other great contemporary delver into the subterrene depths of Christian prehistory. Like Mack, Eisenman discovers a "Christianity" (or perhaps a proto-Christianity, or even a pre-Christianity) for which Jesus had not yet attained centrality. Only, whereas Mack sees the initial germ of the new religion as a variant of Cynicism, Eisenman rejuvenates, even vindicates, Renan's old claim that Christianity began as "an Essenism."

To anticipate the thrust of the book as a whole, let it be said that Eisenman first draws a portrait of the early community of James as a nationalistic, messianic, priestly, and xenophobic sect of ultralegal pietism, something most of us would deem fanaticism. Eisenman shows how "Jewish Christianity" was part and parcel of the sectarian milieu which included Essenes, Zealots, Nazoreans, Nazirites, Ebionites, Elchasites, Sabeans, Mandaeans, etc., and that these categories were no more than ideal types, by no means actually segregated one from the other like exotic beasts in adjacent, well-marked cages in the theological zoo. Over against this sort of "Lubavitcher Christianity," Eisenman depicts Pauline Christianity (plus its Hellenistic cousins Johannine, Markan, Lukan, etc., Christianities) as being root-and-branch a compromising, assimilating, Herodianizing apostasy from Judaism. Greek Christianity gives the Torah, and Jewish identity, the bum's rush. The Pauline Christ, a spiritual redeemer with an invisible kingdom, is of a piece with the christening of Vespasian as the messiah by Josephus.

Of course, these ideas are by no means new. Eisenman is simply filling out the picture in an exhaustive manner undreamt of by S. G. F. Brandon, Robert Eisler, and their successors. The picture of Jesus in the Greek Gospels, eating with tax collectors, lampooning the traditions of his people, welcoming sinners and ridiculing Torah piety are all expressions of Gentile anti-Judaism. Only Gentiles utterly without sympathy to Judaism could profess to see such a Jesus as a noble pioneer of a "higher righteousness." In the same way, the New Testament notion that Jerusalem fell because her people had rejected the messiah, when in fact they were fighting a messianic war against the Roman antichrist, must be judged a piece of cynical Hellenistic Jew-bashing. Christianity as it emerges in the Gentile mission is a product of cultural accommodationism, pro-Roman Quislingism, and intentional assimilation. It is a kind of paganized, syncretic, diluted Judaism not unlike the Sabazius cult.

Armed with a hermeneutic of suspicion, Eisenman shows us how to crack the codes of theological disinformation, to listen to the long-faded echoes, to find handholds up what had seemed an insurmountable climb to a peak from which to view the hitherto-unseen landscape of early Christianity. What are his climbing tools?

First, Eisenman considers a much wider range of historical sources than most think they need to. He plumbs, as we have come to expect, the Dead Sea Scrolls, as well as the Clementine *Recognitions* and *Homilies*, the *Apostolic Constitutions*, Eusebius, the two James Apocalypses from Nag Hammadi, even the Western Text of Acts and the Slavonic Josephus. And Eisenman takes Josephus much more seriously as a source for Luke's Acts than anyone ever has before. All these our author carefully sifts, taking nothing uncritically. Where he differs from most previous scholars is in taking these materials seriously at all as new sources of information, finding the odd clue here or there, about James and Paul. As Richard I. Pervo (*Profit with Delight*) has begun to show, the traditional neglect of these and other related sources (e.g., the apocryphal Acts of the apostles) by supposedly critical scholars is more a matter of canon apologetics than of historical method. Why do New Testament scholars agree that Luke's Acts is in large measure legendary and fictitious—and go right on taking the story at face value? Eisenman, on the other hand, realizes that Luke and the Pseudo-Clementines are more or less on a par. Each must be treated with great reserve, yet with the optimism that, like the Oxyrhynchus alligators, somewhere amid all the stuffing one may at last discover a vital bit of information.

THE NAME GAME

Second, Eisenman has developed a keen sense for the "name game" played in the sources. Most of us have at some time scratched our heads over the tantalizing confusions latent in the strange redundancy of similar names in the New Testament accounts. How can Mary have had a sister named Mary? Is there a difference between Joseph Barsabbas Justus, Judas Barsabbas Justus, and James the Just? Whence all the Jameses and Judases? Who are Simon the Zealot and Judas the Zealot (who appears in some New Testament manuscripts and other early Christian documents)? Is Clopas the same as Cleophas? What's going on with Jesus ben Ananias, Jesus Barabbas, Elymas bar Jesus, and Jesus Justus? What does "Boanerges" really mean? Is Nathaniel a nickname for someone else we know of? And so on, and so on. Most of us puzzle over these oddities for a moment—and then move on. After all, how important can they be, anyway? But Eisenman does not move on till he has figured it out.

In Thomas V. Kuhn's terms, Eisenman has decided to start with the recalcitrant "anomalous data" left to the side by the old paradigm and to construct a new paradigm that will make sense of it, and perhaps in the process wind up making new sense of everything else. Eisenman's efforts here recall those of Bart Ehrman in *The Orthodox Corruption of Scripture*, in which he demonstrated that a great many of the textual alterations which critics traditionally weed out of their texts and then ignore can be counted as theologically motivated attempts to render the text unfriendly to "heretical" exegesis, a kind of built-in "prescription against the heretics," a booby-trapped text. What had been cursorily dismissed by scholars as a pile of random goofs wound up disclosing an apologetical pattern of redactional alteration. As Collingwood might have said, the variant readings turned out not to be evidence for the original text, but that didn't mean they weren't evidence for something *else*. And in just the same way, Eisenman has cracked the code of the strange name lists of the New Testament.

His working hypothesis is that the confusions, alterations, and obfuscations stem from an interest in covering over the importance, and therefore the identity, of the *Desposyni*, the Heirs of Jesus who had apparently functioned at least for Palestinian Christianity as a dynastic caliphate similar to the Alid succession of Shi'ite Islam or the succession of Hasmonean brothers. It is a commonplace that the Gospel texts treating Jesus' mother, brothers, and sisters either severely (Mark and John) or delicately (Luke; cf. the *Gospel according to the Hebrews*) are functions of ecclesiastical polemics over their leadership claims as opposed to Peter and the Twelve (analogous to the Companions of the Prophet in Sunni Islam) or to outsiders like Paul. It is equally well known that the Synoptic apostle lists differ between themselves and between manuscripts of each Gospel. Why? Eisenman connects these phenomena with another, the confusion arising among early theologians over the siblings of Jesus as the doctrine of Mary's perpetual virginity became widespread. They had to be harmonized with the dogma, so brothers and sisters became cousins, step-siblings, etc. And characters became sundered. Mary suddenly had a sister named Mary because the mother of James, Joses, Simon, and Judas could no longer also be the mother of Jesus. And so on.

The Gospels give prominence to an inner circle of three: Peter, John son of Zebedee, and *John's* brother James. And Galatians has the Three Pillars in Jerusalem: Peter, John son of Zebedee, and *Jesus'* brother James. What happened here? Surely the inner group of three in the Gospel narrative is intended as preparatory for the Pillars, to provide a life-of-Jesus pedigree for the Pillars. But then why are there two different Jameses? Mustn't they originally have been the same? Eisenman says they were, but certain factions who wanted to play up the authority of the shadowy college of the Twelve against the earlier authority of the Heirs found it politic to drive a wedge between James the brother of Jesus and the Twelve, so James becomes James the Just on the one hand and James the brother of John on the other.

Another attempt to distance James the Just from the Companions of Jesus would have been the cloning of James the Just as James the son of "Alphaeus," which name Papias says is interchangeable with "Cleophas," who happens to be the father of Simeon, James's successor as bishop of Jerusalem and his brother as well. And eventually James the son of Alphaeus and James son of Zebedee both replace James the Just in the circle of disciples. Meanwhile, Thomas has similarly undergone mitosis into Judas of James, Thaddaeus, Lebbaeus, and Judas Iscariot. Simon the Zealot is Simon bar Cleophas, another brother of Jesus, the successor of James as the leader of the Jerusalem Christians after James's martyrdom. He has been confused with the similar-sounding Simeon Cephas (Simon Peter) as well. Eisenman has worked out a complex and coherent grammar of these processes. He ends up with a much-reduced circle of "the Twelve," most of them being aliases and replacements for the brothers of Jesus. This will outrage some, but others will find the theory ringing true against the otherwise-odd fact that the supposedly important Twelve are such shadowy nonentities in the New Testament.

UNSCRAMBLING THE EGG

Third, Eisenman brings to bear on the narratives of Acts the model of a "mix and match" redactional technique whereby Luke is seen to have composed his stories by recombining the salient features of very different stories from his sources. When Luke finishes, only bits of either the paradigmatic or syntag-mic composition of the originals are left, but there is enough to recognize the one as the mutation of the other. This is the procedure used recently to great effect by a number of scholars, not least John Dominic Crossan (who shows the Passion Narrative to be built up from various Old Testament proof texts), Randel Helms (who in *Gospel Fictions* shows case after case of a Gospel story's derivation from a similar Septuagint story), and Thomas L. Brodie (who unscrambles numerous Lukan tales into their original Deuteronomic compo-nents). Eisenman's originality at this point lies not in the technique but rather in his willingness to take seriously Luke's use of Josephus as a source. (Again, this is something no one who wants an early date for Luke or a historical basis for Acts is likely to consider seriously, but then we have another case of apolo-getics masquerading as criticism.) And Eisenman's redactional analyses of Luke on Josephus is only one of the major advances of *James the Brother of Jesus*. It seems not too much to say that the book ushers in a new era in the study of Acts.

This is not to say, however, that Eisenman limits his use of the technique to Luke and Josephus. Far from it: he is able to distill traditions from various sources and to identify them in their new guises in Luke–Acts and elsewhere in the New Testament. I propose now to provide summaries of a few of Eisen-man's reconstructions, showing in broad outline what he sees Luke (or others) having made of originally quite different traditions.

Various early Christian sources have James being elected by the apostles as bishop of Jerusalem at the behest of Jesus (as in the *Gospel of Thomas*, logion 12). Luke's hellenizing agenda has led him to retell this story not as the instal-lation of James the Just as Jesus' successor, but rather the replacement of the villain Judas Iscariot by the nonentity "Matthias." James the Just has shrunk so small as to hide behind the runner-up for the position, "Joseph Barsabbas called Justus." The name Matthias was suggested, via simple word association, by Mattathias the father of another Judas, Judas Maccabeus. Thus when later we meet James the Just as the head of the Jerusalem Church we are expected to know who he is, though Luke has eliminated what would have been our introduction to him! A telltale sign of the story's originally having dealt with James's election, not as a new twelfth apostle, but as the bishop of Jerusalem, is the proof-text, "his bishopric let another man take." And James has simply been excised from various tales in Acts where we should expect to read of all three Pillars but now read of only the dynamic duo of Peter and John.

As Hans-Joachim Schoeps had already surmised, the stoning of Stephen has in precisely the same way supplanted the stoning of James (actually a confla-tion of James's ultimate stoning at the command of Ananus and an earlier assault on James by Saul on the Temple steps preserved as a separate incident in the *Recognitions*). The name Stephen has been borrowed from a Roman offi-cial beaten by Jewish insurgents whom Josephus depicts ambushing him out-side the city walls. Why this name? Because of a pun: Stephen means "crown" and was suggested both by the long hair of the Nazirite (which James was, according to early church writers) and by the crown of martyrdom. To Stephen has been transferred James's declaration of the Son of Man at the right hand of God in heaven, as well as James's "Christlike" prayer for his persecutors. (Eisenman might have noted, too, that the martyr's original identity as James the Just is signaled by Acts 7:52, "the Just, whose betrayers and murders you have *now* become"!)

We read that a young man named Saul was playing coat check for the executioners of Stephen and, his taste for blood whetted, immediately began to foment persecution in Jerusalem and Damascus. This has been drawn, again, from the lore of James as well as Josephus. The clothing motif was suggested by the final blow to James's head with a fuller's club, while just after his own account of James's death, Josephus tells of the rioting started by a Herodian named Saulus in Jerusalem!

PATCHWORK PROPHETS

Eisenman sees various Jamesian themes floating around to link up in entirely different forms elsewhere in Christian scripture. For instance, the Transfiguration has Jesus glimpsed in heavenly glory as Stephen saw him and James proclaimed him. And of course "James" is there on the scene. The "fuller" element is repeated in the form of Jesus' shining clothes, whiter than any fuller on earth could have bleached them. Again, in the *Recognitions* Saul is pursuing James and the Jerusalem saints out to Jericho (the vicinity of the Qumran "Damascus"), and somehow they are protected by the spectacle of two martyrs' tombs which miraculously whiten every year. There is the whitening element linked with Saul's persecution. Again, at the empty tomb (recalling those martyrs' tombs), we meet a "young man" (the epithet applied to Saul in Acts' stoning of Stephen) who is dressed in white and sitting at the right, this time, of Jesus' resting place (just as Stephen saw Jesus at the right hand of God).

Peter's visit to Cornelius almost qualifies as a parody of Josephus's story of one Simon, a pious leader of his own "assembly" in Jerusalem who wanted to bar Herod Agrippa I from the Temple on account of his Gentile pollutions, whereupon Agrippa invited him to inspect his home at Caesarea and then sent him away with gifts. Luke borrowed the name Cornelius from elsewhere in Josephus where Cornelius is a name of two Roman soldiers, one involved in the siege of the Temple under Pompey, the other in the siege of Jerusalem under Titus. The Roman cohort at Caesarea, where Luke stations his pious Cornelius, were among the most violence-prone in Palestine. The element of conflict between Herod Agrippa I and Simon Peter, of course, has been transferred over to Acts 12, where Herod arrests Peter but Peter escapes, the same basic outcome, but with heightened drama.

What about the always fascinating character Simon Magus? Eisenman indentifies him with a magician named Simon of whom Josephus recounts that he helped Bernice convince her sister Drusilla to dump her husband King Azizus of Emesa, who had gotten circumcised to marry her, so she could take up with the uncircumcised Felix instead. Josephus's magician Simon is a Cypriot, while Acts' Simon Magus is said by later writers to hale from Gitta (Gath) in Samaria, but this actually strengthens the connection, since it was natural to confuse "Gitta" with the "Kittim," or Sea Peoples of Cyprus. Not only so, but Eisenman notes that some manuscripts of Josephus name the magician "Atomus," which Eisenman connects with the Primal Adam doctrine he sees implied in Simon's claim to have been the Standing One reincarnated many times. But there is a closer link still, that Eisenman chanced not to note. Anyone can see that Luke has created the episode of Saul/Paul squaring off against Elymas the sorcerer (Acts 13:8ff.) as a Pauline counterpart to Peter's contest with Simon Magus in Acts 8:9ff. (in fact, Elymas's patronymic "bar-Jesus" as likely as not reflects the claim Simon made to have recently appeared in Judea as Jesus). So Elymas is simply Simon Magus. And, what do you know, the Western Text of Acts gives the name as Etoimas or Etomas instead of Elymas! Thus, Simon Magus = Elymas = Etomas = Atomus = Josephus's Simon = Simon Magus.

Where did Luke find his raw material for the prophecy of Agabus of a great famine to transpire in Claudius's reign, of Paul's trip from Antioch to deliver famine relief funds to Jerusalem, and for the earlier tale of Philip and the Ethiopian eunuch? Again, from Josephus (though perhaps also from other cognate sources of information). It all stems, by hook and by crook, from the story of Helen, Queen of Adiabene, a realm contiguous and/or overlapping with Edessa, whose king Agbar/Abgarus some sources make Helen's husband. Helen and her son Izates converted to Judaism, though initially Izates refrained from circumcision on the counsel of a Jewish teacher who assured him the worship of God was more important than circumcision. His mother, too, advised against it, since his subjects might resent his embracing of such alien customs. But soon a stricter Jewish teacher from Jerusalem, one Eliezer, visited Izates, finding him poring over the Genesis passage on the Abrahamic covenant of circumcision. Eliezer asked if Izates understood the implications of what he was reading. If he did, then why did he not see the importance of being circumcised? And this the prince then agreed to do. Helen and Izates proved the sincerity of their conversion by, among other philanthropies, sending agents to Egypt and Cyrene to buy grain during the Claudius famine and to distribute it to the poor in Jerusalem.

These events have left their mark in the New Testament as follows. Eisenman notes (as of course all commentators do) that there is no room for the famine relief visit in Galatians' itinerary of Paul's visits to Jerusalem, but he ventures to place the event during Paul's sojourn in "Arabia," which in the parlance of the time could include Edessa/Adiabene. Acts knows two Antiochs, those in Pisidia and Syria, but there were others, including Edessa! Eisenman identifies Paul as the first Jewish teacher who tells Izates he need not be circumcised if he has faith in God. (This episode also lies at the basis of the Antioch episode recounted in Galatians, when certain men from James arrived in Antioch to tell Paul's converts they must be circumcised after all.) Paul is one of Helen's agents to bring famine relief to Jerusalem, which he is said to do "from Antioch," in Acts 11.

But we pick up the Helen story again back in chapter 8, with Philip substituted for Paul, where Philip accosts the financial officer of a foreign queen going from Jerusalem down through Egypt by way of Gaza. This is of course the Ethiopian eunuch. Why has Luke transformed Helen the Queen of Adiabene into Candace the Queen of Ethiopia? He has reverted to an Old Testament prototype, making Helen, a convert to Judaism, into a New Testament Queen of Sheba, having come to Jerusalem to hear the wisdom of Solomon. There is also a pun on the root *saba*, denoting baptism, à la the Essenes, Sampsaeans, Sabeans, Masbutheans, and Mandaeans, the type of Judaism Helen would have converted to (given the later Zealot involvements of her sons and her own reputed twenty-one years of Nazirite asceticism). Henry Cadbury pointed out long ago that Luke fell into the same trap as a number of literary contemporaries by taking as a personal name, Candace, the title of all the old Ethiopian queens, *kandake*. But Eisenman also sees a pun on the name of Helen's son Kenedaeos, who gave his life for his adopted people in the Roman War. In any case, there were no Ethiopian queens at this time.

When the prophet Agabus predicts the famine, Luke has derived his name from that of Helen's husband Agbarus. When the eunuch invites Philip to step up into his chariot, we have an echo of Jehu welcoming Jonadab into his chariot (2 Kings 10:15–16). When Philip asks the Ethiopian if he understands what he reads, Luke has borrowed this from the story of Izates and Eliezer, where the question also presages a ritual conversion, only this time the text is Isaiah's prophecy of Jesus, and the ritual is baptism. The original circumcision survives in the form of crude parody (recalling Gal. 5:12) with the Ethiopian having been fully castrated. Even the location of the Acts episode is dictated by the Helen story, as the Ethiopian travels into Egypt via Gaza as Helen's agents must have in order to buy the grain. Luke's substituted motivation for the trip, by contrast, is absurd: a eunuch could not have gone to Jerusalem to worship since eunuchs were barred from the Temple!

The suicide of Judas Iscariot (originally "the Sicarius") represents a mixing of elements that make more sense in their presumably earlier setting in the life of James and Jude. The suicide element (as well as the drawing of lots in the adjacent context in Acts 1) comes from the drawing of lots to begin the suicides of the Sicarii at Masada. The falling headlong comes from James's being pushed from the pinnacle of the Temple, while the gushing out of his bowels reflects the dashing out of James's brains by the evil launderer. Like James, Acts' Judas is buried where he fell.

THE CENTRALITY OF JAMES

Eisenman sees James as integrally involved in some of the episodes Josephus recounts from the same period, such as the building of a wall to cut off Herod Agrippa's dining room view overlooking the sacrificial altar of the Temple, which happened just before James's martyrdom, and the prophecy of Jesus ben-Ananias of Jerusalem's eventual doom that happened just afterward. James had been the bulwark holding off the judgment of God, and with him out of the way, the city's doom was sealed. (Origen had read a version of Josephus in which he said the people ascribed the fall of the city to punishment for the death of James the Just.) This prophecy of Jesus ben Ananias is the basis for both the oracle mentioned by Eusebius that warned the Jerusalem Christians to flee and for Agabus's warning to Paul not to continue on to Jerusalem (Acts 21).

James had been executed for blasphemy on account of his functioning (as early church writers tell us) as an opposition High Priest entering the Inner Sanctum on the Day of Atonement. As an Essene (as shown by his ascetic practices, his linen dress, etc.) he would have celebrated Yom Kippur on a different day, which is how he could manage not to collide with Annanus doing the same thing, and why he would have been executed for ritual irregularity as the Mishnah required for such an infraction.

As Eisenman describes the role of James, it has very little to do with Jesus (about as little as the Epistle of James does, come to think of it!). What of the famous Hegesippus story of James being invited by the High Priest to address the people at Passover, to dissuade them from their growing faith in Jesus, issuing in his surprise confession, "Why do you ask me concerning the Son of Man . . . ?" Eisenman seems to imply that it might be a Christianization of an original in which James was asked to quell, not burgeoning Christianity, but rather the Jewish-messianic excitement of the Passover crowds (a yearly source of eschatological headaches for the Temple and Roman establishments), with no reference to Jesus one way or the other. And James's answer would have been an incitement of messianic expectation, again with no reference to Jesus. (One clue that the story as we read it is a reworking of a pre-Christian original is that we can hardly imagine the Jewish elders being ignorant of James's connection to Jesus if James owed his prominence precisely to his being the brother and vicar of Jesus!) Similarly, the vow of James neither to eat nor to drink till the Son of Man should have risen from among them that sleep (*Gospel According to the Hebrews*) might be a Christian redaction of James's vow to observe Nazirite asceticism till the coming of the Jewish Messiah, not necessarily the resurrection of Jesus.

So Eisenman's James would make sense as a major religious figure in his own right. And this picture comports with another distinctive hypothesis of Eisenman: his identification of James as the Qumran Teacher of Righteousness, a case he argues at length in his earlier books now happily reprinted in the collection *The Dead Sea Scrolls and the First Christians*. He alludes to the possibility of this identification several times in *James the Brother of Jesus*, but the main argument is in no way dependent upon it. But it is irresistible to ask: if James was the Teacher of the Scrolls, how could so little (nothing, really) be said about Jesus in the Scrolls? The answer is simple (though Eisenman does not give it): James the Just has been co-opted by later Christians just as they assimilated John the Baptist, another independent charismatic leader in his own right. Christians tried to attract or undercut their rivals by making their figureheads subservient to the Christian Jesus.

"FOR HE IS NOT A REAL JEW . . ."

Eisenman shows himself willing to take seriously the Ebionite charge that Paul was never a real Jew to begin with. Eisenman adduces the evidence of Paul's Herodian background, something we really do not have to read too far between the lines to see, given his Roman citizenship, his kinship to one Herodion and to the household of Aristobulus. If this is what the Ebionites meant, that Paul was as little a Jew as Herod the Great despite his pretense, then we have a scenario more natural than that which the Ebionite charge might otherwise imply: the idea of Paul as some sort of Greek pagan entering Judaism superficially and from without. As Eisenman notes, Paul protests that he is a Hebrew, an Israelite, even a Benjaminite, but he avoids calling himself a Jew! And Eisenman suggests that, given the strange fact that "Bela" appears both as a chief clan of Benjamin and as the first Edomite king, "Benjaminite" may have been a kind of Herodian euphemism for their oblique relation to Judaism. Eisenman cites the Talmud's notice that the Rechabites (= Nazirites) used to marry the daughters of the High Priests. Though he does not make the particular connection I am about to make, this Talmudic note suggests to me a new and more natural way of understanding the Ebionite slur that Paul had converted to Judaism only because he was smitten by the High Priest's daughter and wanted to curry favor with her father to win her hand. Think of Acts' account of Paul's unsuccessful ruse, feigning Nazirite allegiance by paying for the purification of four of James's zealots (Acts 21:23–26), which backfired on him and led to rioting by (as F. C. Baur recognized) James's "zealots for the Torah" (not some vacationing Jews from Asia Minor, as Luke would have it) over Paul's attempt to profane the Temple (vv. 27–30). As this use of money to underwrite the four men's purification rite seems to be a variant version of the presentation, and rejection, of the Pauline Collection (Rom. 15:31), we may suspect that this final rebuff of Paul as a would-be Nazirite, this decisive rejection of Paul's attempt to curry favor with the party of James, has been figuratively rendered in later Jamesian (i.e., Ebionite) propaganda as Paul's frustrated attempt *to do what Nazirites did*, to "marry the daughter of the High Priest"! Why choose this particular metaphor for Paul as a false prophet?

Because of the resonances of "the suitor" as a seducer (of Israel), a deceiver and false prophet (cf. 2 Cor. 11:1–5, where Paul turns precisely the same charge back on the Jerusalem "super-apostles").

JOHN BAR ZEBEDEE

One question Eisenman leaves open is the true identity lying behind the fictitious John "son of Zebedee." Who can he have been? I think we have a couple of clues. (And I think it is worth pursuing them here by way of demonstrating that Eisenman's case relies not merely upon his own subjective impressions, but rather on a method which may be taken up by others to get their own results. Once one gets the knack of it, the Eisenman method proves itself as scientific as any employed in form and redaction criticism.)

First, since Judas Thomas/Thaddaeus is also called "Lebbaeus," an apparent variant of James's title "Oblias" (the Bulwark = the Pillar), we must suppose that the Heirs of Jesus and the Pillars were synonymous, which in turn makes the Pillar John a brother of Jesus. (Eisenman supposes that there must have been a Pillar named John; it is his connection with the cipher "James son of Zebedee" that presents the difficulty.) Thus there is no problem accepting the Pillar John as the real brother of James the Just and of Judas Thomas and Simeon bar Cleophas. All were counted as Pillars or Bulwarks whose presence in Jerusalem kept the city safe (à la Gen. 18:22–32 and the later Jewish doctrine of the "fifty righteous" for whose sake the world is maintained). And remember the curious business with James and John being christened "Boanerges," taken to mean "sons of thunder," but (with John Allegro) more likely representing the Sumerian *Geshpuanur* (the prefix becoming a suffix as is common in Near Eastern names), meaning "upholder of the vault of heaven," a title of one of the Dioscuri or heavenly twins (Acts 28:11). This is to make James and John at once both brothers and cosmic pillars. And since the two cosmic pillars upholding the roof of Solomon's Temple (symbolic of the firmament of the heavens, as in all ancient temples) were called Boaz and Jachin, one may wonder whether Boanerges has something to do with Boaz, James/Jacob with Jachin. Like James, John is said (by Polycrates) to have worn the priestly ephod, and this would fit the Zealot-like rebel priesthood ideology of James and Judas Thomas (Theudas).

But then why does John not appear in the sibling list of Mark 6:3? I suspect his place has been taken by "Joses." John's original position as a brother of Jesus has been transferred to another John, *John the Baptist*. Luke makes the Baptist both a hereditary priest and a "cousin" of Jesus, just as later tradition made Jesus' brothers Simeon and James his cousins. And an early apocalypse preserved in Chrysostom's *Encomium on John the Baptist* (see E. A. Wallace Budge's *Coptic Apocrypha in the Dialect of Upper Egypt*) is ascribed to "John the Lord's Brother," implying (in the same manner as a striking textual variant) that perhaps someone, somewhere, had remembered the original connection.

But what of Mark's "Joses"? Eisenman suggested this name is a barely disguised reshuffling of none other than *Jesus*, preserved from the original occurence of the list, simply *as* a list of all the brothers including Jesus. This is not unlikely. But I would suggest Joses is a place-holder for John. As for the name itself, it is a vestige of a list that originally would have read, "Is this not the carpenter, the son of Mary and Joses, and brother of James, and John, and Judas, and Simon?" By the time we see it in Mark 6, it has become garbled, Joses becoming one of the brothers and Jesus' father dropping out of the list. Matthew (13:55) thought this unseemly, so he has taken from Jesus the epithet "the carpenter" and made the carpenter into the father of Jesus (anonymous here but implicitly equated with the Joseph of Matthew's Nativity story). Originally, à la Eisenman and Hugh J. Schonfield, the appellation "Jesus son of Joseph" had nothing to do with the name of Jesus' father (who must actually have been Cleophas if Jesus' brother Simeon was "bar Cleophas") but rather is a historicizing of the Galilean/Ephraimite title "Messiah ben Joseph."

As for the designation "bar Zebedee," I wonder if we can kill two birds with one stone. In *The Essene Odyssey*, Hugh J. Schonfield puzzled over the inclusion of one "Yochanan ben Zabda" (= John bar Zebedee) as the partner of physician Asaph ben Berechiah in the ancient *Sepher Refu'ot* (Book of Medicines), a writing with Qumran affinities. Schonfield wondered how this Christian character wound up in such a Jewish writing. I wonder if it might not have been the reverse: If Yochanan son of Zabda were already renowned as a Jewish healer in the early Christian period, it is easy to see that, once Christians began to try to distance Jesus from his relatives, another identity would be sought for his brother John. And so he became (con)fused in the early Christian mind with a (possibly contemporary) Jewish healer named Yochanan ben Zabda.

If Eisenman's *James the Brother of Jesus* often seems too circuitous and redundant, this is the result of his having to keep a great number of balls in the air at once. He has to begin explaining something here, put it on hold, go on to something else that you'll need to plug into the first explanation, then return to it, go on to another, and another, then back to the earlier items, remind you of them, and then finally assemble the whole complex device. Eisenman is like the Renaissance scientists who had to handcraft all the intricate parts of a planned invention. The book is an ocean of instructive insight and theory, a massive and profound achievement that should open up new lines of New Testament research.

Index of Scripture and Other Ancient Sources

Hebrew Bible books are listed in the order of the Tanakh; New Testament books are in canonical order; all other books or authors are in alphabetical order.

Index of Modern Authors